Contributions to Economics

More information about this series at http://www.springer.com/series/1262

Daniel Oto-Peralías • Diego Romero-Ávila

Colonial Theories of Institutional Development

Toward a Model of Styles of Imperialism

Springer

Daniel Oto-Peralías
School of Management
University of St. Andrews
St. Andrews, United Kingdom

Diego Romero-Ávila
Department of Economics, Quantitative Methods and Economic History
Pablo de Olavide University
Seville, Spain

ISSN 1431-1933 ISSN 2197-7178 (electronic)
Contributions to Economics
ISBN 978-3-319-54126-6 ISBN 978-3-319-54127-3 (eBook)
DOI 10.1007/978-3-319-54127-3

Library of Congress Control Number: 2017936137

Printed on acid-free paper

This Springer imprint is published by Springer Nature
The registered company is Springer International Publishing AG
The registered company address is: Gewerbestrasse 11, 6330 Cham, Switzerland

Preface

Diego Romero-Ávila would like to dedicate this book to the memory of his father, Pedro José Romero de Ávila Aguilar, for encouragement and support throughout his career. The authors are particularly indebted to Luis Ángeles, Jesús Crespo-Cuaresma, Joaquín Maudos, Carlos Usabiaga, and Simon Wren-Lewis for valuable comments and suggestions. We also thank seminar participants at Pablo de Olavide University, St. Andrews University, and Vienna University of Economics and Business for valuable comments and suggestions. The authors acknowledge financial support from the Spanish Ministry of Science and Technology (grant ECO2009-13357), the Spanish Ministry of Economics and Competitiveness (grant ECO2012-35430), and the Andalusian Council of Innovation and Science (Excellence Project SEJ-4546).

St. Andrews, UK
Sevilla, Spain

Daniel Oto-Peralías
Diego Romero-Ávila

About This Book

This study analyzes the role played by initial endowments and colonizer identity in the explanation of institutional development in former colonies. After a brief review of the literature, a model of two styles of imperialism is presented that integrates the *colonial origin* and *endowment views* explaining current institutions. We argue that Britain and Portugal adopted an "economically oriented" style, which was pragmatic and sensitive to initial conditions. For this style of imperialism, the *endowment view* is applicable, because in territories with large endowments European powers established extractive institutions, with negative consequences for subsequent institutional development. In contrast, France followed a "politically oriented" style of imperialism, in which ideological and political motivations were more present. This led to a uniform colonial policy largely independent of initial endowments. The Spanish case is a hybrid between both models. Formally Spain implanted the same institutions across the New World colonies, but in practice, due to the limited resources of the metropolis, the intensity of colonial penetration varied depending on the possibilities to extract rents. Our empirical analysis finds remarkable heterogeneity in the relationship of endowments and colonizer identity with current institutions. This result can be read in two ways: the impact of colonizer identity varies with the level of endowments, and the relationship between endowments and institutions is very different across former colonial powers. A couple of important consequences can be derived from this finding. First, the *endowment view* is not universally applicable. Negative effects of endowments on institutions are only observed for former British colonies and to a lower extent for Spanish and Portuguese colonies but not for the rest. Second, former British colonies are not always associated with better institutions since former French colonies at least equal the British when the level of endowments is sufficiently high. The form of colonial rule appears to mediate between colonies' initial endowments and their interaction with metropolis' domestic conditions and current institutional levels.

Contents

Chapter 1
Introduction

> *"The central issue of economic history and of economic development is to account for the evolution of political and economic institutions that create an economic environment that induces increasing productivity"*
> Douglass C. North (1991, p. 98)

Abstract Institutions are seen as a fundamental requirement for economic development, since they form the incentive structure of economic agents and are considered essential for the proper functioning of the economy. The immediate question that follows is what factors explain the quality of institutions. Many scholars have sought the answer to this question in colonialism. Our study is rooted in this renewed interest. Several factors have been highlighted to explain this different legacy of colonialism on subsequent institutional development. A first group of authors emphasizes the identity of the colonizer, with the hypothesis that certain colonial powers (particularly Britain) implemented more benign colonial policies and transferred better institutions to their colonies than others, which led to higher institutional development. A second group focuses on the initial conditions existing in colonized territories, arguing that factors such as the disease environment, indigenous population density or resources abundance determined the colonial strategy of all Western powers in largely similar ways, thereby shaping the incentives to create different types of institutions. In this debate we advocate an intermediate (*eclectic*) *view*, since historical examples and systematic analysis of the data show that colonial origin and endowments as well as their interaction should be important factors in the formation and subsequent development of institutions. This analysis is framed within a simple model of two styles of imperialism that integrates the *colonial origin* and *endowment views*.

1.1 On the Importance of Institutions

Institutions are seen as a fundamental requirement for economic development. Since the work of North and Thomas (1973) and North (1981, 1991), many economists have been concerned about the economic impact of institutions,

D. Oto-Peralías, D. Romero-Ávila, *Colonial Theories of Institutional Development*, Contributions to Economics, DOI 10.1007/978-3-319-54127-3_1

which form the incentive structure of economic agents and are considered essential for the proper functioning of the economy. This argument has received extensive support in the literature. Among others, we highlight the early contributions made by Knack and Keefer (1995), Mauro (1995), La Porta et al. (1998), Hall and Jones (1999), Acemoglu et al. (2001, 2002, 2005), Easterly and Levine (2003), and Rodrik et al. (2004). The importance of institutions for economic development has been widely accepted not only by academics but also by international organizations such as the World Bank.[1]

Following North (1991, p. 97), institutions can be defined as "humanly devised constraints that structure political, economic and social interaction". When thinking about institutions, one usually relates them to laws, property rights protection and constitutions, but they can also refer to informal constraints such as sanctions, taboos, and codes of conduct. The first type can be called formal or de jure institutions, while the second type relates to informal or de facto institutions. For instance, in a study about productivity differences in the Americas, Acemoglu and Dell (2010) mention law enforcement, fairness of elections, control of political elites, and the efficiency of the judiciary as examples of de facto institutions. Therefore, the concept of institutions is very broad, including dimensions such as corruption, political decentralization, check and balances on the executive, electoral system, etc.

In this study, we operationalize institutions as the degree to which *rule of law* governs the economic and political life of a country. In our view, *rule of law* is a concept that reflects well the institutional environment conducive to economic development since it captures important aspects such as property rights protection, contract enforcement, legal certainty, and an independent judiciary. We use the rule of law indicator from Kaufmann et al. (2009), which ranges from −2.5 to 2.5, where higher scores indicate better institutions. Figure 1.1 shows a map with the score of each country corresponding to the year 2000 (the baseline year of this study). Variation in institutional quality across countries is huge. There are countries like the Democratic Republic of Congo and others in sub-Saharan Africa with rampant corruption, weak rule of law, and pervasive violence, while others like the Scandinavian countries are consolidated democracies with efficient bureaucracies.

Institutional quality goes hand-by-hand with economic prosperity. Figure 1.2 shows a map with the distribution of the average level of GDP per capita during the period 2011–2015. It is worth noting that areas with high income levels overlap with regions characterized by high institutional quality. The correlation between institutional quality in 2000 and the log of GDP per capita one decade later is as high as 71.5%. This strong relationship is shown in the scatterplot

[1]The World Development Report 2002 is clear about the importance of institutions in economic growth: "The ability of the state to provide those institutions that support growth and poverty reduction—often referred to as good governance—is essential to development. Countries that have failed in this respect have seen incomes stagnate and poverty persist." (World Bank 2002, p. 115).

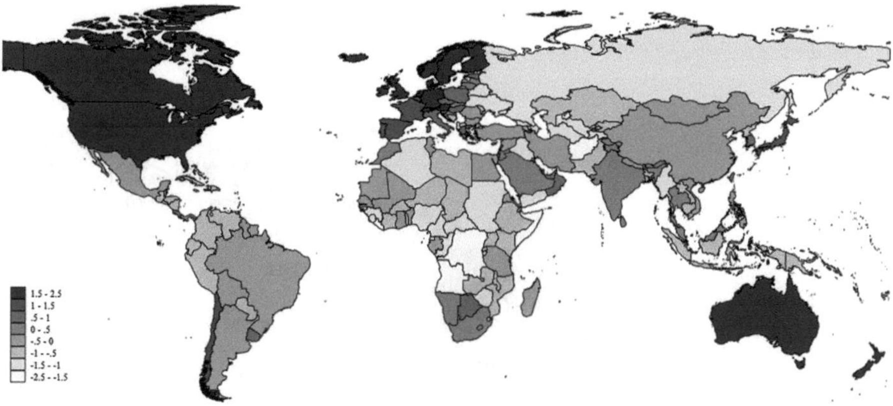

Fig. 1.1 Quality of institutions around the world: Rule of Law. *Notes*: Indicator of rule of law from Kaufmann et al. (2009). *Darker colors* indicate more institutional quality. Year 2000. Countries without data do not appear in the map

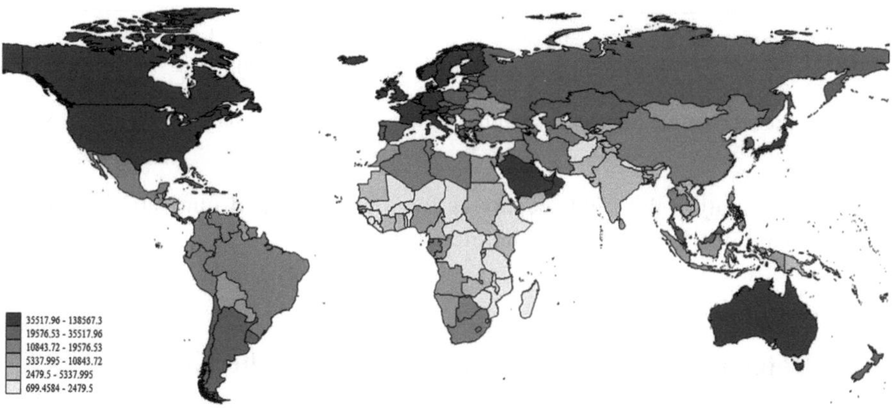

Fig. 1.2 Income levels around the world: GDP per capita. *Notes*: GDP per capita, PPP. *Darker colors* indicate a higher value. Average 2011–2015. Countries without data do not appear in the map (Data source: World Bank Open Databases)

depicted in Fig. 1.3. This stylized fact has fuelled the interest of economists in establishing the determinants of institutions.

It is worth mentioning that institutions are a highly persistent feature of countries. For instance, the correlation between the rule of law indicator in 2000 and the same indicator 15 years later (in 2015) is 89%. This high correlation means that institutions are very difficult to change. The development of a legal and judicial system that both protects individual and collective rights and enforces the law in a fair and efficient manner is a long-term process. Vested interests and political capture may prevent the development of good institutions, undermining the prospects for economic development. A proper institutional

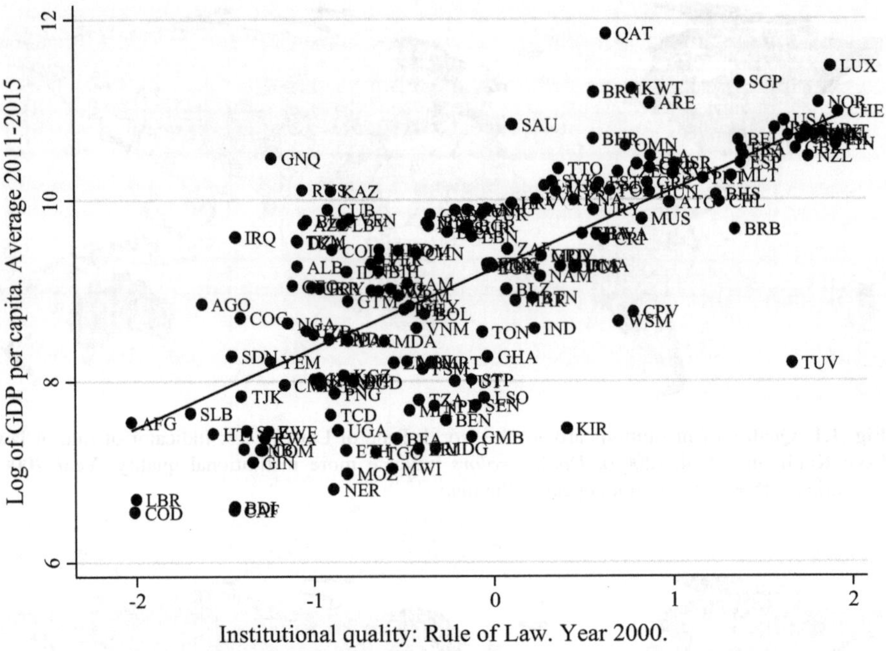

Fig. 1.3 The relationship between institutional quality and income levels

framework creating the right incentives for investment and innovation is one of the preconditions for modern economic growth.

1.2 Determinants of Institutional Quality: The Key Role of European Colonialism

The importance of institutions for economic development, along with the large variation that exists around the world, has raised the question as to which factors explain the quality of institutions. Many scholars have sought the answer to this question digging deeper into history since institutional development is considered a long-term process. Of all historical events studied, colonialism has been the one attracting more attention in the past years (Nunn 2009). This is not surprising, since colonialism was a historic event of extraordinary importance. In 1914, the territory occupied by European powers and their new and former colonies extended over approximately 85% of the global surface (Fieldhouse 1966). This meant an enormous influence of Europe around the world, leading to the implantation of different systems of colonial government, policies and institutions.[2] In addition, colonialism is seen as a kind of natural experiment and, therefore, as a source of exogenous variation that has been widely used to study the economic effect of institutions (Acemoglu et al. 2001, 2002; Easterly and Levine 2003; Rodrik et al. 2004).[3] Moreover, the increasingly consolidated notion of the tendency for institutions to persist over time (the concept of path dependency) gives historical phenomena such as colonialism additional interest, since current institutions of former colonies are largely seen as a product of their colonial past.[4]

Our study is rooted in this renewed interest in explaining current institutions through colonial past. There is ample evidence suggesting that the legacy of colonialism was very different from one country to another. Some former colonies enjoy high-quality institutions, such as Australia, Chile, and the U.S. Others, however, have very weak institutions that seriously hinder their economic development (e.g., Angola, Congo or Haiti). An interesting debate has emerged about the factors that explain this different legacy of colonialism on subsequent institutional development.

A first group of authors emphasizes the identity of the colonizer, with the hypothesis that certain colonial powers (particularly Britain) implemented more benign colonial policies and transferred better institutions to their colonies than others, which led to higher institutional development. This *colonial origin view* is largely supported by North (1991), Grier (1999), Bertocchi and Canova (2002), and Klerman et al. (2011). Another group of scholars focuses on the initial conditions existing in colonized territories, arguing that factors such as the disease environment, indigenous population density or resources abundance determined the colonial strategy of all Western powers in largely similar ways, thereby shaping the incentives to create different types of institutions. This *endowment view* is strongly supported by Engerman and Sokoloff (1997, 2000) and Acemoglu et al. (2001, 2002).

In this debate we advocate an intermediate (*eclectic*) *view*, since historical examples and systematic analysis of the data show that colonial origin and endowments as well as their interaction should be important factors in the formation and subsequent development of institutions. Indeed, some scholars point out the

---

[2]Even in states not formally colonized, such as China, the influence of European imperialism was clear, as evidenced by the trade liberalization that followed the Opium Wars (1840–1842; 1856–1860).

[3]European countries were thrown to the conquest of much of the world and implemented in their colonies different systems of government, policies and institutions. This source of exogenous variation that is attributed to colonialism is key to the analysis of the economic consequences of institutions.

[4]Institutions, and more generally colonial policies, established by European empires had a powerful influence on the subsequent institutional development of colonized territories. This central statement can be found in North (1991), Engerman and Sokoloff (2000), and Acemoglu et al. (2001).

compatibility of the *colonial origin* and *endowment views* (Levine 2005; Lange et al. 2006). We contribute to this debate by developing an informal model on styles of imperialism as well as by conducting a regression-based analysis in which we interact the identity of the colonizer with the level of endowments. Our empirical analysis provides extensive empirical support for the marked difference in the way the British and the French approached colonialism on the basis of their distinct response to initial endowments.

1.3 Toward a Model of Styles of Imperialism

This study provides a simple model of two styles of imperialism that integrates the *colonial origin* and *endowment views*. First, the 'economically-oriented' style is characterized by a strategy that aims to exploit colonial resources in order to satisfy the economic needs of the metropolis. Consequently, this style of imperialism renders a pragmatic empire, with purely economic goals and sensitive to the initial conditions of each territory, since the specific colonial policy required to maximize rents and satisfy metropolitan needs will depend on the particular characteristics of each colony. The second style of imperialism, labeled as 'politically-oriented', is characterized by a colonial strategy that consists of expanding the territorial domains of the colonizing power for non-economic reasons, such as the glory or prestige of the nation or religious-ideological motives. In this case, the lack of an economic calculus and the desire to impose political dominion lead to a uniform colonial policy insensitive to initial conditions.

Importantly, colonial powers tend to adopt one style of imperialism or the other depending on their domestic circumstances. We argue that the specific conditions prevailing in Britain such as its insularity and liberal economic and political regimes favored the development of an 'economically-oriented' style of imperialism. In contrast, the centralist state tradition, the ideological heritage of the Great Revolution and military defeats led France to adopt a 'politically-oriented' style. These different models of imperialism were well reflected in the diverging characters of the British and French empires as well as in the different colonial policies adopted. France was characterized by a colonial philosophy based on the consideration of the colonial empire as an intrinsic part of the Republic and the ideal of *assimilation*. That led to a more centralized system of government and a more homogeneous colonial administration across the empire (Fieldhouse 1966). As a consequence, France conducted a colonial strategy largely insensitive to initial conditions, which implies that institutional development in former French colonies is independent of precolonial endowments.

In contrast, the government system in the British Empire was more decentralized and varied substantially from one colony to another. We can distinguish, on the one hand, the colonies of settlement with constitutional systems and a high level of self-government (the U.S., Canada and Australasia). On the other, the remaining colonies had various systems of rule. The system known as *indirect rule* was widespread among extractive colonies, particularly in sub-Saharan Africa and some parts of Asia, although implemented in different degrees depending on their initial endowments. Between the extremes of *settlement* and *indirect colonialism*, we find *direct colonialism* prevalent in strategically trade-oriented colonies (Hong Kong and Singapore) and plantation colonies (West Indies), in addition to *hybrid colonialism* present in colonies like South Africa, Zimbabwe or India (Lange et al. 2006). Thus, the British empire had a high variability in government systems as a response to different initial endowments in colonized territories.[5] We further argue that Portugal followed an 'economically-oriented' style of imperialism and Spain a hybrid between the two styles.

Our model of colonial empires predicts that the *endowment view* is applicable to the 'economically-oriented' style of imperialism, but not to the 'politically-oriented' style. Therefore, only in the first case but not in the second do we expect to observe a negative relationship between precolonial endowments and the current institutional level. Interestingly, it is *colonial origin* what determines whether endowments influence or not colonial policies, since domestic conditions in the colonizing country and the resulting style of imperialism adopted are responsible for the sensitivity of colonial policies to initial endowments.

1.4 Preliminary Empirical Evidence

Table 1.1 provides preliminary evidence supporting our thesis. Rows present former colonies classified into five groups: British, French, Spanish, Portuguese and other empires (residual group). The first two columns show the mean values of our main institutional indicator (*rule of law*) for colonies with population density in 1500 below and above the median.[6] The third column reports the *t*-statistic of mean differences. For the full sample of colonies, those with greater precolonial population density have on average worse institutions (−0.66 vs. −0.07), with the mean difference being highly significant. Thus, without distinguishing across colonial empires the data fit well the *endowment view*. Moreover, the last column shows that former British colonies exhibit better institutions than the other groups of former colonies, which is also consistent with the *colonial origin view*. However, the

[5]In India the British made use of the land revenue system that was in place upon their arrival and enjoyed the potential of the Indian market. In the West Indies, the British used slave labor as a main input into the plantation system. The system of indirect rule that was prevalent in large parts of sub-Saharan Africa provided the British with a low-cost means of administering large and populated territories, while taking advantage of the potential economic benefits. Hence, we observe how the British could vary their system of colonial rule in order to exploit the indigenous and natural resources of the colonies.

[6]According to Acemoglu et al. (2002), population density in 1500 accounts for the level of precolonial development and prosperity. They postulate that colonizers implanted "extractive" institutions in more prosperous territories, while settler colonies in less developed areas.

Table 1.1 Colonial empires, endowments and institutions

	Rule of law (WGI): mean values			
	Less than or equal to the median of population density (1500)	Greater than the median of population density (1500)	*t*-statistic of mean differences	All colonies
All colonies	**−0.07**	**−0.66**	[3.62]	**−0.35**
	54	*48*		*102*
Colonies classified by colonial empires				
British colonies	**0.53**	**−0.62**	[5.39]	**0.08**
	28	*18*		*46*
French colonies	**−0.95**	**−0.64**	[−1.50]	**−0.76**
	9	*14*		*23*
Spanish colonies	**−0.39**	**−0.50**	[0.35]	**−0.44**
	10	*9*		*19*
Portuguese colonies	**−0.48**	**−1.39**	[n.a.]	**−0.66**
	4	*1*		*5*
Other empires colonies	**−1.48**	**−0.96**	[−1.08]	**−1.13**
	3	*6*		*9*

Notes: Rule of law ranges from −2.5 to 2.5, where a higher value indicates better institutions. Its year of measurement is 2000. Variable descriptions are provided in Table A.1. The sample contains non-European countries colonized by Western powers (Table A.2). The number of countries appears in italics

picture is quite different when we consider colonial empires and endowments simultaneously. Interestingly, only former British colonies match well with the *endowment view,* as given by the statistically significant lower institutional development for a level of endowments above the median. This contrasts with the fact that former French and other empires' colonies display better institutions when endowments are large, whereas Spanish and Portuguese colonies follow a similar pattern to the British. In these four cases, mean differences are statistically insignificant.

This heterogeneity in the relationship between endowments and institutions across colonial empires is clearly shown in Fig. 1.4. The *endowment view* fits well the case of former British colonies, for which a highly significant negative relationship is found. Former Spanish and Portuguese colonies also show a negative relationship between endowments and institutions, though it is not significant. In sharp contrast, former French colonies show a positive relationship, whereas for the other empires the relationship appears very weak. Returning to Table 1.1, another interesting observation can be made: former British colonies do not always exhibit the best institutions. For colonies above the median of population density, Spanish colonies slightly exceed the British (−0.50 vs. −0.62), while French colonies have almost the same score.

Our results have two important implications for the extant literature. First, the *endowment view* cannot be generalized to all colonial empires. A negative relationship between endowments and institutions is only observed for former British,

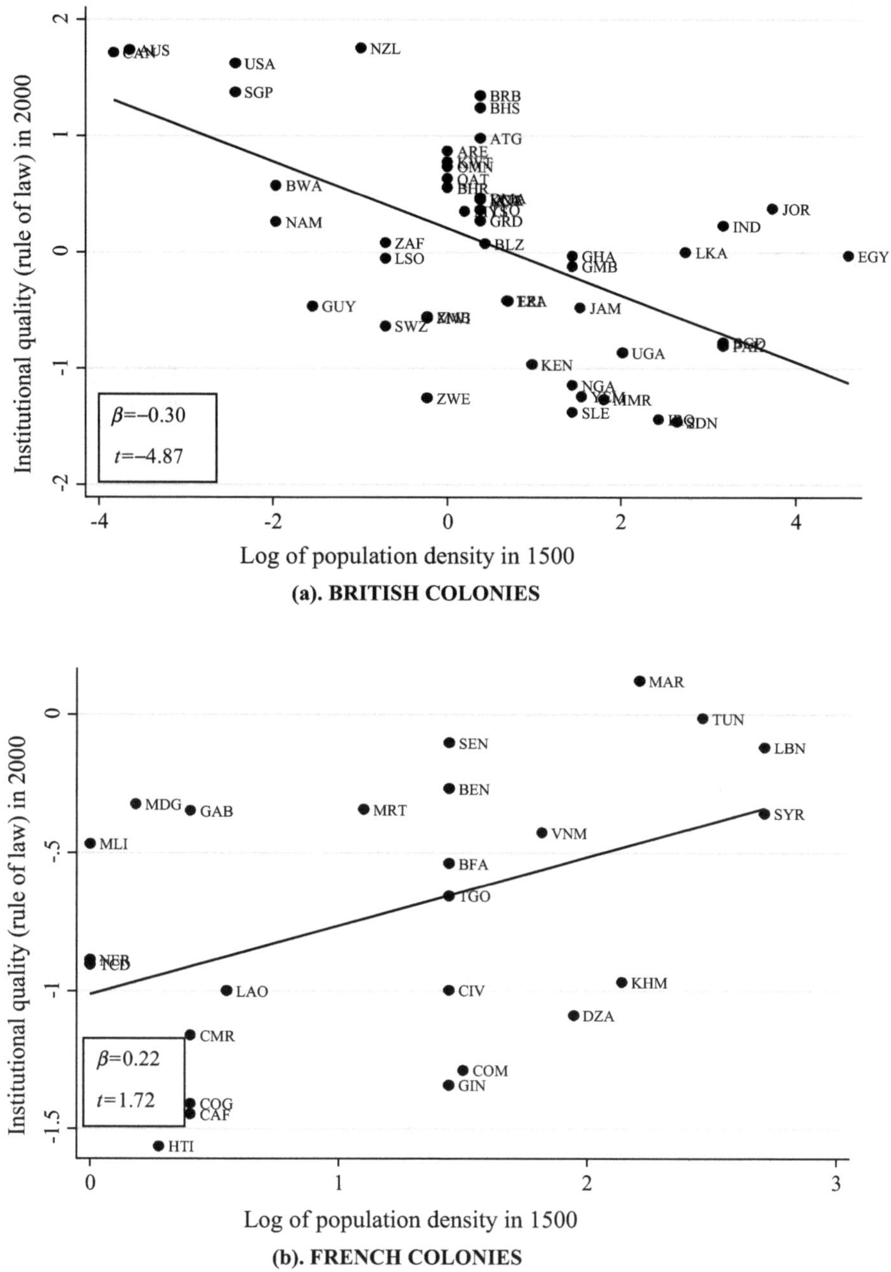

Fig. 1.4 The relationship between log of population density in 1500 (x-axis) and rule of law in 2000 (y-axis)

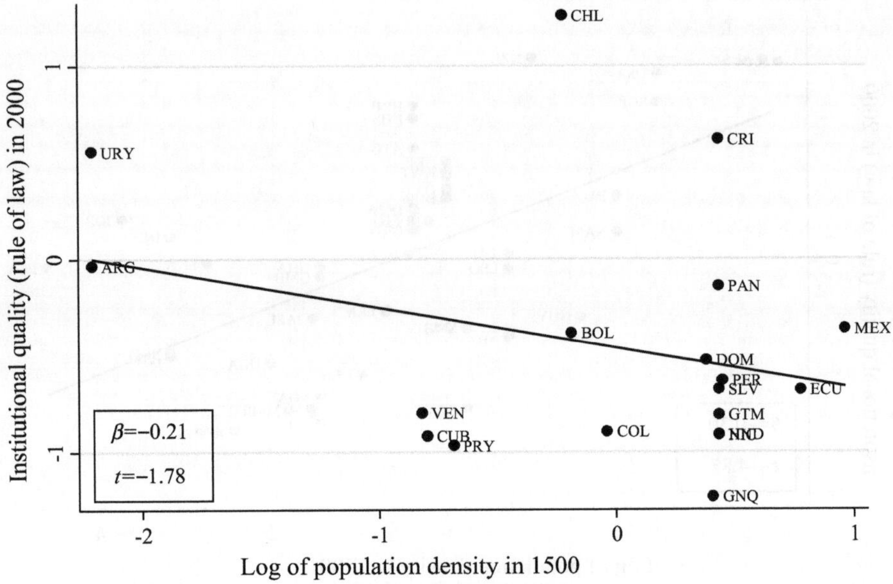

(c). SPANISH COLONIES

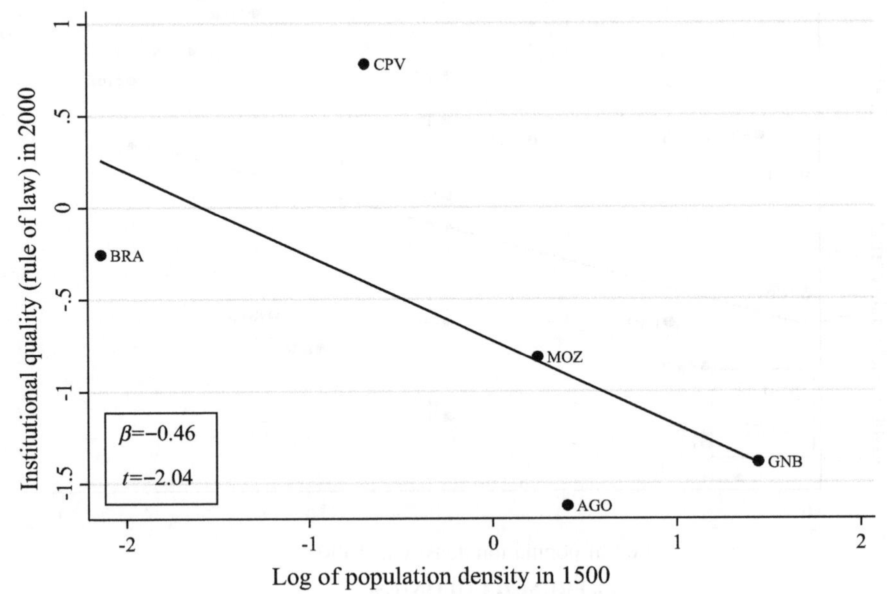

(d). PORTUGUESE COLONIES

Fig. 1.4 (continued)

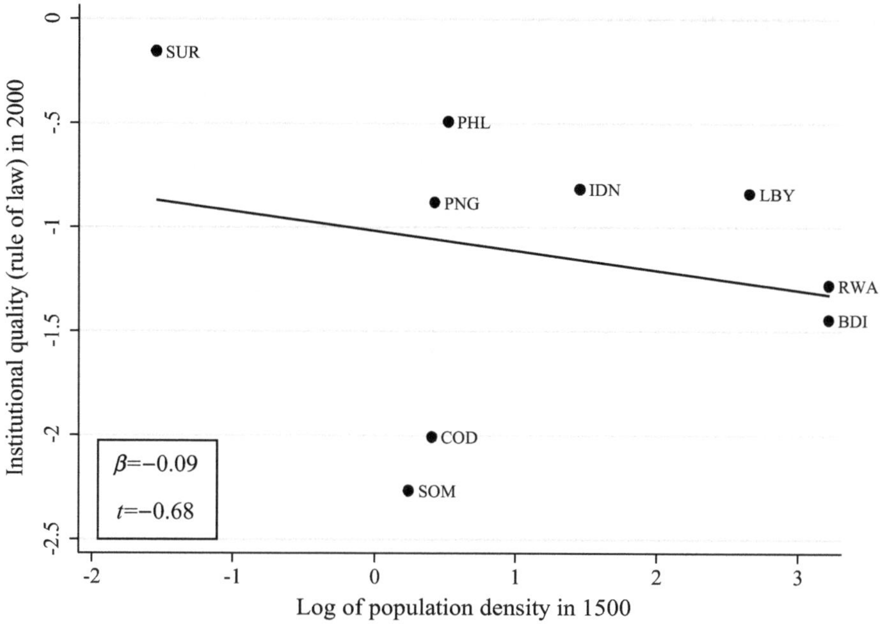

(e). OTHER COLONIES

Fig. 1.4 (continued)

Portuguese and to a lesser extent Spanish colonies, but not for the French, which implies that—according to our model—the style of imperialism matters. Second, the relative effect of colonizer identity on institutions depends on the level of endowments. Thus, British colonies exhibit better institutions at low levels of initial endowments, but not in those territories where endowments were large. In the rest of the study we analyze these results through an interaction model for a cross-section of 102 former colonies. Institutions are explained by endowments, colonizer identity and their interaction. We find that the contrast between former British and French colonies is particularly robust, even after controlling for a wide variety of alternative explanations of current institutions.

In addition, we make a first attempt to shed light on the channels through which the interaction between colonizer identity and endowments affect current institutions. We find that factors like education, inequality and to a lesser extent social conflict are relevant channels through which colonial policies have affected institutional development. Institutional development emerges as a complex picture that is the result of a wide range of factors and processes launched during the colonial period, which continue to exert strong influence on institutions even decades and in many cases centuries after independence.

1.5 Structure of the Study

The remainder of the study is organized as follows. Chapter 2 outlines the existing views linking colonialism with institutions and reviews the literature on the study of the long-term legacies of historical events. Chapter 3 presents our theoretical framework of two styles of imperialism and how it applies to the colonial experiences of European powers. Chapter 4 describes the empirical methodology employed to test the predictions of our model and then presents the basic regression evidence. Chapter 5 examines the robustness of our findings to alternative theories and Chap. 6 conducts further sensitivity analyses. Chapter 7 explores the key mechanism of colonial rule linking colonies' initial endowments and their interaction with domestic conditions in the metropolis to current institutions. Chapter 8 conducts an exploratory analysis of the effect of European colonialism on several relevant determinants of institutional development. The final chapter puts forward some implications and concludes.

Chapter 2
Views Linking Colonialism with Institutions

Abstract Nowadays there is widespread consensus on the importance of institutions for economic progress. Many social scientists have seen the imprint of colonial past in countries' current institutions. Some scholars focus on the identity of the colonizing nation, considering that Britain implemented better policies and institutions in their colonies than the other European powers. Others emphasize the initial conditions encountered by Europeans, arguing that colonial policies implemented in environments with large endowments or high potential mortality led to pernicious institutions. A third group advocates that both factors are relevant for the institutional development of former colonies. A review of these three strands of the literature is provided, along with a more general description of the literature that deals with the study of the long-term legacies of historical events.

This chapter briefly summarizes the two views on institutional development in former colonies: the *colonial origin view*, which stresses the identity of the colonizer country, and the *endowment view*, which is based on the characteristics of the colonial territory and the precolonial conditions before the arrival of Europeans. We then present the *eclectic view* that emphasizes the need for taking into account the interaction between both factors. Finally, we provide an overview of other related studies on the long-term legacy of historical events.

2.1 The *Colonial Origin View*

Advocates of the *colonial origin view* were typically the first to study the influence of colonial history on institutional and economic development. According to their view, colonial policies of European powers had a lasting influence on colonized territories. Metropolis with better institutions, such as Britain, implemented and transferred more benign policies and institutions to their colonial dominions than colonial powers like Spain, with a domestic absolutist regime.

North (1989, 1991) explains the institutional development of North America and Latin America in relation to the characteristics of European powers in the colonial period. In England there was some degree of polyarchy, with disputes of power between the Parliament and the Crown. By contrast, in Spain the conquest of America

D. Oto-Peralías, D. Romero-Ávila, *Colonial Theories of Institutional Development*, Contributions to Economics, DOI 10.1007/978-3-319-54127-3_2

coincided with the decline of the Castilian Cortes and the gradual concentration of power by the Catholic Monarchs and their heirs to the throne. The political situation of the metropolis had important consequences for the colonies. According to North, these different starting points marked the emergence of very divergent institutional paths of development in the New World.

Historians have pointed out the existence of considerable differences in the policies implemented by the different colonial empires. For example, Fieldhouse (1966) describes how the French empire was more centralized than the British, and was ruled with a very different ideology (the French ideal of "assimilation"). While France preferred the system of *direct rule*, Great Britain opted for a system of colonial administration with more flexibility, variability to local conditions, and local autonomy, which in many parts of the empire took the form of indirect rule. Landes (1998) considers the influence of European powers in a broad sense, including political elements, culture and human capital as possible determinants of the subsequent development of colonies.[1] From an empirical point of view, Grier (1999), Treisman (2000), Bertocchi and Canova (2002), and Klerman et al. (2011) observe systematic differences across the colonies of the different European powers, finding that British colonies are associated with better institutions and economic performance.

There is a group of scholars who stress the legal tradition transplanted by Europeans in their colonies. Hayek (1960) has long emphasized the advantage of English common law versus French civil law, and more recently La Porta et al. (1998, 2008) have underlined the relationship between legal tradition and financial development. The pioneering papers of La Porta et al. (1997, 1998) analyze the effect of legal traditions on the legal protection of corporate shareholders and creditors, finding that common law countries have stronger investor and creditor rights than civil law countries. The common law is also found to be superior to the French civil law in terms of financial development (La Porta et al. 1998; Beck et al. 2003a). This is explained by the lower judicial formalism and the greater ability for the common law to evolve as a response to changing circumstances (Beck et al. 2003b).[2] Unlike civil law, common law is thought to better guarantee individual rights, limit to a greater extent the power of the state and promote the independence of the judiciary.[3]

[1]In a passage on the contrast between North and Latin American colonies, Landes writes "when one compares English ebullience and diversity with the Counter-Reformation orthodoxy and superstitious enthusiasms of Spain and Portugal—the power of ideas and initiatives in North America as against discontents in the Spanish and Portuguese dominions—one can understand the political outcome." (Landes 1998, p. 312).

[2]See Beck and Levine (2005) and La Porta et al. (2008) for authoritative reviews of the legal origins literature.

[3]Subsequent work has confirmed these initial findings for a larger sample of countries, improved indicators of legal rules and over a wider time interval (La Porta et al. 2006; Djankov et al. 2007, 2008b). Related research has shown that common law countries are associated with lower legal formalism, more efficiency of contract and debt enforcement, higher judicial independence and, in general, higher quality of legal systems (Djankov et al. 2003, 2008a; La Porta et al. 2004; Balas et al. 2009). All this literature advocates that the British common law is associated with better rules and

Therefore, according to this group of scholars who emphasize the legal tradition or origin of each country, former colonies that received their legal system from Britain have stronger protection of property rights and more efficient judicial systems. Likewise, former colonies within the common law tradition are better off in terms of financial development. Given the importance of a well-functioning legal and financial system for the health of the economic and political system, the Legal Origins Theory has very relevant implications for institutional and economic development.

Whether the distinguishing characteristic brought by European powers to their colonies is just the legal tradition or also some other factors like culture, religion, human capital or institutions themselves, is a controversial issue. Irrespective of that distinction, the common assumption in the *colonial origin view* is that the diverse orientations of each colonizing nation influenced the subsequent political and economic institutions of their former colonies.

2.2 The *Endowment View*

Proponents of the *endowment view* first draw attention on the enormous diversity in terms of wealth and institutions among colonies of the same European power (e.g., when comparing Canada with Sudan, both former British colonies). This diversity does not fit at all with the *colonial origin view* and leads them to focus on the conditions of the territories before the arrival of Europeans. Depending on these precolonial conditions or *endowments*, the European powers established a certain type of political and institutional organization that determined the subsequent path of development of colonial societies. Within this view, we highlight the work of Acemoglu et al. (2001, 2002) and Engerman and Sokoloff (1997, 2000).

Acemoglu et al. (2001) assert that the disease environment is a key factor to understand the colonization strategy of European powers. The presence of malaria and yellow fever, among other diseases, conditioned the feasibility of settlements and influenced the type of established institutions. In hospitable territories where the expected mortality was low—as in the U.S., Canada and Australasia—Europeans were able to settle en masse and implanted institutions guaranteeing political and civil freedoms and the enforcement of property rights. At the other extreme, in places like sub-Saharan Africa, where the expected European mortality was extremely high, the number of settlers was very low, which encouraged the establishment of extractive institutions in which a minority was able to control and exploit the colonial dominion.[4]

---

outcomes than the French civil law in many areas of the legal system. It has also been shown that governments in common law countries intervene and regulate to a lesser extent the economy (La Porta et al. 2002; Djankov et al. 2002; Botero et al. 2004).

[4]Using newly constructed data on colonial European settlement, Easterly and Levine (2016) find a strong, positive link between current levels of economic development and colonial European settlement, which is robust to controlling for the current share of European population. This

Acemoglu et al. (2002) offer a more complete theory of the colonization strategy of European powers. They state that precolonial wealth was a fundamental factor that fostered the establishment of extractive institutions, which led to a subsequent "reversal of fortune" in the colonies. In the territories where Europeans found more prosperous and densely populated societies, they had incentives to build institutions to exploit indigenous resources.[5] However, the relevant factor was not the short-run effects of exploitation policies, but the long-run consequences of "extractive institutions", which had as a distinguishing feature "a high concentration of political power in the hands of a few who extracted resources from the rest of the population" (Acemoglu et al. 2002, p. 1264). This structure of power concentration persisted over time, hindering the emergence of appropriate institutions for economic development.

Engerman and Sokoloff (1997, 2000) also emphasize the importance of pre-existing conditions in the colonies. They differentiate three types of colonies in the New World: plantation economies (sugarcane, tobacco and cotton), which used slaves as labor force (the Caribbean, for example); rich mineral resource economies with substantial numbers of natives (Meso-America); and sparsely populated territories lacking suitable conditions for large plantations (North America). In the first two cases, the concentration of economic and political power in the hands of the elite led to institutions that precluded much of the population from economic opportunities. So, large endowments in the form of scale-economies plantations and high mineral-resource abundance originated a vicious cycle of inequality and institutions biased to privilege the elite.[6] Only the third type of colonies, based on smallholder farmers of European descent, established institutions conducive to economic development.[7]

Easterly and Levine (2003) test the hypothesis whether economic development depends on geographic endowments like temperate versus tropical location, which

---

applies even to those colonies in which European settlers were a minority, thus suggesting that any adverse effect on extractive institutions was more than offset by other factors Europeans brought with them, such as human capital and technology. This result would stand in favor of the early findings by Glaeser et al. (2004) supporting the human capital channel through which colonial European settlement affects current development.

[5]The "economic profitability of alternative policies" and "whether Europeans could settle or not" are the factors that explain the colonial strategy followed by the European powers. The abundance of mineral resources, for example, favored the lucrative exploitation of the Amerindians (the case of Spanish America). The pre-existence of well-articulated hierarchical societies allowed the use of indigenous tribute systems and coercive labor. A high population density hindered European settlements, thus reducing the pressure for "institutions of private property" (Acemoglu et al. 2002).

[6]In the words of the authors: "the greater inequality in wealth contributed to the evolution of institutions that protected the privileges of the elites and restricted opportunities for the broad mass of the population to participate fully in the commercial economy even after the abolition of slavery" (Engerman and Sokoloff 2000, p. 221).

[7]Along these lines, Engerman and Sokoloff (2005) show that regions with scarcity of labor force, which were characteristic of frontier areas or areas with small native populations, had an incentive to extend political rights to attract immigrants.

condition the ecological environment shaping diseases and the suitability for producing grains or certain cash crops. Their evidence shows that tropics, germs, and crops affect economic development through institutions, instead of directly through channels other than institutions, thus supporting the *endowment view*.

More recently, Hariri (2012) points out that a country's precolonial tradition of statehood may affect current democracy levels. Territories with more developed precolonial state institutions were less likely to be colonized and, in the event of colonization, there was less European influence through settlement, and they were more likely to be colonized through indirect forms of colonialism. Indirect forms of rule were likely to lead to autocracy because "(a) there was only limited European diffusion, (b) there was limited European settlement and ideational diffusion, and (c) the incorporation of indigenous political institutions would often reinforce the existing authoritarian authority structures" (Hariri 2012, p. 475).[8]

2.3 The *Eclectic View*

The *colonial origin* and *endowment views* may not be necessarily exclusive. Thus, one should be cautious about statements such as "it is not the identity of the colonizer or legal origin that matters, but whether European colonialists could safely settle in a particular location" (Acemoglu et al. 2001, p. 1373). We argue that both the identity of the colonizer and endowments are important in explaining the institutional development of former colonies. More interestingly, there is evidence of heterogeneity in the relationship between endowments and institutions across colonial empires. Britain introduced worst institutions and policies in more prosperous precolonial territories, as did also Spain, while France did not condition its colonial strategy to the level of endowments. The French empire was more centralized and homogeneous than the British, which can be explained by the French colonial philosophy of assimilation.

Previously, other scholars have also argued in favor of this *eclectic view*. Levine (2005) in a review of the recent literature sees no reason to reject either the *colonial origin view* (in its legal origin version) or the *endowment view*. Specifications with property rights as the dependent variable render statistically significant negative coefficients on endowments (settler mortality) and French legal origin (see also Beck et al. 2003a). In an important contribution, Lange et al. (2006) take into account the economic models of the colonizing nations as well as the initial conditions of the territories. In doing so, they give a different explanation of the reversal of fortune observed in Acemoglu et al. (2002). "Mercantilist Spain" tended

[8]European influence is measured by Hariri (2012) as the fraction of native population speaking a main European language, and the extent of indirect rule as the number of customary court cases over the total number of court cases (which is available only for 33 former British colonies—from Lange 2004).

to colonize most extensively territories that were populous and developed, with negative consequences for subsequent development. Conversely, "liberal Britain" tended to colonize most extensively regions that were sparsely populated and underdeveloped, which exerted positive effects on subsequent development. "Thus, both Spain and Britain reversed the fortunes of precolonial regions, but in largely opposite ways" (Lange et al. 2006, p. 1412).

More recently, in a study that focuses on the law and finance nexus, Oto-Peralías and Romero-Ávila (2014a) state that Britain and France differed in their strategies of implanting their legal systems in the colonies. In sparsely populated and politically unorganized territories the British could effectively implant the common law, which was conducive to high financial development (in terms of both higher private credit and stock market capitalization). However, in places with large indigenous population (that often featured well-established customary law) the common law was superficially introduced. By contrast, France implanted its civil code more rigidly and uniformly across its colonies.[9]

Oto-Peralías and Romero-Ávila (2014b) went one step further and assessed thoroughly the mechanisms linking precolonial conditions and their interaction with legal traditions to postcolonial legal outcomes. In addition, that paper differed from Oto-Peralías and Romero-Ávila (2014a) in that, instead of analyzing the determinants of financial development, it brought additional insights into the core of the Legal Origins Theory. They argued that the process of distribution of legal traditions from origin countries to colonies was crucial to understand the relationship between legal origins and legal rules. Legal families were transferred from only few mother European countries to the rest of the world. An assumption made by the Legal Origins Theory is that the essential characteristics of each legal tradition remain both in origin and transplanted countries, and also implicitly that the implantation was homogeneous across countries within the same legal tradition. However, Oto-Peralías and Romero-Ávila (2014b) showed that the relative legal rules and outcomes (in terms of creditor and investor rights, credit information, legal system efficiency and regulatory burden) of the British common law vs. the French civil law are associated with the colonial strategies followed by mother countries when implanting their legal systems in their colonial dominions. They argued that the distribution of legal traditions was highly heterogeneous, with initial endowments in colonized territories being the key factor explaining this diversity. In addition, the form of colonial rule in British colonies was found to mediate between endowments and postcolonial legal outcomes.

[9]The relatively poorer performance of the common law at high levels of endowments can be related to the findings of Acemoglu and Johnson (2005), who find that property rights institutions (instrumented by population density in 1500 and settler mortality) are more central to economic development, investment, and financial development than contracting institutions (instrumented by legal origin). Acemoglu and Johnson's evidence indicates that endowments matter much more for financial development than having a common law tradition, since in the presence of large endowments the adverse effect on financial development dominates the positive effect from being a common law colony.

We follow this line of research. There are now good reasons to believe that both initial conditions and colonizer identity are relevant factors. European powers had different orientations toward colonization, resulting in different policies which did not always depend on initial endowments in the same way. The next chapter develops a simple model of styles of imperialism that is able to integrate the *colonial origin* and *endowment views*.

2.4 Other Related Literature

Besides the aforementioned studies, more generally a growing body of literature addresses the study of the long-term legacies of historical events (Nunn 2014; Spolaore and Wacziarg 2013). This renewed interest in history tries to find in the past the key to understand the mechanisms of economic development. It is studied how some historical events influence specific economic and social factors, and how these factors persist over time and ultimately affect current economic outcomes. In this context, historical events are considered critical junctures which create some kind of path dependence. Many factors associated with economic prosperity such as political and economic institutions, legal rules, inequality or human capital levels are largely the result of historical processes whose origins go far back in time (Nunn 2009). This literature started with Engerman and Sokoloff (1997, 2000) and Acemoglu et al. (2001, 2002), who—as seen above—focused on European colonialism as a crucial event to explain institutional and economic development in former colonies. This section conducts a brief (and non-comprehensive) review of the historical development literature. We first focus on other studies on colonialism, then on those works analyzing the impact and determinants of precolonial institutions, and finally on articles investigating the legacy of other historical events.

2.4.1 Additional Studies on Colonialism

Banerjee and Iyer (2005) exploit the particularities of the British colonial policy in India in order to analyze the effect of colonial institutions such as the land revenue system on current economic outcomes. They show that regions in which property rights in land were given to landlords have worse outcomes in terms of agricultural productivity, health and education than regions in which these rights belonged to the cultivators. Relatedly, Iyer (2010) compares the direct and indirect systems of colonial rule in India by the British. She finds that regions under direct rule have lower development outcomes in the postcolonial period than those under indirect rule.

Using an indicator of land suitability for plantation crops as an instrument for inequality, Easterly (2007) tests the Engerman and Sokoloff hypothesis that initial endowments predict inequality, which in turn leads to underdevelopment. He finds confirmatory evidence for a large cross-section of countries.[10] Feyrer and Sacerdote (2009) consider the European colonization of islands around the world as a natural experiment and take advantage of wind patterns as an instrument for the length of colonization. Their analysis shows a robust positive effect of the number of years spent as a colony on current income measured through GDP per capita.

Naritomi et al. (2012) explore the consequences of the sugarcane plantations and gold mining in colonial Brazil on the efficiency of local institutions and the distribution of de facto political power in the form of land. They find that municipalities created during the sugar-cane colonial period (and therefore characterized by an oligarchic social structure) have today a more unequal land distribution, while municipalities created during the gold colonial period (and with strong presence of the Portuguese state) have worse institutional quality today. Acemoglu et al. (2008) provide evidence for the case of the municipalities of Cundinamarca in Colombia that political inequality rooted in colonial times reduces current secondary school enrolment rates.

Gallego (2010) finds that cross-country differences in schooling are related to differences in democracy and political decentralization, which are affected by colonial factors. Focusing on within-country variation across the Americas, Bruhn and Gallego (2012) showed that colonial activities that relied heavily on labor exploitation (mining and sugar plantation) led to lower economic development, relative to colonial activities that were performed in sparsely populated areas and did not require the exploitation of labor. In a path-breaking paper, Dell (2010) utilizes a spatial regression discontinuity design to analyze the long-term impact of the forced mining labor system (known as the *mita*) operating in some parts of Peru and Bolivia between 1573 and 1812, finding a negative effect on current consumption levels, the prevalence of stunted growth in children, and education and roads provision.

Using a new database of colonial investment in French West Africa at the district level, along with a regression discontinuity estimation strategy, Huillery (2009) finds strong evidence that early colonial investments in education, health and infrastructures appear to exert persistent effects on current levels of schooling, health outcomes, and access to electricity and water. The results hold even between neighboring districts only. The high persistence of the effect of early colonial investments stems from the fact that those regions with higher investments in colonial times continue to be those in which more resources are invested nowadays.

Acemoglu et al. (2014b) show that in those places in Sierra Leone in which paramount chiefs were more powerful and faced less competition because chieftaincies were concentrated in fewer ruling families, several developmental

[10]Using 1860 U.S. census data to examine the Engerman and Sokoloff (1997, 2000) inequality channel, Nunn (2008a) does not find any evidence supporting the negative relationship between initial economic inequality and current levels of economic development across the U.S. states and counties.

outcomes such as education, child health and the fraction of the population working in other sectors outside agriculture are found to be significantly lower. Their evidence points to the ability of powerful chiefs to control people's access to land, as a main mechanism through which to extract rents at the expense of the provision of public goods.

Most of the works in this literature argue that extractive institutions established in the distant past have negative consequences for modern day institutions (Acemoglu et al. 2001). However, recent studies provide a more nuanced perspective. For instance, Broms (2017) focuses on former British colonies and documents a positive link between colonial revenue level during the early twentieth century and current government quality. The author further shows that this positive relationship is stronger when the neo-Europes (Canada, Australia and New Zealand in his sample) are excluded. The evidence of positive effects of revenue extraction on institutional development partially qualifies the extractive institutions hypothesis. More specifically, it requires being precise when defining what exactly an "extractive institution" is, since apparently "institutions for revenue extraction" may have positive consequences (Broms 2017, p. 2).

Also related to the literature on colonialism is a recent paper by Oto-Peralías and Romero-Ávila (2016). They provide evidence that the way the Christian kingdoms colonized the land conquered from the Muslims in the Iberian Peninsula during the Middle Ages had lasting consequences for economic development. They find that the speed of the Reconquest was a crucial factor affecting the type of colonization conducted in each territory, with a fast rate being associated with imperfect colonization characterized by an oligarchic political equilibrium. The authors argue that the Spanish Reconquest gives clues about the subsequent colonization of the New World. When Spain undertook the colonization of America, it had all the experience gathered in the Reconquest and the policies implemented in the occupation of Muslim lands. For instance, the *encomienda* was first used in Spain by Castile during the Reconquest process and later exported to the New World.

2.4.2 Studies about the Importance of Precolonial Institutions

Partly as a reaction to the previous literature that strongly emphasizes the crucial role of the colonial policies and institutions implemented by European powers, there is a group of scholars pointing to the importance of indigenous institutions, that is, those organizational structures in place before the arrival of Europeans. In pioneering work, Gennaioli and Rainer (2007) argue that in territories where centralized ethnic groups are prevalent, the hierarchical structure of rule facilitates the local accountability of chiefs to a higher-level traditional authority. This fosters policy coordination among local chiefs, which renders a better provision of public goods. In contrast, when ethnic groups are politically fragmented, policy coordination among local chiefs and individual chief accountability are usually weak or absent. Consistent with their argument, they find that ethnic groups' precolonial centralization is positively related to the provision of public goods such as education and health.

Combining information on the spatial distribution of ethnicities prior to colonization with regional variation in current economic performance measured through satellite images of light density at night, Michalopoulos and Papaioannou (2013) provide strong evidence of a positive link between precolonial ethnic political centralization and regional economic development in Africa. The fact that this finding holds even within pairs of adjacent ethnic homelands with different colonial legacies calls into question the prevalence of the effect of colonial institutional arrangements versus that of precolonial ethnic institutions. Along similar lines, Michalopoulos and Papaioannou (2014) find no evidence of a statistically significant effect of national institutions on African economic development. In doing so, they exploit the fact that the political boundaries at the eve of African independence partitioned more than 200 ethnic groups across adjacent countries subject to different formal institutions. The consequences of ethnic partitioning in Africa are further investigated in Michalopoulos and Papaioannou (2016), who find evidence that political violence and military interventions from neighboring countries are more prevalent in partitioned homelands.

In a recent article, Angeles and Elizalde (2017) explore the effects of precolonial institutions on current socioeconomic outcomes in Latin America. They argue that indigenous institutions survived through Amerindian rural communities, which explains their evidence of a positive association between more advance precolonial institutions and current outcomes. Their finding of highly persistent effects of precolonial institutions is remarkable, given the pervasive impact that European powers had on Latin America after three centuries of colonialism, which includes the decimation of the Amerindian population because of diseases brought by European settlers.

The evidence on the importance of precolonial institutions has led some scholars to investigate the determinants of indigenous institutions. Focusing on the origins of colonial forced labor across 439 subnational territories in the Americas, Arias and Girod (2014) find evidence that colonizers employed local, indigenous forced labor in those territories featuring an indigenous political administration that was already coercing labor prior to the arrival of the European powers. In addition, foreign forced labor in the form of African slavery was used in those territories where indigenous labor was unorganized and natural resources were present. This suggests that differences in political and economic development today are likely to predate European colonialism. Alsan (2015) investigates the effect of the tsetse fly, which is unique to Africa and constitutes a vector for a harmful parasite to humans and livestock. Interestingly, she finds that ethnic groups living in regions suitable for the tsetse fly were less likely to use domesticated animals and the plow, featured a lower population density, and exhibited lower political centralization.

With a focus on African societies, Fenske (2013) links the existence of large tracts of unoccupied land and low population density (and in turn labor scarcity) to a lack of price and rights over the land as well as to the prevalence of slavery and other forms of coerced labor across the African continent. Using a cross-section of global societies, Fenske (2013) also finds evidence of the persistence of precolonial institutions by linking them to current land transactions, polygamy and the provision of public goods.[11] In a related study, Fenske (2014) analyzes the determinants of pre-colonial African states and finds that ecological diversity—by increasing trade across ecological boundaries—leads to more precolonial centralization.

Using data from the Standard Cross-Cultural Sample, Osafo-Kwaako and Robinson (2013) provide strong evidence that neither population density, nor inter-state warfare and trade, can explain the level of political centralization across African societies, thus rejecting the empirical validity of standard models of Eurasian state formation in Africa. This evidence appears to follow the tradition initiated by social anthropologists such as Evans-Pritchard and Fortes (1940).[12]

2.4.3 Other Work on the Historical Roots of Comparative Development

There is a growing number of studies investigating the consequences of other historical events. In general, the main objective of this branch of the literature is to identify by means of historical sources of exogenous variation the effect on economic development of factors such as inequality, forced conversions and expulsions, religious reformations, weather shocks, armed conflicts, institutions and breakthrough technological innovations. In a seminal contribution, Nunn (2008b) explores the long-term effects of Africa's slave trades. He estimates the number of slaves exported from each country and shows a negative relationship between slaves taken from a country and current economic development. This result can be explained by the theoretical model of Nunn (2007), which exhibits multiple equilibria and path-dependence. One equilibrium features secure property rights

[11]The evidence provided by Fenske (2012) for the Egba of south-western Nigeria over the period 1830–1914 supports the empirical validity of this land abundance view. It was only when the Egba were confined to a small region of initial settlement that they developed rights over the land, particularly over especially productive plots like those involving tree crops. This in turn would also help improve the functioning of credit markets, since land per se was of no value to be used as collateral.

[12]More generally, Michalopoulos (2012) and Ahlerup and Olsson (2012) investigate the origins of ethnic diversity and ethnolinguistic diversity, respectively. The former finds within- and cross-country evidence of a geographic origin, particularly through geographic variability measured by variation in regional land quality and elevation. In addition, the latter show that such factors as a long duration of human settlements since prehistoric times, the proximity to the equator and the short length of historical state experience are responsible for the current high level of ethnic diversity in Africa. To the extent that high ethnic fragmentation is associated with lower growth prospects (Easterly and Levine 1997), the fundamental factors explaining present-day ethnic fractionalization may account for a fraction of Africa's dismal growth performance.

and a high level of production, while the other equilibria are poverty traps with insecure property rights and low production. In the event of sufficiently high external extraction (during for instance the slave trade or colonial rule), a society can shift from the high production to the low production equilibrium, in which the country will remain trapped even after the period of external extraction ceases. In subsequent work, Nunn and Wantchekon (2011) find that the origins of mistrust in Africa are partially explained by slave trades. More specifically, they show that "individuals whose ancestors were heavily raided during the slave trade are less trusting today" (Nunn and Wantchekon 2011, p. 3221).

Using historical data on urbanization rates, per capita incomes and executive constraints, Acemoglu et al. (2005) explain the rise of Europe on the basis of the rise of the nations directly engaged in the Atlantic trade (i.e., Britain, France, Holland, Portugal and Spain). The mechanism at work is related to the shift in the balance of power from the monarchy to the merchant class enriched with the lucrative Atlantic trade. This institutional change, which only took place in those countries that initially had non-absolutist political regimes, would exert permanent changes on long-term economic development.

Acemoglu et al. (2011a) exploit the exogenous variation introduced by the French Revolution and the drastic reforms imposed by France on German territories, finding that institutional reforms positively affected subsequent economic growth in the affected territories within Germany. Acemoglu et al. (2011b) show that mass displacement and execution of Jews population during World War II appears related to slower population growth and per capita income 50 years later. Bai and Kung (2011) show that nomadic incursions into settled Han Chinese territories for an extended period of more than two millennia are correlated with weather shocks associated with the level of rainfall. Chaney (2013) provides evidence that deviant Nile floods reduced the replacement probability of Egypt's highest-ranking religious authority. Dell (2012) analyzes the effect of historical drought on current development through the insurgency channel during the Mexican revolution. Chaney (2008) and Chaney and Hornbeck (2016) investigate the impact of the expulsion of about 120,000 *moriscos* in 1609 from the Kingdom of Valencia in Spain.[13]

There is also a bunch of studies focusing on the effect of religious reformations. Becker and Woessmann (2009) test Weber (1976)'s hypothesis and find evidence of a positive effect of Protestantism on economic development for a cross-section of Prussian counties in 1871. The effect can be entirely attributed to existing

[13]Chaney (2008) finds that it was the creation of more extractive economic institutions rather than lower human capital levels in former *morisco* districts that reduced overall development and in turn the size of their "productive" non-agricultural sector. Chaney and Hornbeck (2016) show that in former *morisco* districts, output fell after the shock but recovered faster than total population over the next 100 years, thus rendering sustained increases in per capita output. They explain this fact on the basis of the persistence and even accentuation of pre-expulsion extractive institutions, which sharply reduced demographic responses to labor scarcity and fostered labor-saving production adjustments through raising farm size and shifting to cash crops cultivation.

differences in literacy between Protestants and Catholics. More recently, Andersen et al. (2017a) cast doubts on the literacy channel by developing a theory and empirics of the pre-Reformation roots of the Protestant ethic. More specifically, they argue that the proximate source of the values of hard work and thrift, which have constituted the basis for the Protestant ethic, is the Catholic order of Cistercians in England during the early modern period. Conditional on a relevant set of exogenous controls, their evidence indicates that English counties with a higher presence of Cistercian monasteries exhibited faster population growth between 1377 and 1801. They also find that the values of work ethic and thrift are more present today in those regions of Europe with a higher historical presence of Cistercian monasteries; legacy that has left its imprint in present-day employment rates across European sub-regions. The results are remarkable given that these monasteries were dissolved in the 1530s.[14] In a similar spirit to Becker and Woessmann (2009), Bai and Kung (2015) provide evidence that Protestantism promoted economic prosperity (measured through urbanization rates) in China via knowledge diffusion activities associated with the construction of schools and hospitals by Protestant missionaries. In contrast to the above evidence, Cantoni (2015) finds no effect of Protestantism on economic growth using population figures for 272 cities in the Holy Roman Empire over the period 1300–1900.

Some research has also been conducted on the long-term consequences of other religious denominations. Botticini and Eckstein (2005, 2007) assign key importance to the requirement for all Jewish males to read the Torah since the burning of the Second Jewish Temple by the Romans in 70 AD. The subsequent accumulation of human capital, generations upon generations, gave rise to higher literacy and numeracy. This would be responsible for the long-term path of economic success in business of the Jewish people.

There is also a branch of the literature on the long-term impact of breakthrough innovations. Dittmar (2011) provides evidence of the long-term effect of the printing press, which was first established in Mainz between 1446 and 1450. Using the distance from Mainz as an instrument for the adoption of the printing press in the fifteenth century, he finds that European cities adopting the printing press in the interval 1450–1500 experienced higher rates of population growth between the sixteenth and nineteenth centuries. Along similar lines, Baten and van Zanden (2008) find evidence that the production of printed books in eight western European countries over the period 1450–1800 appears highly correlated with literacy rates, thus having an impact on early-modern growth trajectories. Technological innovations in agriculture such as the adoption of the plough have been shown to exert long-term effects on cultural patterns and economic development. Linking cross-cultural ethnographic data with contemporary measures of gender role attitudes, Alesina et al. (2013) show that traditional plough agriculture,

[14]With respect to the diffusion of Protestantism in Europe, Iyigun (2008) shows that Protestantism spread as a result of the Ottoman military incursions into continental Europe between the mid-fifteenth and late sixteenth centuries.

through the cultural traits formed around traditional gender division of labor, appears related, even nowadays, with less equal beliefs about the roles of men and women in society. Andersen et al. (2017b) find evidence that the adoption of the heavy plough, which was necessary to take proper advantage of the fertile clay soils of Northern Europe, is correlated with greater population growth and higher urbanization rates for a sample of 316 European regions over the period 500–1300, with observations every 100 years. Similar evidence is found using a high quality dataset for Denmark.

Another interesting branch in this literature analyzes the long-term effects of historical political boundaries. Typically, articles exploit the institutional and political heterogeneity introduced by borders that no longer exist. Becker et al. (2016) compare municipalities on both sides of the former Habsburg Empire frontier in order to analyze the legacy of the Empire with respect to attitudes toward the state. They find that historical Habsburg affiliation increases current levels of trust and reduces corruption in courts and police. Grosjean (2011a) studies the institutional legacy of the Ottoman Empire on financial development by exploiting within-country variation in six south-eastern European countries that were only partly occupied by the Ottomans, and Grosjean (2011b) applies a gravity approach to studying the influence of living under a common historical Empire (Ottoman, Habsburg, Russian or Prussian) on cultural integration.

Finally, it is worth mentioning a nascent literature on the long-term consequences of historical frontiers. A recent example is a paper by Oto-Peralías and Romero-Ávila (2017) that explores the political economy that leads frontier regions to be unequal. By focusing on the presence of a stable frontier between Castile and the Nasrid Kingdom of Granada in the late Middle Ages, they show how a historical border may generate differences in inequality that can become extremely persistent. They argue that the dynamics of being a militarily insecure frontier region may bias the political equilibrium in favor of the military elite, thereby creating the conditions for an oligarchic society, with negative consequences for long-term development. This finding is consistent with the "conditional frontier thesis" proposed by García-Jimeno and Robinson (2011).[15]

[15] According to the conditional frontier hypothesis, the contrasting outcomes obtained from the different frontier experiences in the American continent must be sought in the initial political equilibrium existing in society at the time when the expansion of the frontier occurred. When the political equilibrium was biased toward the oligarchies with political power as occurred in most of Latin America, frontier land was allocated on an inegalitarian basis to white immigrants and members of the oligarchy as a way to remain in power.

Chapter 3
A Model of Two Styles of Imperialism

Abstract This chapter provides a simple model of two styles of imperialism that integrates the *colonial origin* and *endowment views*. First, the 'economically-oriented' style is characterized by a strategy that aims to exploit colonial resources in order to satisfy the economic needs of the metropolis. Consequently, this style of imperialism renders a pragmatic empire, with purely economic goals and sensitive to the initial conditions of each territory, since the specific colonial policy required to maximize rents and satisfy metropolitan needs will depend on the particular characteristics of each colony. The 'politically-oriented' style of imperialism is characterized by a colonial strategy that consists of expanding the territorial domains of the colonizing power for non-economic reasons, such as the glory or prestige of the nation or religious-ideological motives. In this case, the lack of an economic calculus and the desire to impose political dominion lead to a uniform colonial policy insensitive to initial conditions. Importantly, colonial powers tend to adopt one style of imperialism or the other depending on their domestic circumstances. We argue that the specific conditions prevailing in Britain such as its insularity and liberal economic and political regimes favored the development of an 'economically-oriented' style of imperialism. In contrast, the centralist state tradition, the ideological heritage of the Great Revolution and military defeats led France to adopt a 'politically-oriented' style. These different models of imperialism were well reflected in the diverging characters of the British and French empires as well as in the different colonial policies adopted. Our model of colonial empires predicts that the *endowment view* is applicable to the 'economically-oriented' style of imperialism, but not to the 'politically-oriented' style. Therefore, we expect to observe a negative relationship between precolonial endowments and the current institutional level in the first case but not in the second.

D. Oto-Peralías, D. Romero-Ávila, *Colonial Theories of Institutional Development*, Contributions to Economics, DOI 10.1007/978-3-319-54127-3_3

3.1 The Theoretical Framework

We present a simple model of colonial empires that integrates the *colonial origin* and *endowment views*. Our model assumes two styles of imperialism, the 'economically-oriented' and the 'politically-oriented'.[1] The former conceives the empire as a way to satisfy the economic needs of the metropolis. There is a variety of these needs, such as natural resources including valuables like gold and silver (which can be obtained through own exploitation via coercive labor or through trade monopolies), markets for industrial exports, investment opportunities, land for settlements, etc.[2] It is an empire with purely economic goals, in which colonial policy is an instrument to extract rents and resources from colonized territories as well as to achieve other economic objectives. There could be secondary purposes, but economic interests prevail. Therefore, this style of imperialism is characterized by a colonial strategy based on an economic calculus. This implies a pragmatic colonial policy, which must be sensitive to initial conditions, since the specific policy that maximizes rents will vary on the basis of the particular circumstances encountered in each territory by Europeans upon their arrival. Consequently, policies and institutions established by the metropolitan power will be diverse, since they respond to the specific characteristics of each colony. Sometimes the best policy may be—for example—to create settler colonies to cultivate fertile lands and serve as an outlet for overpopulation in the metropolis, while other times to establish extractive colonies aimed at exploiting indigenous population through forced labor in mining or plantations. Thus, in the case of 'economically-oriented' imperialism, institutions implanted by the colonizer depend on initial conditions or endowments. This makes the *endowment view* fully applicable, since European powers—guided by economic incentives—are likely to establish extractive institutions in places with large endowments.

'Politically-oriented' imperialism is very different.[3] The imperial power is guided by certain ideals, an ideology or a religion that it aims to expand all over

[1]The rich literature on the determinants of European imperialism considers many factors behind this phenomenon. Initially, the works of Hobson (1902) and Lenin (1917), among others, made the economic explanations of imperialism very popular. Over time this view was highly criticized and a number of alternative explanations emerged that considered factors as diverse as domestic politics, popular pressure, geopolitics or crises on the periphery (see Fieldhouse 1973; Hobsbawn 1987). Although the historiographical discussion is mainly focused on nineteenth-century European imperialism, many of the arguments are applicable to colonialism in general.

[2]See Fieldhouse (1973) for an overview of the different economic theories on imperialism.

[3]Bringing to the debate this non-economic side of imperialism is to some extent novel because the recent economic literature on the consequences of European colonialism has emphasized much more economic explanations of colonial strategies than other kinds of explanations (e.g., Acemoglu et al. 2001, 2002; Engerman and Sokoloff 1997, 2000; Lange et al. 2006). As noted by Hobsbawn (1987), economic motivations are important for imperialism, but there are also political, emotional, ideological and patriotic impulses.

the world. The main feature of the colonial strategy consists of expanding the territorial domains of the empire for non-economic reasons such as the glory or prestige of the nation or religious-ideological motives. There may be also economic exploitation of colonial territories through tributes or other methods, but the distinctive feature is that the imperial enterprise cannot be explained by economic goals. The primary source behind imperial expansion is different. The metropolitan power pursues to expand its influence, enlarge the empire and bring its civilization to many parts of the world. The lack of an instrumental-economic calculus and the goal of extending the metropolitan political dominion lead to a uniform colonial policy insensitive to initial conditions. In this style of imperialism the metropolitan power will be disinclined to grant local autonomy in government to its subjects. Centralism and uniformity in colonial policies and institutions are the hallmarks of this type of empire. Consequently, similar institutional arrangements—which try to resemble those of the metropolis—are implanted in all colonies of the empire, irrespective of their particular characteristics. Therefore, in this style of imperialism the *endowment view* is not applicable.

Domestic conditions in the metropolis determine in each case the style of imperialism adopted.[4] Since domestic conditions or national circumstances may change in space (among countries) and time (over periods or epochs), two countries in the same period may adopt different styles of imperialism and, also, one country may change its style along different periods. It is impossible to exhaustively list what specific conditions lead to one style of imperialism or another. However, we can make some reasonable assumptions. First, the political regime is a very important element to take into account. On the one hand, we can consider a liberal polity characterized by several centers of power and a number of diverse interests represented by different segments of the population, which have the capacity to influence political action of the government. As a result, colonial policy probably aims to satisfy the diverse interests existing in society (some of them of economic nature). Arguably, this political regime leads to an 'economically-oriented' style of imperialism. On the other hand, we can consider a monolithic, centralistic and bureaucratic political regime, in which few social interests influence government action and a high degree of military pressure and large doses of ideology are present. This other regime is more associated with the features of 'politically-oriented' imperialism, as described above.

Second, the economic model of the metropolis also matters.[5] Arguably, the more important the role of the market and the private initiative, the more pronounced the

---

[4]Domestic conditions do not only matter for the style of imperialism adopted (as we define it), but also for many other aspects related to colonial policies such as the quality of the legal system transplanted and so on. However, our focus here is on the relationship between domestic conditions and the style of imperialism, leaving aside their other implications.

[5]This point has been emphasized by Lange et al. (2006), who differentiate between 'mercantilist' and 'liberal' economic models. In both cases the implications are a colonial policy sensitive to initial endowments. We depart from these authors by trying to identify those features of the economic regime that can affect the style of imperialism.

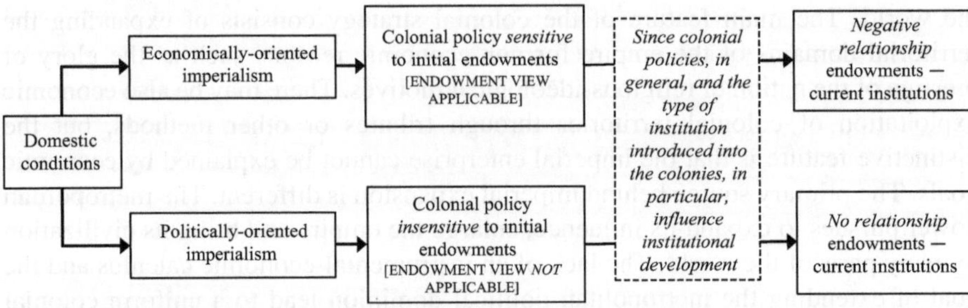

Fig. 3.1 A model of two styles of imperialism

'economically-oriented' character of the empire, since colonial policy will be more influenced by private economic agents seeking profit. On the contrary, the more prevalent the role of the state in allocating resources and the public initiative, the more pronounced the 'politically-oriented' character of the empire and the higher the chances that a uniform colonial policy is adopted.

Third, geographic conditions are also important. For instance, islands and small coastal countries are more dependent on outside resources to satisfy economic needs and—at the same time—have greater opportunity of overseas contacts, which may favor an 'economically-oriented' style of imperialism. Following this argument, continental powers are not so externally dependent and have lower incentives to seek resources abroad. Also, from a military point of view, continental countries require larger armies to defend borders. Since armies are closely associated with discipline, centralization and bureaucracy, it is plausible to consider a link between military requirements derived from geographical location and political centralization and absolutism, which are factors associated with the 'politically-oriented' style of imperialism. Finally, other historical contingencies may be even more important, such as the success of a revolution, a military defeat, threat to national security, international competition and so on. In short, the chances to adopt a 'politically-oriented' style of imperialism will be higher when the presence of the following elements is more pronounced: ideology, religion, centralism, bureaucratism, absolutism, militarism, economic statism, interventionism, little inclination to grant local government autonomy and the character of the mainland (continental, larger country area, etc.).

As a corollary, the identity of the colonizing country (i.e., *colonial origin*), which implies a particular style of imperialism derived from its domestic conditions, is what ultimately determines whether endowments play or not a role in shaping colonial policies and institutions. Since colonial policies, in general, and the type of institution introduced into the colonies, in particular, influence subsequent institutional development, the predictions of our model are: (1) endowments are negatively related to current institutions among former colonies of an 'economically-oriented' empire, and (2) endowments are *not* related to current institutions among colonies of a 'politically-oriented' empire. This is shown in Fig. 3.1, which represents schematically our theoretical framework. The model presented is useful because it helps explain how domestic conditions in the metropolis and initial endowments in the colonies influenced the impact of European colonialism on institutional development. One more thing should be noted. The 'economically-oriented' and the 'politically-oriented' styles of imperialism are ideal types and as such they are not strictly observable in the real world. They can be considered as two extreme cases, between which there is a continuous line in which historical colonial experiences can be placed. We next try to apply the model to the real colonial experiences of the main European powers in an attempt to determine how close, if any, they are to either style of imperialism.

3.2 An Application to European Colonial Empires

3.2.1 The British Empire

Concerning the case of Britain, their domestic conditions led this country to follow a style of imperialism closer to the 'economically-oriented' type.[6] Britain had a liberal political and economic regime in which the private initiative and the power of the bourgeoisie played an important role in society. Also, its insularity and limited territory increased the dependence on outside resources. In this sense, the West Indies were a leading source of raw cotton for the British industry in the late eighteenth century and Canada became the supplier of timber for building Britain's powerful navy. In fact, "energy efforts were made to create resource pools within the empire" (Cain and Hopkins 1980, p. 473). Thus, the main purpose of British colonial policy was to satisfy the economic needs of the metropolis, which could consist of resources, markets or land for settlements. Hobsbawn (1987) points out that Britain was the country where imperialism was more important, since its economic supremacy hinged on the special relation with overseas markets and sources of raw materials. Accordingly, it was essential for the British economy to preserve its privileged access to the non-European world.

[6]Although in our theoretical framework we raise the possibility that domestic conditions can change over time and so the style of imperialism, in the discussion that follows we consider that domestic conditions were essentially persistent so that each imperial power can be characterized by one style of imperialism. This assumption seems stronger for colonial empires spanning over several centuries, but it is still a reasonable assumption according to historical evidence. For example, Cain and Hopkins (1980) state that their interpretation about the close relationship between domestic economy and British imperial expansion in the interval 1750–1914 is applicable to the entire history of British colonial expansion. Notwithstanding, in the empirical analysis we control for the year of colonization of each colony in order to reduce the possible impact derived from a change in domestic conditions in the metropolis.

There is a close connection between the British presence abroad and the economic needs of the metropolis (Cain and Hopkins 1980).[7]

Instrumented through an 'economically-oriented' style of imperialism, the British conducted a pragmatic colonial policy that was adapted to the particular conditions found in the territories upon their arrival. Britain opted for a "flexible" colonial administration system, which was variable to local conditions and featured a high degree of local autonomy. Institutional arrangements sharply varied across colonies and the particular purposes for their occupation determined their character and function (Fieldhouse 1966). As suggested by Lange et al. (2006), where Britain found relatively advanced, densely populated territories, they did not settle massively and instead they created extractive states in many instances instrumented through *indirect colonialism*. Even though this system constituted a low-cost means of administering large territories, which was important due to Britain's reluctance to subsidize the colonies (Fieldhouse 1973), it empowered indigenous leaders and incorporated customary institutions into the overall structure of colonial domination, thereby entailing a low level of institutional transfer from Britain (Lange 2004).[8] In Mamdani's (1996) words, Britain's wide application of indirect rule in Africa and in some parts of Asia generated a "bifurcated state", in which two separate and incompatible forms of ruling coexisted. One dominated by the colonial administration, and another one controlled by a large network of unconstrained chiefs. This implied that the rural areas could be controlled and ruled by chiefs, whereas a tiny colonial administration could only control the colonial capital city but was unable to broadcast power over the countryside. Indirect rule thus promoted

[7]The overseas expansion "between 1750 and 1914 can be explained satisfactorily by linking it with the process of modernization in Britain"; the various phases of the imperial expansion "were closely connected with the development of the domestic economy, the shifting balance of social and political forces which this development entailed, and the varying intensity of Britain's economic and political rivalry with other powers." (Cain and Hopkins 1980, p. 489). This connection between economy and colonial empire is sometimes not apparently evident. Thus, many colonies were occupied for strategic reasons, but it is important to note that most of the times the strategic motivation was related to controlling the access to different regions considered vital for trading and shipping interests. In this sense, India was the center of British global colonial strategy precisely because it was of vital importance to the British economy (Hobsbawn 1987). This colony was crucial for British exports as well as for maintaining its international financial position. Within this global strategy, the trade-oriented colonies of Hong Kong and Singapore were also key to articulating overseas exchange.

[8]Despite the fact indirect rule was previously applied in some parts of India, Lord Lugard is known to be the colonial administrator that theorized it. Lugard (1919, p. 298) argues for "a single Government in which the native chiefs have well-defined duties and an acknowledged status equalling with the British officials" (see also Lugard 1922). Indirect rule was thus based on cooperation, rather than subordination as in the French case (Crowder 1964; Betts 1985). Along similar lines, Lange (2004, p. 906) argues that the most commonly view for indirect rule is that of Fisher (1991) who describes it as "the incorporation of indigenous institutions—not simply individuals—into an overall structure of colonial domination. From this view, direct rule differs from indirect rule in that it involves the construction of a complete system of colonial domination that lacks any relatively autonomous indigenous component, yet which might be staffed overwhelmingly by indigenous actors."

decentralized despotism and lack of centralized control, which led to ineffective central administrations unable to provide the necessary public goods and services to raise economic prosperity (Lange 2004).[9]

In contrast, where the British encountered sparsely populated territories and less complex societies, they settled massively and built their own political and institutional arrangements featuring high levels of self-government, without having to replace pre-existing organizational structures (e.g., the U.S., Canada and Australasia). This colonial system constitutes an extreme form of direct rule. Therefore, British colonial policy was sensitive to initial conditions. This makes the *endowment view* broadly applicable, since better (worse) institutions were introduced in places with scarce (large) endowments.

3.2.2 The French Empire

Unlike Britain, France adopted a style of imperialism closer to the 'politically-oriented' type. Its character of continental power, the historical centralism and bureaucratism, the revolutionary ideological exaltation and some contingencies such as the military defeat in the Franco-Prussian war led France to follow this style of imperialism. On ideological grounds, French colonialism was rooted in the ideal of assimilation and the consideration of the colonies as an intrinsic part of the Republic (Fieldhouse 1966). The objectives of the empire were the creation of *La Plus Grande France* and the extension of the benefits of *la civilisation française* to the colonial population. Even as late as after World War II, these aspirations dominated French official thinking (Lewis 1962).[10] Unlike the British, French

[9]Lange (2004) provides evidence for 33 former British colonies that indirect rule is strongly and negatively associated with several proxies for postcolonial political development. Comparing the direct and indirect rule systems within India, Iyer (2010) shows that directly ruled areas of British India exhibit significantly lower levels of postcolonial development, as measured through schooling or health provision. A key to understanding why the natives states, which were indirectly ruled, led to better outcomes lays in the fact that hereditary kings had incentives to properly govern their territories, since they could be removed in the event of misrule. In the case of directly ruled areas, it is also important the land revenue system in place. Whenever the ruler was in charge of collecting the revenue directly from cultivators (cultivator-based land revenue system), public good outcomes were superior to those cases in which revenue collection was carried out by landlords (landlord-based land revenue system). The good performance of the indirect rule exercised by hereditary kings in the native states contrasts with that of the indirect rule applied by landlords in British India. This is because, unlike hereditary kings, landlords in British India were not subject to removal in the case of misrule. Therefore, Iyer's overall results are not that different from those obtained for indirectly ruled areas in Africa. Whenever the incentives faced by the local administrator are not appropriate, indirect rule can lead to poor institutional governance, with negative repercussions on postcolonial development.

[10]As a matter of fact, the Brazzaville statement of 1944 was "a reaffirmation of the ideal of 'assimilation' to the French nation as the logical outcome of the French 'mission civilisatrice'" (Lewis 1962, p. 129). Indeed, colonial subjects became citizens of France in 1946.

interest in the African continent was mainly driven by political pressures rather than by economic motives (Fieldhouse 1966, 1973; Fage 2002). Conquest of African territories was seen as a way to compensate for the humiliating defeat against the Germans in 1871 and constituted a great opportunity for military promotion (de Sousa and Lochard 2012). According to Crowder (1968, p. 70), for France the occupation of extensive areas was more important than the quality of the land occupied, whereas "Britain gained the smaller but richer part of West Africa".[11]

Therefore, the ideological peculiarities and the leading role played by political and military motives are responsible for the features of the French style of imperialism, with important implications for the colonial policies adopted and institutional arrangements established. The French empire was characterized by a relatively uniform administrative-institutional system that was not sensitive to the particularities of the colonial territories. Compared to the British, it was more based on direct rule and a centralized bureaucratic control of colonial dominions (Fieldhouse 1966). The colonial empire had clear formal rules and chain of command, and indigenous chiefs were not an autonomous part in the system of colonial control (Crowder 1964). The ultimate goal of assimilating (integrating) the colonies into a "Greater France" implied centralism, lack of local autonomy and uniformity in order to assimilate indigenous institutions and culture to those of the mother country (Fieldhouse 1966; Blanton et al. 2001). In fact, French assimilation has been associated with "applying a uniform set of rules in all colonies without taking into account differences in size, distance from France, social organization, religious patterns, economic development, etc." (Lewis 1962, p. 131). All this implies a colonial policy largely insensitive to initial conditions, which makes the *endowment view* inapplicable.[12]

As our theoretical framework suggests, French and British imperialism needs to be related to their domestic history (Kumar 2006). Indeed, referring to British indirect rule, Perham (1934, p. 332) pointed out that it "derives partly from our conservatism, with its sense of historical continuity and its aristocratic tradition. Our experience has not taught us to believe in fresh constitutional starts, or in the

[11]According to Fieldhouse (1973), economic factors played little role in the French decision to occupy Algiers in 1830, which must be explained by domestic political factors, in particular, the desire to improve government prestige. Importantly, Algeria provides useful hints for the understanding of subsequent French imperialism, which was a model of colonial expansion due mainly to political and military considerations rather than to the economic needs of the metropolis. However, despite the limited economic importance of colonies for a continental power like France, supporters of imperialism gave economic justifications for them and, obviously, once territories were occupied France tried to obtain some economic advantage, though with little success.

[12]Our view is also broadly supported by Zweigert and Kötz (1998, p. 113) who claim that "French colonial policy always sought in the long-run to assimilate the native populations. English policy was different: true to the principle of 'Indirect Rule', English colonial administrators relied as much as possible on existing native rulers, kept the local courts decentralized, [. . ..]. The French, on the other hand, inspired by egalitarian ideals of the Great Revolution and a belief in the superiority of 'civilisation française', constantly strove to lead the native population step by step to the higher level of metropolitan culture".

existence of political principles of universal applicability". Indirect rule "derives equally from our liberalism with its respect for the freedom of others". Regarding French higher reliance on direct administration, Whittlesey (1937, p. 371) points out that "[i]t is a method of political control which happens to fit the character and traditions of the French people. Their feeling for logical systems and order would not accept a scheme of government which varied from place to place".

3.2.3 The Spanish Empire

Regarding the Spanish empire, its categorization as 'economically' or 'politically' oriented is more problematic. Several domestic conditions, such as its character of continental power, the religious fervor and the increased power of the centralized monarchy, favored a 'politically-oriented' style of imperialism. However, other factors, such as the limited demographic and financial resources of the metropolis and the need for valuable commodities such as silver and gold to finance European wars, acted in favor of an 'economically-oriented' style. Thus, on the one hand, Spain "formally" conducted a homogeneous colonial policy in the New World. The same legal rules were applicable to all colonies (e.g., *Recopilación de las Indias* published by Charles II in 1680) and the same general institutional organization was imposed on all of them. During three centuries, Spanish American colonies were ruled by a common legislation, a central administration consisting of a centralized and bureaucratic government, and a single religion and culture (Fieldhouse 1966). But, on the other hand, Spain's resources were limited and Spaniards were particularly interested in those territories where the extraction of rents could be larger. These places were the Aztec and Inca empires, in which the intensity of Spanish colonialism was higher.[13] As suggested by Lange et al. (2006), Spain conducted intensive colonialism in more prosperous, densely populated and hierarchical societies with the aim of extracting resources through coercive labor without having to alter radically pre-existing economic structures. In other places of Latin America, particularly in the Southern Cone, the attractiveness of extracting rents was lower, which led to a less intensive level of Spanish colonialism. This translated into less pervasive effects from exploitation policies, which gave rise to the construction of more egalitarian societies, thereby leaving more room for subsequent institutional development.

An important difference with respect to the other empires is that Spanish colonialism, with some minor exceptions, was concentrated in the sixteenth, seventeenth and eighteenth centuries. This period corresponds to that identified by Olsson (2009) as the 'mercantilist' wave of colonialism, which had quite different

[13]The Spaniards employed a system of coercive labor known as *encomienda* with the aim of exploiting the densely populated territories of the Aztec and Inca empires, which was accompanied by a complex system of monopolies and trade regulations set up with extractive purposes.

characteristics relative to the subsequent 'imperialist' period.[14] Besides, since almost all Spanish American colonies achieved their independence at the beginning of the nineteenth century, other factors over this long postcolonial period may also have influenced their institutional development. These include the waves of European immigrants in the nineteenth and early twentieth centuries that affected mainly the Southern Cone countries.[15] To sum up, the Spanish empire is a hybrid between the 'economically-oriented' and the 'politically-oriented' categories, which makes the *endowment view* partially applicable.[16]

3.2.4 The Portuguese Empire

Portugal had an important colonial empire that with ups and downs spanned from the late fifteenth century, with the occupation of Cape Verde, to the late twentieth century, with the independence of the African colonies. This makes the Portuguese colonial empire the lengthiest. Portugal is a small coastal country opened to the Atlantic and, possibly, this fact influenced its style of imperialism, which sought to meet the economic needs and overcome the limitations of the metropolis. Its first colonial empire was trade-oriented and consisted mainly of a number of seaports located on the route to the East Indies. The second empire was more profitable since it rested on plantations and mines in Brazil, its huge colony in South America (Clarence-Smith 1985). The Portuguese presence in Atlantic slave trade was very important, with Cape Verde constituting a prominent enclave for that. They were actually the ones who invented the plantation system employing slaves as labor

[14]Differences across both periods range from innovation in tropical medicine to colonists' incentives and choice sets (i.e., institutions of European countries in both waves were very different and so was the range of options about the type of institution to implant). This fact, along with the possibility that domestic conditions change over time, supports the inclusion of the year of colonization in the empirical analysis.

[15]This suggests that these postcolonial flows of Europeans may be partly responsible for the better outcomes observed nowadays in these countries. However, the fact of choosing Argentina, Uruguay and Chile as major destinations responds, among other reasons, to their better socio-institutional features inherited from the colonial period.

[16]Some authors like Grafe and Irigoin (2006) and Irigoin and Grafe (2008) argue against conventional wisdom that supports that the Spanish Empire had a purely extractive character. On the one hand, they claim that the system of governance in colonial Spanish America was highly negotiated rather than absolutist, since the colonial tax system depended to a large extent on regional and local decision-making and the Crown could hardly control the system. On the other, their evidence on the functioning of colonial fiscal systems points to the fact that the aim of the metropolis was not to extract revenues from the colonies for its own benefit. Rather, it aimed at redistributing the revenues to those regions with insufficient revenues as well as at making the colonies self-sufficient and autonomous in deciding how to allocate these interregional transfers. According to these authors, an alignment in fiscal policy between the interests of the elites and the Crown by fostering economic growth may explain why the empire survived as a single political unit over a period of 300 years.

force in Brazil (Fieldhouse 1966). In addition, Portugal created an important colonial empire in Africa. As in earlier periods, the driving force behind the imperial expansion of the nineteenth and twentieth centuries in Africa was to satisfy domestic economic needs, particularly, the search for markets and the need for foreign exchange (Clarence-Smith 1985; de Sousa Ferreira 1974).[17] Therefore, it can be argued that Portugal followed an 'economically-oriented' style of imperialism and adopted a colonial strategy that aims to extract rents from colonized territories, which—according to our framework—is sensitive to initial conditions.

3.2.5 The Remainder Empires

Regarding the other colonial empires, the small number of former colonies belonging to each of these empires prevents us from conducting a deep analysis. However, it is interesting to provide at least a brief overview. We begin with the Italian colonial empire that was a clear case of nineteenth-century chauvinism and can thus be considered as 'politically-oriented'. This newly reunified country tried to occupy very unattractive territories from an economic point of view, such as large tracts of desert and mountains in Africa, only with the aim of strengthening its position as a great power (Hobsbawn 1987). Since it was too weak to compete in Europe, Italy directed its aspirations to North Africa as the heir of ancient Rome (Fieldhouse 1973). In contrast, the Netherlands adopted a style of imperialism much closer to the 'economically-oriented'. For this liberal and small coastal country, its colonial empire was very important from an economic perspective (Hobsbawn 1987). Over three centuries, the Dutch obtained good economic benefits from their colony in South Asia, Indonesia, where they extensively introduced the plantation system and applied indirect rule. Regarding Belgian possessions, the reason for the creation of the Congo Free State by Leopoldo II was, indeed, to imitate the Dutch example and make profits. Thus, this colony, which until 1908 was the king's private asset, had a clear economic purpose. Initially, it was ruled by a minimal government that treated the native population very rudely and later, when it became an official colony, indirect rule was widely applied (Fieldhouse 1966).

It remains to review the main features of two major continental powers. Germany had a brief colonial empire that was a clear outcome of the partition of Africa in the Berlin Conference of 1885. German African colonies offered few economic opportunities and their occupation responded to domestic reasons such as prestige for a recently unified nation, popular pressure and the search for electoral support

[17]According to de Sousa Ferreira (1974, p. 33), "[t]he colonies played a particular and very important role in the Portuguese economy. First, they provided a protected market, supplying raw materials at cheaper prices than world market rates and buying Portuguese products for which, in general, foreign demand is low. Secondly, their foreign exchange earnings from exports and services alleviated the chronic deficit on Portugal's balance of trade". All this occurred despite the alleged civilizing mission that Portuguese authorities attributed to the colonial enterprise.

and alliances (Hobsbawn 1987; Fieldhouse 1973). In this sense, Bismarck said: "All this colonial business is a sham, but we need it for the elections" (von Strandmann 1969, p. 146). Therefore, German imperialism style is clearly 'politically-oriented'. Finally, regarding the Russian imperial expansion in the nineteenth and twentieth centuries, the decisive factor was the defense of the existing imperial domains against possible threats from rival powers, whereas economic interests played a limited role. Russian impulse to territorial expansion derived from historical ideas close to the Schumpeter's (1919) model of atavistic behavioral patterns, i.e., the state's disposition to an unlimited expansion of borders (Fieldhouse 1973). Hence, we can also label Russian imperialism as 'politically-oriented'.

3.3 Some General Observations Between Domestic Conditions and the Style of Imperialism

Our model implies that domestic conditions in the metropolis determine the style of imperialism. For illustrative purposes, Table 3.1 shows the value of some indicators related to domestic conditions in the European colonial powers and their style of imperialism. The domestic conditions considered are the continental character of the metropolis measured by its surface area, the openness of the political regime in

Table 3.1 Domestic conditions and styles of imperialism

Country	Surface area	*Polity2* (average nineteenth century)	Population density (average nineteenth century)	Style of imperialism
Belgium	30,530	6.4	159.1	Economically oriented
France	549,190	4.4	67.1	Politically oriented
Germany	540,857	1.6	69.0	Politically oriented
Italy	301,340	3.0	87.5	Politically oriented
Netherlands	41,530	2.9	83.8	Economically oriented
Portugal	92,120	2.6	45.2	Economically oriented
Russian Federation	17,098,240	0.0	3.0	Politically oriented
Spain	505,000	3.6	30.6	Hybrid
United Kingdom	243,610	6.0	124.1	Economically oriented

Notes: *Polity2* variable is rescaled, taking values from 0 (strongly autocratic) to 10 (strongly democratic). Regarding Germany, it is considered the German Empire that lasted from 1871 to 1914. Variable descriptions are provided in Table A.1

the nineteenth century (polity2) and the demographic pressure for resources in the nineteenth century measured by population density. Consistent with our model, the four countries with the lowest surface area followed an 'economically-oriented' style of imperialism, the others—with the exception of Spain (a hybrid style)—followed a 'politically-oriented' style. Also, partially consistent with our argument, the two more politically opened regimes (Belgium and Britain) followed an 'economically-oriented' type, whereas the two less opened regimes adopted a 'politically-oriented' type, with the correlation being less clear in the intermediate positions. Regarding population density, countries with higher values are generally associated with an 'economically-oriented' style (Belgium, the Netherlands and Britain).

Chapter 4
Empirical Methodology and Baseline Regression Results

Abstract This chapter describes the estimation methodology and the data. The model of colonial empires contains testable predictions. Among former colonies of European powers that adopted an 'economically-oriented' style of imperialism a negative relationship between initial endowments and current institutions is expected, whereas for colonial empires adopting a 'politically-oriented' style no such relationship is expected. These hypotheses are tested via an interaction model in which the effect of endowments on current institutions for each colonial empire can be differentiated. As far as the data are concerned, among all possible indicators of institutional quality, we choose *rule of law*. Regarding the measure of endowments, we choose population density in 1500, which represents the precolonial level of development and a crucial factor of production in colonial times. The estimation of a basic additive model provides evidence that institutions depend significantly on colonizer identity and endowments, which is consistent with the *endowment* and *colonial origin views*. However, since heterogeneity in the relationship between endowments and current institutions across colonial empires is expected, we estimate a baseline interaction model. The evidence indicates that not all colonial powers reacted in the same way to the level of precolonial endowments. Britain followed an 'economically-oriented' style of imperialism and, as such, we observe that the evidence fits well the *endowment view*, since there is a negative and highly significant relationship between initial endowments and current institutions among British colonies. France, by contrast, adopted a 'politically-oriented' style of imperialism and, as such, we find that the *endowment view* does not hold, as reflected in the insignificant coefficient on the interaction term. Regarding the Spanish colonial empire, which is a hybrid between both styles, our model predicts partial applicability of the *endowment view*, which is congruent with a reported negative coefficient on the interaction term that is smaller (in absolute terms) than that on British colonies and only marginally significant. Portuguese former colonies also show a pattern consistent with the categorization of the empire as 'economically-oriented', since endowments exert a negative effect on institutions.

D. Oto-Peralías, D. Romero-Ávila, *Colonial Theories of Institutional Development*, Contributions to Economics, DOI 10.1007/978-3-319-54127-3_4

4.1 Empirical Strategy and Data Description

The model of colonial empires presented in the previous chapter contains testable predictions (see Fig. 3.1). Among former colonies of European powers that adopted an 'economically-oriented' style of imperialism we expect to find a negative relationship between initial endowments and current institutions, whereas for colonial empires adopting a 'politically-oriented' style no such relationship is expected. The best way to test these hypotheses is by using an interaction model in which we can differentiate the effect of endowments on current institutions for each colonial empire. Thus, we estimate the following equation that allows for the possibility of heterogeneity in the coefficient on endowments:

$$\begin{aligned} \mathit{instit}_i = {} & \alpha + \beta_1 \cdot \mathit{french}_i + \beta_2 \cdot \mathit{spanish}_i + \beta_3 \cdot \mathit{portug}_i + \beta_4 \cdot \mathit{other}_i + \beta_5 \\ & \cdot \mathit{uk} \times \mathit{endow}_i + \beta_6 \cdot \mathit{french} \times \mathit{endow}_i + \beta_7 \cdot \mathit{spanish} \times \mathit{endow}_i \\ & + \beta_8 \cdot \mathit{portug} \times \mathit{endow}_i + \beta_9 \cdot \mathit{other} \times \mathit{endow}_i + \beta_{10} \cdot \mathit{year\_colon}_i \\ & + \varepsilon_i \end{aligned} \tag{4.1}$$

where instit_i is our measure of institutions, α is a constant term, french_i, $\mathit{spanish}_i$, portug_i and other_i are dummy variables representing whether the colonizer is France, Spain, Portugal or other powers (Britain being the reference group, reflected in the constant term), endow_i represents the endowments indicator, $\mathit{year\_colon}_i$ stands for years since colonization, and ε_i is the error term.

Among all possible indicators of institutional quality, we choose *rule of law*, from the World Bank Institute (Kaufmann et al. 2009). Compared to other sources, this one has a wider coverage of countries and entails indicators that are built on the basis of a very elaborate and careful methodology (Arndt and Oman 2006). Compared to other indicators of the same source, *rule of law* better reflects the institutional environment that promotes economic development. Many authors have emphasized the importance of property rights, contract enforcement, legal certainty and independent judiciary, as prerequisites for economic prosperity (North 1991; Knack and Keefer 1995; Levine 2005). Arguably, these concepts are part of what is known as rule of law. More specifically, according to Kaufmann et al. (2009), rule of law aggregates several indicators "capturing perceptions of the extent to which agents have confidence in and abide by the rules of society, and in particular the quality of contract enforcement, property rights, the police, and the courts, as well as the likelihood of crime and violence".[1]

[1]Other studies such as Dollar and Kraay (2003), Rodrik et al. (2004), and Bardhan (2005) have already used *rule of law* as an indicator of essential institutions for economic development. In contrast, Easterly and Levine (2003) use the average of the six indicators of Kaufmann et al. However, we prefer not to do that because the aggregation of composite indicators (i.e., indicators that result from the aggregation of other indicators) is inadequate, because at the end one does not know what the aggregate indicator exactly represents. Also, taking a simple average implies the loss of the statistical advantages of the aggregation method used by Kaufmann et al. (see Arndt and Oman 2006).

We create five groups of colonies, depending on whether they belonged to the British, French, Spanish, Portuguese or other empires. The identity of the colonizer is obtained from the classification of Teorell and Hadenius (2005), contained in the Quality of Government Dataset (Teorell et al. 2011). It is important to note that the Portuguese empire contains only five colonies in our sample. Hence, in the subsequent empirical analysis the evidence obtained for this colonial empire must be taken as highly suggestive or preliminary, but not as conclusive. Besides, we justify the creation of a residual group of 'minor' empires on the basis of the small number of observations belonging to each of these empires (this group contains nine former colonies for a total of five different colonizers).[2] In addition, by creating this group we do not mix these countries with former British, French, Spanish and Portuguese colonies, which allows for a clearer analysis of the effect of colonialism in these empires. An implication of the creation of this residual (and heterogeneous) group is that, for these colonial empires, we cannot test the relationship between endowments and institutions since what matters—according to our approach—is to examine this relationship *within* empires. Figure 4.1 shows the distribution of European colonial empires around the world.

Regarding the measure of endowments, we choose population density in 1500, which comes from Acemoglu et al. (2002) and represents the precolonial level of development. Population density is an important endowment indicator often quoted and widely used in the literature (e.g., Fieldhouse 1966; Engerman and Sokoloff 2000; Mahoney 2003; Lange 2004; Lange et al. 2006; Bruhn and Gallego 2012). It is available for a larger cross-section of countries than other indicators. Acemoglu et al. (2002) argue that population density is an adequate proxy for precolonial prosperity because only rich territories could afford to be areas with large populations.[3] In their view, colonial strategies depended largely on pre-existing wealth, since extractive institutions were established in more prosperous places. In addition, indigenous population represented a crucial factor of production in colonial times. According to Acemoglu and Robinson (2012), the key factor behind the different colonial strategies followed by Spain and England in the New World was the presence or not of native population that could be used as forced labor.

---

[2]We would also like to mention that we did not pursue the separation of German, Dutch, Italian and Belgian colonies, which are now grouped into 'other empires'. This is because German, Italian and to a lower extent Belgian colonization had a relatively short duration; and applicable to these four colonial powers, their colonization efforts led to the occupation of very few colonies each, whereas major colonial powers' colonialism was more widespread and generally involved much more extension. In statistical terms, the extremely short number of colonies for each of the 'minor' colonial powers and the potential loss of degrees of freedom prevent us from pursuing this any further.

[3]Compared to other possible indicators of precolonial prosperity, we prefer to use indigenous population density. As a matter of fact, precolonial urbanization rate may be a better proxy for pre-existing wealth, but it implies a drastic reduction of the sample (for example, it does not include sub-Saharan Africa).

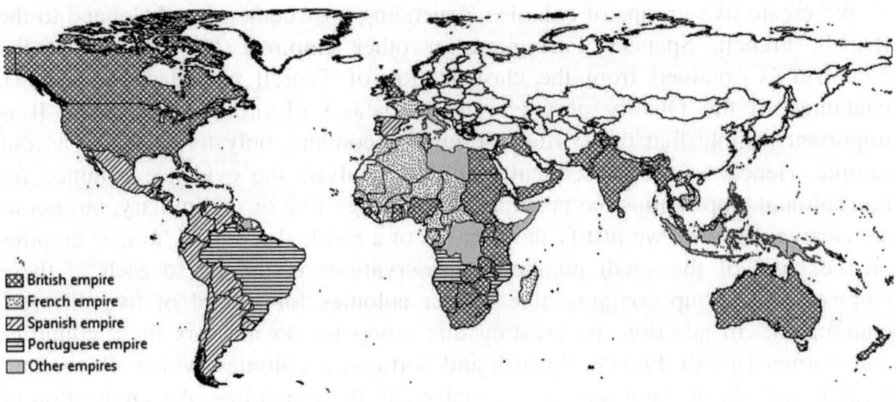

Fig. 4.1 European colonial empires. *Notes*: This map represents former European colonies as included in our baseline sample. *Source*: Teorell and Hadenius (2005)

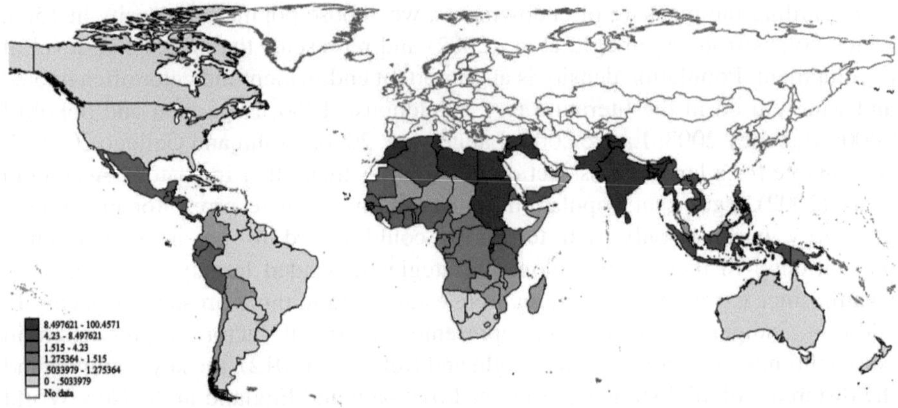

Fig. 4.2 Population density in 1500 in former European colonies. *Notes*: Population density in 1500. *Darker colors* mean higher population density. *Data source*: Acemoglu et al. (2002)

Figure 4.2 depicts a map with the values of the indicator of population density in 1500 for our sample of former colonies.

Our reference model also includes the variable 'years since colonization', which is obtained from Olsson (2009). We find it necessary to control for this factor since European colonialism was a historical phenomenon that lasted for five centuries, and circumstances existing at the beginning of the colonial enterprise were very different from those in subsequent periods (Olsson 2009). In addition, domestic conditions may change over time, which influence the style of imperialism adopted by the colonizer. Therefore, by controlling for 'years since colonization' we partially mitigate both problems.

The sample is restricted to overseas former colonies of Western powers, which excludes for example the Russian and Japanese empires and colonies within the European continent. There are a total of 102 ex-colonies for which data on the variables included in our reference model are available. Throughout the analysis, we use ordinary least squares (OLS) and report heteroscedasticity-consistent standard errors. We refer the reader to Table A.1 in the Appendix for descriptions and sources of the rest of the variables, to Table A.2 for a list of the colonies categorized by colonizer identity, and to Table A.3 for the descriptive statistics of all the variables used in the empirical analysis.

4.1.1 Alternative Endowment Variables

Following the *endowment view* literature, endowments are referred to as those initial conditions in colonized territories that were crucial in accounting for the colonial strategies followed by European powers. Even though the body of the study uses precolonial population density (indicating the extent of indigenous labor abundance and precolonial prosperity) as the main endowment variable, one needs to conceive endowments in a broad sense, also considering other aspects such as the tropical disease environment (endowments of *germs* in the terminology of Easterly and Levine 2003). Toward this end, we complement the analysis with the use of the potential mortality rate of European settlers, with the results being remarkably robust to the endowment indicator employed. This should not be surprising because the *endowment view* emphasizes that high levels of European settler mortality and indigenous population density are both generally associated with low European settlement and the predominance of extractive colonial strategies conducive to political structures aimed at exploiting indigenous resources, rather than building sound property rights (Acemoglu et al. 2001, 2002; Levine 2005). This is the case of most sub-Saharan African countries. In contrast, territories with favorable germ conditions and low indigenous population density like North America and Australasia attracted more European settlement, which led to inclusive institutions. Interestingly, the data indicate that even the African countries with a lower precolonial population density (Botswana and Namibia) were more densely populated and urbanized than Australia, Canada and the U.S. in precolonial times, coinciding with African historiography (Austin 2008). Also, some South Asian, Latin American and North African countries exhibit relatively high levels of population density and intermediate levels of European settler mortality. Besides, there are practically no countries displaying high settler mortality and low indigenous population density (see Fig. 4.3). Conceptually, we can thus safely relate *high levels of endowments* to those territories with high precolonial population density and medium/high potential settler mortality rates (thus implying adverse

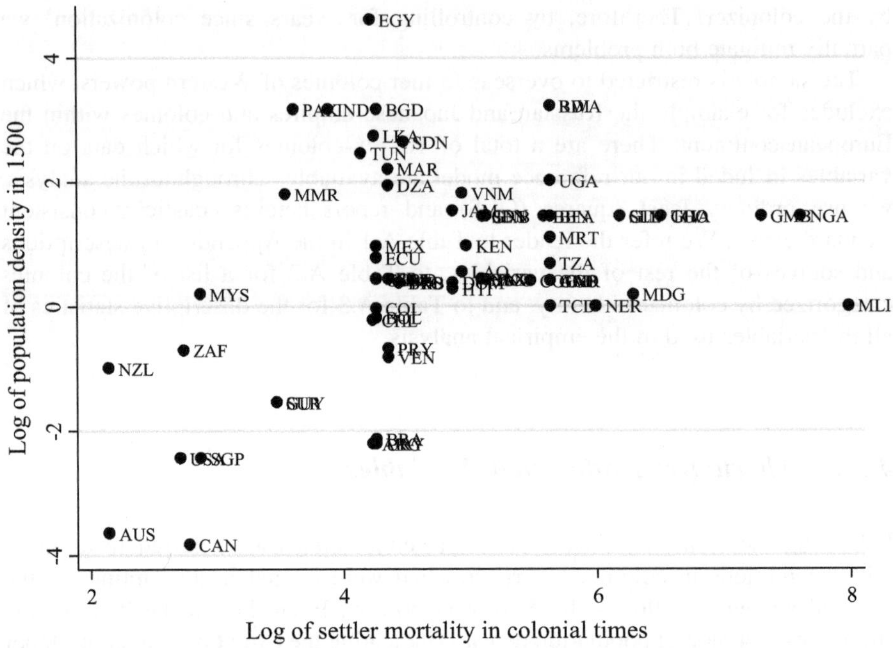

Fig. 4.3 Correlation between population density and settler mortality

endowments). Likewise, *low levels of endowments* can be associated with low indigenous population density and a favorable disease environment.

For robustness purposes, the sensitivity analysis also considers other alternative endowment variables: among others, the level of population density before colonization (since the level of precolonial population density in 1500 may be less relevant for the second wave of colonialism in the nineteenth century), measures of land suitability for sugar versus wheat (as emphasized by Engerman and Sokoloff 1997, 2000), measures of mineral resources abundance, and the natural log of the state antiquity index in the first year of colonization—as a measure of a long tradition of statehood (Bockstette et al. 2002). For illustrative purposes, Figs. 4.4 and 4.5 provide a map with the distribution of the potential mortality rate of European settlers and the sugar/wheat ratio in former colonies—as a measure of the suitability of land for sugarcane relative to wheat (Easterly 2007), respectively.

As a preliminary analysis of the empirical validity of the *endowment view* for some of the alternative endowment measures, Figs. A.1, A.2, A.3, and A.4 in the Appendix present scatterplots of rule of law against the level of population density in the year of colonization, the potential mortality rate of European settlers, the sugar-wheat ratio, and the log of the state antiquity index in the year of colonization, respectively. The figures also contain the coefficient and t-statistic of the relevant coefficient on the respective endowment. As depicted in Fig. A.1, the *endowment view* fits well the case of former British colonies, as reflected in a highly

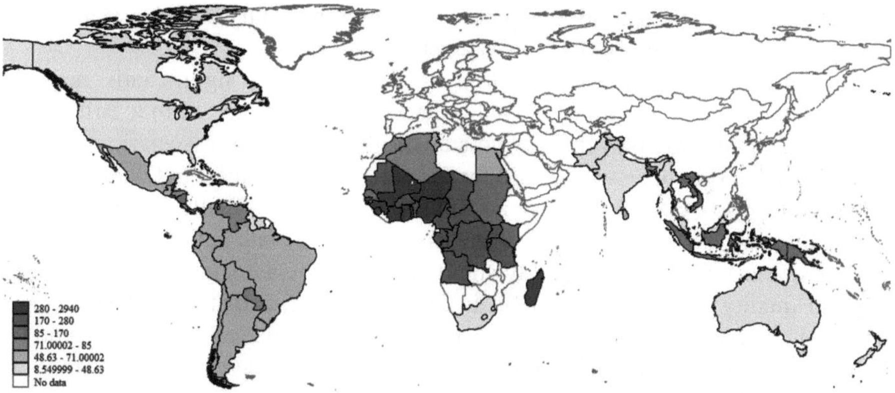

Fig. 4.4 Settler mortality rates in former European colonies. *Notes*: Settler mortality rates per thousand. *Darker colors* mean higher rates. *Data source*: Acemoglu et al. (2002)

Fig. 4.5 Sugar/wheat ratio in former European colonies. *Notes*: Sugar/wheat ratio (in levels). *Darker colors* mean higher ratios. *Data source*: Easterly (2007)

significant negative correlation between institutional quality and population density in the year of colonization. For Portuguese and Other Empires' colonies, there is also a highly significant negative correlation between rule of law and population density in the year of colonization, whereas the correlation is negative but statistically insignificant for Spanish colonies. By way of contrast, the *endowment view* does not hold at all for former French colonies, since there is a positive and statistically insignificant correlation between institutional quality and population density at the time of colonization for this group.

Similar evidence is found when the potential mortality rate of European settlers is used in Fig. A.2. On the one hand, there is a statistically significant negative correlation between rule of law and settler mortality for former British, Portuguese and Other Empires' colonies, thus supporting the *endowment view*. On the other, the relationship between institutional quality and settler mortality is highly statistically insignificant for former French and Spanish colonies.

Concerning the sugar-wheat ratio, Fig. A.3 depicts a significantly negative correlation between institutional quality and endowments for former British and Spanish colonies, whereas there is no statistically significant association between rule of law and the sugar-wheat ratio for former French colonies. In Other Empires' colonies, the association is positive and highly significant.[4] Finally, Fig. A.4 depicts the relationship between rule of law and the log of the state antiquity index at the time of colonization. A statistically significant negative association between institutional quality and early statehood is found for former British and Portuguese colonies, whereas the relationship is negative but statistically insignificant for Spanish and Other Empires' colonies. Again, the *endowment view* does not hold for the French, since there is a positive and statistically insignificant correlation between current institutional quality and early statehood.

In all, we observe clear-cut evidence of the *endowment view* across the four alternative endowment variables in former British and Portuguese colonies, and in some instances in former Spanish and Other Empires' colonies.[5] In sharp contrast, the *endowment view* does not hold for the French across the four endowments considered, as given by a highly insignificant correlation between rule of law and endowments.

4.2 Initial Results: Additive Model Versus Interaction Model

We begin by estimating a simple additive model in column 1 of Table 4.1, in which institutions depend on colonizer identity, endowments and years since colonization. The results indicate that endowments and all colonial dummies carry highly significant negative coefficients, which are consistent with the *endowment* and *colonial origin views*. On the one hand, a higher level of endowments reduces institutional quality as postulated by the great reversal hypothesis of Acemoglu et al. (2002). On the other, former British colonies have better institutions than others. The variable 'years since colonization' shows a positive and significant coefficient, which means that territories colonized earlier have developed in general better institutions.

However, since we suspect the existence of heterogeneity in the relationship between endowments and current institutions across colonial empires, we estimate our reference model in column 2. The results are in line with those outlined in

[4]For this endowment variable, there were not sufficient observations to construct the scatterplot in the Portuguese colonies' group.

[5]This evidence for the Other Empires' group would capture the 'economically-oriented' styles of imperialism of the Dutch and Belgium empires.

Table 4.1 Reference model

Dependent variable is rule of law (WGI)		
	Additive model	Reference model
	(1)	(2)
Endowments	−0.23*** (0.05)	
British colonies (Reference group)		
French colonies	−0.51*** (0.18)	−1.00*** (0.24)
Spanish colonies	−0.99*** (0.2)	−1.02*** (0.2)
Portuguese colonies	−1.15*** (0.31)	−1.19*** (0.31)
Other empires colonies	−0.96*** (0.24)	−1.22*** (0.31)
UK × Endowments		−0.3*** (0.07)
French × Endowments		0.21 (0.15)
Spanish × Endowments		−0.24* (0.14)
Portuguese × Endowments		−0.32* (0.16)
Other empires × Endowments		−0.02 (0.12)
Years since colonization	0.17*** (0.06)	0.17*** (0.06)
Constant	−0.25 (0.19)	−0.23 (0.19)
R^2	0.45	0.50
Number of observations	102	102

Notes: Rule of law ranges from −2.5 to 2.5, where a higher value indicates better institutions. Its year of measurement is 2000. The endowments indicator is log population density in 1500, from Acemoglu et al. (2002). Variable descriptions are provided in Table A.1. The sample contains non-European countries colonized by Western powers (Table A.2). Robust standard errors are in parentheses. *, ** and *** denote statistical significance at the 10, 5 and 1% level, respectively

Table 1.1 and Fig. 1.1 and indicate that not all colonial powers reacted in the same way to the level of precolonial endowments. According to our historical review, Britain followed an 'economically-oriented' style of imperialism and, consistent with our theoretical framework, we observe that the evidence fits well the *endowment view*, since there is a negative and highly significant relationship between initial endowments and current institutions among British colonies. France, by contrast, adopted a 'politically-oriented' style of imperialism and, consistent with our hypothesis, we find that the *endowment view* does not hold, as reflected in the insignificant coefficient on the interaction term. Regarding the Spanish colonial empire, which is a hybrid between both styles, our model predicts partial applicability of the *endowment view*, which is congruent with a reported negative coefficient on the interaction term that is smaller (in absolute terms) than that on British colonies and only marginally significant. Portuguese former colonies also show a pattern consistent with the categorization of the empire as 'economically-oriented', since endowments exert a negative effect on institutions.[6]

The reference model also allows us to analyze the relative effect of each colonial empire on current institutions. Since we use an interaction model, the effect of colonial identities on institutions should be calculated relative to the level of endowments. Toward this end, Fig. 4.6 plots the predicted value of institutions for each group of colonies and for a varying level of endowments. The figure shows that at low levels of endowments former British colonies enjoy better institutions than the other groups, particularly in relation to former French colonies. But as the level of endowments rises, the difference between British and French colonies vanishes. This becomes clearer in Fig. 4.7 that provides 95% confidence intervals. For values of the log of population density in 1500 lower than 1, British colonies exhibit superior institutions to French colonies, whereas for values above 1, the difference would no longer be statistically significant. The figures convey two important messages. On the one hand, there is clear heterogeneity in the relationship between endowments and institutions across different colonial empires; on the other, former British colonies do not always have better institutions than other empires. These findings partly qualify the *endowment view,* which is not applicable to all colonial empires. The evidence also questions a simplistic *colonial origin view*, since the effect of colonizer identity is conditional on the level of endowments.[7]

These results indicate that not all colonial powers reacted in the same way to the level of precolonial endowments. At the one extreme, in British and Spanish colonization the response to a high level of precolonial prosperity was the creation of extractive institutions that would hinder subsequent development. As suggested by Lange et al. (2006), mercantilist Spain conducted intensive colonialism in more prosperous, densely populated and hierarchical societies with the aim of extracting resources through coercive labor without having to alter radically pre-existing economic structures. In the case of a liberal power like Britain, in those territories where the British encountered relatively advanced, densely populated territories, they did not settle *en masse* and instead they created extractive states in many instances instrumented through *indirect colonialism.* This system empowered indigenous leaders and incorporated customary institutions into the system of

[6]However, as stressed above, this evidence must be taken as suggestive given the small number of Portuguese colonies in the sample.

[7]We also employ formal tests of differences in the effects of endowments in different empires. Wald tests clearly reject at the 1% level the null hypothesis of equality of coefficients between the interaction terms for British and French colonies. We also reject the equality of coefficients between the interaction terms for Spanish or Portuguese colonies relative to French colonies. Rejection of equality of coefficients at the 5% level or better generally holds even after controlling for a wide variety of factors, as done in the next chapter.

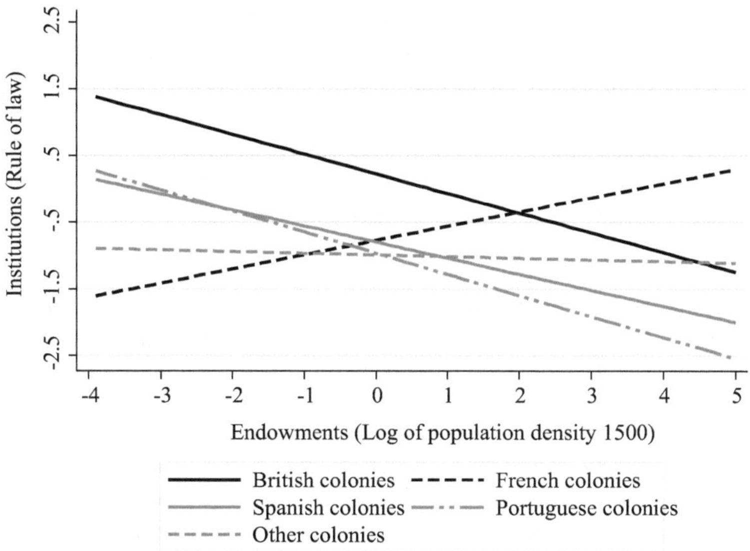

Fig. 4.6 Predicted values of rule of law by the level of population density and colonial empires. *Notes*: Predicted values correspond to column 2 of Table 4.1, using the mean value of the variable 'years since colonization'

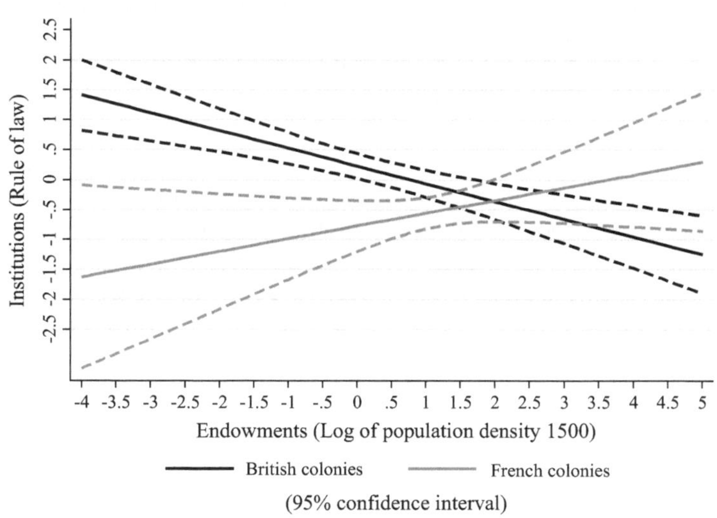

Fig. 4.7 Predicted values of rule of law by the level of population density for British and French colonies. *Notes*: Predicted values correspond to column 2 of Table 4.1, using the mean value of the variable 'years since colonization'

colonial administration, which led to a low level of institutional transfer from Britain (Lange 2004). Britain's wide application of indirect rule in Africa and in some parts of Asia generated a "bifurcated state", which promoted local despotism and lack of centralized control, thus leading to ineffective central administrations unable to provide the necessary public goods and services to raise economic prosperity. In contrast, in those places where the British encountered sparsely populated territories and less complex societies, they settled massively and build their own political and institutional arrangements, without having to replace pre-existing establishments (e.g., the U.S., Canada and Australasia).

At the other extreme, we find that for French colonialism the level of endowments is not related to institutional development. The lack of fit with respect to the *endowment view* can be explained by the peculiarities of French colonialism, which were rooted in the French ideal of assimilation and the consideration of the colonies as an intrinsic part of the Republic. The French empire was relatively more based on direct rule and a centralized bureaucratic control of colonial dominions. It had clear formal rules and chain of command, and indigenous chiefs were not an autonomous part in the system of colonial control. All these features led to a more homogeneous colonial administration largely invariant to the level of endowments. Indeed, conquest of African dominions was mainly driven by political pressures, since it was seen as a way to make up for the humiliating defeat against the Germans in 1871 and constituted a great opportunity for military promotion (de Sousa and Lochard 2012). Thus, the higher role played by political and military motives may also contribute to the more homogeneous French colonial system. These contrasting ways of implementing colonial strategies by the different Western powers in response to initial endowments can largely explain the variation in institutional development across colonies.

To summarize, our results so far show that although a simple additive model is able to illustrate that both endowments and colonizer identity matter, it fails to explain the heterogeneity in the relationship among colonial origin, endowments and institutions. The interaction model reveals the two sides of this heterogeneity: the impact of colonizer identity varies with the level of endowments and the relationship between endowments and institutions is very different across the former colonial empires. These findings have two major implications. First, the *endowment view* is not universally applicable, since it fails to fit the experience of former French colonies and 'Other Empires' colonies. Second, former British colonies are not always associated with better institutions since former French colonies equal the British when the level of endowments is high.

Chapter 5
Sensitivity to Alternative Theories

Abstract This chapter exhaustively controls for all possible factors framed within alternative theories that can explain postcolonial institutional development, which may be relevant omitted variables for the baseline interaction model. These factors comprise (1) distance to the metropolis of Western colonial powers to account for differences in transportation costs from the metropolis to the colonies, (2) geographic costs of control of colonial dominions, (3) time variation in the colonial strategies of different colonial powers within the two main waves of colonization, (4) religion, (5) ethnolinguistic fractionalization and the existence of several precolonial native cultures, (6) the possibility that precolonial political centralization affected the strategies of colonizers beyond its effect on the accountability of local chiefs, and (7) climate and other geographical factors. The evidence indicates that the alternative explanation associated with the timing and duration of colonialism fails to overturn our results regarding the sharp contrast across colonial powers in the effect of endowments on current institutions. Concerning the inclusion of sociological and anthropological factors, current institutional levels are driven by the institutional arrangements imposed externally by the colonizers in the colonies (which in turn differed on the basis of the initial level of endowments) rather than by the degree of precolonial centralization or ethnic homogeneity encountered by European colonial powers upon their arrival. In addition, our results do not appear to be simply caused by a correlation between institutions and colonies concentrated in areas with certain geographic or climatic features.

The validity of our approach can be called into question if other factors potentially correlated with our interaction terms between colonizer identity and endowments also affect current institutions. Therefore, in this chapter we exhaustively control for all possible factors framed within alternative theories that can explain postcolonial institutional development, which may be relevant omitted variables for the interaction model in column 2 in Table 4.1 that only includes indicators of endowments and colonial identity. These factors comprise (1) distance to the metropolis of Western colonial powers to account for differences in transportation costs from the metropolis to the colonies, (2) geographic costs of control of colonial dominions that may differ across colonial powers, which appear closely related to (1), (3) time variation in the colonial strategies of different colonial powers within the two main waves of colonization (Mercantilist vs. Imperialist), (4) religion,

D. Oto-Peralías, D. Romero-Ávila, *Colonial Theories of Institutional Development*, Contributions to Economics, DOI 10.1007/978-3-319-54127-3_5

(5) ethnolinguistic fractionalization and the existence of several precolonial native cultures, (6) the possibility that precolonial political centralization affected the strategies of colonizers beyond its effect on the accountability of local chiefs, and (7) climate and other geographical factors.

5.1 Timing and Duration of Colonization

Although our basic specification already controls for 'years since colonization', in the remainder columns of Table 5.1 we carefully consider the timing of colonization to account for the two different waves in the history of colonialism as well as for the possible variation in the intensity and extension of colonial domination (Grier 1999; Feyrer and Sacerdote 2009; Olsson 2009). In the reference model in column 1, the variable 'years since colonization' enters with a significantly positive coefficient, which may reflect the weak institutions of former African colonies whose colonization was delayed. Column 2 interacts 'years since colonization' with colonizer identity. The coefficients on this interaction for British and 'other empires' are significantly and positively related to current institutions, whereas our previous results regarding heterogeneity in the relationship between endowments and institutions across colonial empires appear fairly robust.

In addition, we incorporate several other variables related to the timing and duration of colonialism. First, it has been argued that a long post-colonial period allows countries to develop institutions according to their needs and eliminate inefficiencies from their colonial past (Olsson 2009; Levine 2005). This is captured by 'years since independence'. A second variable is the duration of colonial rule, which is thought to affect positively post-colonial development (Grier 1999; Feyrer and Sacerdote 2009; Olsson 2009). As a third variable that accounts for the two waves of colonization, we include the dummy 'colonization after 1850'. There are several reasons leading Olsson (2009) to choose 1850 as the cut-off year between both periods. The incentives of colonizers differed markedly in the two periods. Mercantilist colonization was mainly driven by the accumulation of valuables such as silver and gold—particularly for the Spanish and Portuguese–, whereas the British and Dutch were attracted by the attainment of monopoly positions through sugar plantations and the slave trade. By the early 1800s, the situation dramatically changed, since most former American colonies of Spain had gained independence and the United States and France had gone through a revolution. In addition, the mid 1800s constituted a period of rapid innovation in tropical medicine, with the generalization of quinine. This together with the increasing nationalistic rivalry among European powers, which led to the pre-emptive occupation of territories, ended up with the Scramble of Africa from around 1880 until the mid-1900s.

Columns 3, 5 and 7 control for 'years since independence', duration of colonial rule and a 'colonization after 1850' dummy, respectively. Column 9 includes a variable related to the colonies' economic potential: the number of years between when a territory was first sighted by Western Europeans and when it was first

Table 5.1 The timing of colonization

	Dependent variable is rule of law (WGI)										
	Additional control variables										
	Reference model	Years since colonization	Years since independence		Duration of colonization		Colonization after 1850		Gap between first sighted and colonized		All controls together
	(1)	(2)	(3)	(4)	(5)	(6)	(7)	(8)	(9)	(10)	(11)
Endowments											
British colonies (Reference group)											
French colonies	−1*** (0.24)	−0.64* (0.37)	−1.03*** (0.25)	−0.49* (0.28)	−1.03*** (0.25)	−0.88*** (0.32)	−0.99*** (0.24)	−1.56*** (0.36)	−0.98*** (0.24)	−1.22*** (0.3)	−1*** (0.24)
Spanish colonies	−1.02*** (0.2)	−0.73 (0.84)	−1.17*** (0.29)	−1.4*** (0.37)	−1.17*** (0.29)	−0.17 (0.65)	−0.98*** (0.2)	−0.98*** (0.22)	−1.01*** (0.21)	−1.22*** (0.25)	−1.12*** (0.29)
Portuguese colonies	−1.19*** (0.31)	−1.21* (0.71)	−1.18*** (0.31)	−0.51 (0.57)	−1.18*** (0.31)	−1.55** (0.6)	−1.14*** (0.32)	−1.26*** (0.43)	−1.18*** (0.32)	−1* (0.57)	−1.12*** (0.33)
Other empires colonies	−1.22*** (0.31)	−1.58*** (0.56)	−1.21*** (0.32)	−1.06** (0.52)	−1.21*** (0.32)	−1.61*** (0.55)	−1.2*** (0.31)	−0.97*** (0.27)	−1.22*** (0.32)	−1.04*** (0.36)	−1.2*** (0.32)
UK × Endowments	−0.3*** (0.07)	−0.29*** (0.07)	−0.29*** (0.07)	−0.27*** (0.07)	−0.29*** (0.07)	−0.29*** (0.07)	−0.3*** (0.06)	−0.29*** (0.07)	−0.3*** (0.07)	−0.29*** (0.07)	−0.29*** (0.07)
French × Endowments	0.21 (0.15)	0.23* (0.13)	0.23 (0.15)	0.17 (0.14)	0.23 (0.15)	0.26* (0.15)	0.21 (0.15)	0.23* (0.13)	0.19 (0.16)	0.07 (0.16)	0.2 (0.17)
Spanish × Endowments	−0.24* (0.14)	−0.23* (0.13)	−0.24* (0.14)	−0.23* (0.14)	−0.24* (0.14)	−0.16* (0.09)	−0.23* (0.13)	−0.22* (0.13)	−0.24* (0.14)	−0.04 (0.16)	−0.22* (0.13)
Portuguese × Endowments	−0.32* (0.16)	−0.31 (0.21)	−0.27 (0.2)	−0.71 (0.43)	−0.27 (0.2)	−0.21 (0.19)	−0.32* (0.17)	−0.46* (0.28)	−0.32* (0.16)	−0.21 (0.17)	−0.27 (0.2)
Other empires × Endowments	−0.02 (0.12)	0.04 (0.14)	−0.03 (0.13)	−0.03 (0.13)	−0.03 (0.13)	0.05 (0.14)	−0.02 (0.12)	0.07 (0.13)	−0.02 (0.13)	−0.05 (0.13)	−0.02 (0.13)
Years since colonization	0.17*** (0.06)		0.16** (0.06)	0.15** (0.07)	0.3 (0.21)	0.33 (0.22)	0.12 (0.09)	0.06 (0.11)	0.18*** (0.06)	0.16*** (0.06)	0.25 (0.22)
Additional control variable			0.14 (0.23)		−0.14 (0.23)		−0.2 (0.26)		0.00 (0)		[0.809]
UK × Additional control		0.19** (0.07)		0.45* (0.25)		−0.17 (0.24)		−0.5 (0.34)		0.00 (0.00)	

(continued)

Table 5.1 (continued)

	Dependent variable is rule of law (WGI)										
	Additional control variables										
	Reference model	Years since colonization	Years since independence		Duration of colonization		Colonization after 1850		Gap between first sighted and colonized		All controls together
	(1)	(2)	(3)	(4)	(5)	(6)	(7)	(8)	(9)	(10)	(11)
French × Additional control		−0.07 (0.2)		−0.56*** (0.17)		−0.37 (0.32)		0.29 (0.28)		0.000 (0.00)	
Spanish × Additional control		0.12 (0.18)		0.38 (0.24)		−0.53* (0.3)		n.a.		0.01** (0.00)	
Portuguese × Additional control		0.19 (0.21)		−0.89 (0.72)		−0.07 (0.26)		0.21 (0.73)		0.000 (0.01)	
Other empires × Additional control		0.34** (0.13)		0.13 (0.55)		0.03 (0.3)		−0.91* (0.52)		0.000 (0.00)	
Constant	−0.23 (0.19)	−0.26 (0.22)	−0.27 (0.19)	−0.39* (0.21)	−0.27 (0.19)	−0.28 (0.22)	−0.01 (0.35)	0.26 (0.41)	−0.29 (0.21)	−0.15 (0.26)	−0.1 (0.39)
R^2	0.5	0.52	0.51	0.54	0.51	0.52	0.51	0.54	0.5	0.53	0.51
Number of observations	102	102	102	102	102	102	102	102	102	102	102

Notes: Rule of law ranges from −2.5 to 2.5, where a higher value indicates better institutions. Its year of measurement is 2000. The endowments indicator is log population density in 1500, from Acemoglu et al. (2002). Variable descriptions are provided in Table A.1. The sample contains non-European countries colonized by Western powers (Table A.2). Robust standard errors are in parentheses. The last column reports the p-value of the joint significance test of all the additional controls. *, ** and *** denote statistical significance at the 10, 5 and 1% level, respectively

colonized by a European power, with a shorter gap implying that the territory was more valuable for the colonizer relative to the cost of colonizing it (Woodberry 2004, 2012). In all cases, these controls are statistically insignificant, thereby leaving our baseline findings fairly unaltered. In addition, columns 4, 6, 8 and 10 interact the respective additional control with colonizer identity, and column 11 includes all the individual controls simultaneously. In all cases, our baseline results remain unchanged.

In order to account for the possibility that one country changes its style of imperialism along the two main waves of colonialism, we estimate a triple interaction model in which the baseline interaction terms between colonizer identity and endowments are further interacted with a post-1850 colonization dummy to account for the distinct effect of the second wave of colonialism of the nineteenth century versus the first wave beginning at the end of the fifteenth century. These results presented in Table 5.2 provide evidence of (1) the distinct response of colonial powers to endowments (with higher institutional development the lower the level of endowments in the British colonies) and (2) lower institutional development for those British colonies colonized during the second wave of colonialism. However, the triple interaction term between colonizer identity, endowments and the post-1850 dummy appears statistically insignificant for the British and other main colonial powers. Therefore, this result stands against the possibility that either Britain or the other main European colonial powers changed their style along the two main waves of imperialism.

In all, the alternative explanation associated with the timing and duration of colonialism fails to overturn our results regarding the sharp contrast across colonial powers in the effect of endowments on current institutions.

5.2 Sociological and Anthropological Factors

Columns 1–10 of Table 5.3 control for sociological and anthropological factors that may affect institutions. These include religion, ethnic fragmentation measured through ethnolinguistic fractionalization and number of precolonial cultures, the degree of precolonial centralization as a key dimension of precolonial institutions, and a variable capturing the vulnerability of the indigenous population to European diseases, which could affect colonial policies (Easterly and Levine 2016).

Let us now give some intuition to these alternative theories. From the work of Max Weber (1976), religion is seen as a potential determinant of key capitalistic institutions, and more recently, La Porta et al. (1999) use religion as a proxy for culture to explain the quality of institutions. Column 1 introduces the fractions of population professing the different confessions in current times, which fail to enter significantly.

Another factor stressed in this literature is the level of social fragmentation. Alesina et al. (1999, 2003) associate ethnolinguistic fractionalization with the

Table 5.2 Triple interaction: Colonial origin, Endowments and Post 1850 colonization

Dependent variable is rule of law (WGI)	
	(1)
British colonies (Reference group)	
French colonies	−1.37** (0.64)
Spanish colonies	−0.99*** (0.22)
Portuguese colonies	−1.28*** (0.44)
Other empires colonies	−0.95*** (0.13)
UK × Endowments	−0.34*** (0.06)
French × Endowments	0.06 (0.41)
Spanish × Endowments	−0.22* (0.13)
Portuguese × Endowments	−0.46 (0.28)
Other empires × Endowments	−0.22*** (0.03)
Years since colonization	0.06 (0.11)
UK × Colonization after 1850	−0.55* (0.33)
French × Colonization after 1850	0.05 (0.67)
Spanish × Colonization after 1850	n.a.
Portuguese × Colonization after 1850	n.a.
Other empires × Colonization after 1850	−1.16** (0.51)
UK x Endowments × Colonization after 1850	0.13 (0.14)
French x Endowments × Colonization after 1850	0.21 (0.43)
Spanish x Endowments × Colonization after 1850	n.a.
Portuguese x Endowments × Colonization after 1850	0.15 (0.51)
Other empires x Endowments × Colonization after 1850	0.41*** (0.15)
Constant	0.27 (0.4)
R^2	0.56
Number of observations	102

Notes: Rule of law ranges from −2.5 to 2.5, where a higher value indicates better institutions. Its year of measurement is 2000. The endowments indicator is log population density in 1500, from Acemoglu et al. (2002). Variable descriptions are provided in Table A.1. The sample contains

(continued)

Table 5.2 (continued)

non-European countries colonized by Western powers (Table A.2). Robust standard errors are in parentheses. *, ** and *** denote statistical significance at the 10, 5 and 1% level, respectively

provision of public goods and the quality of institutions.[1] Column 3 shows a significantly negative coefficient on this variable. When interacted with colonial origin, column 4 presents significantly negative coefficients for the interaction terms for the British and the Portuguese, thereby leaving our baseline findings fairly unaltered. As an alternative measure of ethnic fragmentation, we consider the number of precolonial native cultures, which—according to Gallego (2010)—may affect the colonization strategy in former colonies. Western powers may have established centralized governments in colonies with one strong ethnic group, whereas decentralized systems of administration in colonies with several competing ethnic groups. We use a dummy variable that takes a value of unity for the case of more than one precolonial ethnic group and zero otherwise. The inclusion of this variable allows us to test the competing hypothesis that the key to explaining the different colonization strategies of Western powers was the degree of precolonial fragmentation rather than initial endowments (as we hold). As shown in columns 5 and 6, the measure 'several precolonial cultures' appears highly insignificant when entered alone or interacted with colonial origin and is unable to overturn our main results. This enables us to discard the possibility that the reason for the more homogeneous and centralized form of colonial administration implemented by the French—which makes it largely invariant to initial endowments—is that they occupied (possibly more centralized) territories with higher precolonial ethnic and cultural homogeneity.

Related to the previous factor, we consider a variable measuring the level of precolonial centralization. As stressed by Gennaioli and Rainer (2007), this was a key dimension of precolonial institutions. The competing hypothesis we aim to test here is whether the level of precolonial centralization would be the key factor to explain the institutions of the colonies and their subsequent postcolonial development, as opposed to the different colonization strategies implemented by European powers as a response to initial endowments. To measure the degree of political centralization, we employ the share of each country's native population belonging to centralized groups. We construct this variable following the methodology devel-

[1]La Porta et al. (1999) relate ethnic fractionalization to the State's predisposition toward greater redistribution. It is assumed that in heterogeneous societies, groups in power are more likely to privilege themselves and exclude the other ethnic groups.

Table 5.3 Control variables II: Sociological and anthropological factors

	Dependent variable is rule of law (WGI)										
	Additional control variables										
	Religion		Ethnic fractionalization		Several precolonial cultures		Precolonial centralization		Indigenous mortality		All controls together
	(1)	(2)	(3)	(4)	(5)	(6)	(7)	(8)	(9)	(10)	(11)
British colonies (Reference group)											
French colonies	−0.97*** (0.22)	−0.77*** (0.25)	−0.87*** (0.29)	−2.05*** (0.47)	−1.16*** (0.3)	−1.29*** (0.36)	−1.04*** (0.26)	−1.45*** (0.3)	−0.96*** (0.26)	−0.79*** (0.22)	−0.67** (0.31)
Spanish colonies	−0.95*** (0.26)	−0.95 (1.08)	−1.03*** (0.19)	−1.03* (0.56)	−0.81*** (0.23)	−0.9*** (0.29)	−1.05*** (0.22)	−1.26*** (0.27)	−1.11*** (0.21)	−1.11*** (0.14)	−0.33 (0.65)
Portuguese colonies	−1.16*** (0.31)	−1.61** (0.78)	−1.06*** (0.29)	2.48*** (0.45)	−1.83*** (0.19)	−1.77*** (0.2)	−1.18*** (0.29)	−0.83** (0.39)	−0.99*** (0.3)	−0.57 (0.4)	−1.15** (0.48)
Other empires colonies	−1.23*** (0.34)	−1.32*** (0.43)	−1.15*** (0.29)	−1.22*** (0.44)	−1.14*** (0.35)	−0.84*** (0.24)	−1.57*** (0.3)	−1.26*** (0.17)	−1.23*** (0.29)	−1.42*** (0.43)	−1.61*** (0.34)
UK × Endowments	−0.31*** (0.07)	−0.3*** (0.07)	−0.28*** (0.06)	−0.28*** (0.06)	−0.31*** (0.07)	−0.31*** (0.07)	−0.28*** (0.07)	−0.26*** (0.07)	−0.26*** (0.07)	−0.25*** (0.07)	−0.3*** (0.06)
French × Endowments	0.17 (0.14)	0.1 (0.14)	0.09 (0.18)	0.33** (0.17)	0.29* (0.15)	0.36** (0.18)	0.29* (0.16)	0.08 (0.13)	0.24 (0.15)	0.17 (0.14)	0.10 (0.17)
Spanish × Endowments	−0.24* (0.14)	−0.23* (0.14)	−0.2 (0.13)	−0.17 (0.15)	−0.25* (0.13)	−0.24 (0.15)	−0.14 (0.14)	−0.12 (0.12)	−0.21 (0.13)	−0.21 (0.13)	0.02 (0.11)
Portuguese × Endowments	−0.34* (0.17)	−0.16 (0.43)	−0.28* (0.15)	0.25** (0.1)	−0.53*** (0.01)	−0.53*** (0.01)	−0.29* (0.16)	−0.1 (0.17)	−0.26 (0.2)	−0.85** (0.41)	−0.48** (0.18)
Other empires × Endowments	−0.01 (0.13)	−0.02 (0.13)	−0.07 (0.13)	−0.09 (0.14)	−0.15 (0.11)	−0.19*** (0.05)	0.18 (0.12)	0.33*** (0.06)	0.02 (0.11)	0.11 (0.15)	0.11 (0.18)
Years since colonization	0.19*** (0.06)	0.19*** (0.06)	0.15** (0.06)	0.14** (0.06)	0.07 (0.08)	0.07 (0.08)	0.16*** (0.06)	0.16*** (0.06)	0.1* (0.06)	0.09 (0.07)	0.03 (0.08)
Additional control variable	[0.601]		−0.63* (0.32)		0.09 (0.19)		−0.25 (0.16)		0.41** (0.2)		[0.030]
UK × Additional control		0.00 (0.00)		−1.03** (0.42)		0.02 (0.32)		−0.46* (0.24)		0.57** (0.23)	

French × Additional control		−0.01 (0.01)		0.61 (0.43)		0.48 (0.3)		0.67** (0.27)		−0.88*** (0.21)	
Spanish × Additional control		0.00 (0.01)		−1.04 (0.97)		0.24 (0.35)		0.14 (0.22)		0.52** (0.23)	
Portuguese × Additional control		0.01 (0.02)		−6.25*** (0.68)		n.a.		−1.33** (0.67)		−1.66 (1.04)	
Other empires × Additional control		0.00 (0.01)		−0.85 (0.7)		−0.46 (0.36)		−1.2*** (0.18)		1* (0.57)	
Constant	−0.22 (0.45)	−0.22 (0.2)	0.17 (0.27)	0.39 (0.35)	0.05 (0.32)	0.07 (0.35)	−0.08 (0.2)	0 (0.22)	−0.22 (0.18)	−0.23 (0.2)	0.71 (0.84)
R^2	0.51	0.51	0.53	0.59	0.54	0.55	0.53	0.59	0.52	0.56	0.66
Number of observations	101	102	101	101	68	68	97	97	102	102	66

Notes: Rule of law ranges from −2.5 to 2.5, where a higher value indicates better institutions. Its year of measurement is 2000. The endowments indicator is log population density in 1500, from Acemoglu et al. (2002). Variable descriptions are provided in Table A.1. The sample contains non-European countries colonized by Western powers (Table A.2). Robust standard errors are in parentheses. *, ** and *** denote significance at the 10, 5 and 1% level, respectively. In column 1 and 11, we report the p-value of the joint significance test. In column 2, colonial origin dummies are interacted with the percentage of catholics

oped by Gennaioli and Rainer (2007).[2] Columns 7 and 8 introduce the precolonial centralization measure alone and interacted with colonial identity. It is worth noting that precolonial centralization is insignificant when entered alone and statistically significant when interacted with colonizer identity for the case of former British, French, Portuguese and other empires' colonies. Again, our baseline results remain unchanged. Therefore, current institutional levels appear to be mainly driven by the institutional arrangements imposed externally by the colonizers in the colonies (which in turn differed on the basis of the initial level of endowments) rather than by the degree of precolonial centralization or ethnic homogeneity encountered by the colonial powers upon their arrival.

Column 9 introduces indigenous mortality, which is a dummy variable indicating whether the country belongs to the New World (North America, the Caribbean and Latin America) or Oceania, where the contact with European colonizers caused a more dramatic decline in native population due to their vulnerability to European diseases (Easterly and Levine 2016). This variable enters with a positive and statistically significant coefficient. When interacted with colonial origin dummies, column 10 shows that the interaction terms for indigenous mortality appear statistically significant for former British, French, Spanish and other empires' colonies. In the case of British, Spanish and other empires' colonies, the higher the indigenous mortality rate, the better the institutional level, whereas the opposite occurs for the French. Again, the inclusion of this factor does not overturn our baseline results. Finally, column 11 includes all sociological and anthropological factors together, which enter jointly significant while leaving our baseline findings unaltered.

5.3 Geographic and Climatic Factors

Columns 1–10 of Table 5.4 introduce factors related to differences across colonial powers in transport costs as well as in geographic costs of controlling colonial dominions.[3] These are 'distance from metropolis',[4] country landlockedness, distance to the sea, altitude (Bruhn and Gallego 2012) and an indicator variable for being an island (Acemoglu et al. 2002). Arguably, in colonial times "producing

[2]They used anthropological data from Murdock (1967), who assigned a number of jurisdictional levels beyond the local community to each ethnic group in a certain area. A value of 0 was assigned to groups "lacking any form of centralized political organization", 1 to "petty chiefdoms", 2 to "large permanent chiefdoms/small states" and 3 or 4 to "large states". Gennaioli and Rainer (2007) employed these scores to build two categories: fragmented ethnic groups scoring 0 and 1 and centralized ethnic groups falling into categories 2, 3 or 4.

[3]Lang (1975) discusses the increase in transportation costs due to higher distance from the metropolis for the case of Spanish and British colonies in the Americas, and its effect on commerce.

[4]We construct distance from metropolis following the great circle formula in order to capture the differences in transportation costs across European colonial powers. In addition, all else kept equal, the higher the distance from metropolis, the greater the cost of controlling colonies.

Table 5.4 Control variables III: Transportation costs

	Dependent variable is rule of law (WGI)										
	Control variables										
	Distance from metropolis		Landlocked		Distance from the coast		Altitude		Island		All controls together
	(1)	(2)	(3)	(4)	(5)	(6)	(7)	(8)	(9)	(10)	(11)
British colonies (Reference group)											
French colonies	−0.99*** (0.24)	−0.41 (0.48)	−0.89*** (0.25)	−1.26*** (0.32)	−0.83*** (0.28)	−1.32*** (0.4)	−0.89*** (0.26)	−0.99* (0.5)	−1.03*** (0.24)	−0.79*** (0.21)	−0.75** (0.3)
Spanish colonies	−1.02*** (0.2)	−2.55** (1.04)	−0.97*** (0.2)	−1*** (0.22)	−0.96*** (0.21)	−0.94*** (0.27)	−0.77*** (0.22)	−1.45*** (0.33)	−0.82*** (0.22)	−0.6** (0.24)	−0.72*** (0.23)
Portuguese colonies	−1.17*** (0.32)	0.3 (0.65)	−1.2*** (0.31)	−1.23*** (0.31)	−1.13*** (0.28)	−0.51** (0.21)	−1.26*** (0.22)	−1.16*** (0.25)	−1.05*** (0.27)	−1.13*** (0.23)	−1.17*** (0.25)
Other empires colonies	−1.22*** (0.31)	−0.93 (0.64)	−1.28*** (0.35)	−1.34*** (0.34)	−1.21*** (0.31)	−1.17*** (0.33)	−1.08*** (0.35)	−1.25*** (0.39)	−1.13*** (0.33)	−1.01*** (0.37)	−1.1*** (0.38)
UK × Endowments	−0.29*** (0.07)	−0.27*** (0.07)	−0.31*** (0.06)	−0.32*** (0.06)	−0.3*** (0.07)	−0.31*** (0.07)	−0.28*** (0.07)	−0.3*** (0.07)	−0.28*** (0.06)	−0.28*** (0.07)	−0.26*** (0.08)
French × Endowments	0.22 (0.15)	0.18 (0.13)	0.11 (0.17)	0.26 (0.18)	0.09 (0.17)	0.25 (0.2)	0.23 (0.15)	0.2 (0.17)	0.25 (0.15)	0.19 (0.13)	0.19 (0.19)
Spanish × Endowments	−0.24* (0.14)	−0.14 (0.13)	−0.25* (0.13)	−0.25* (0.13)	−0.27** (0.13)	−0.28** (0.14)	−0.22 (0.14)	−0.28* (0.17)	−0.22 (0.14)	−0.23* (0.12)	−0.21 (0.14)
Portuguese × Endowments	−0.31* (0.17)	−0.51*** (0.16)	−0.35** (0.17)	−0.36** (0.17)	−0.44*** (0.16)	−0.98*** (0.15)	−0.24** (0.1)	−0.26*** (0.06)	−0.34** (0.13)	−0.27*** (0.09)	−0.24* (0.13)
Other empires × Endowments	−0.02 (0.13)	−0.03 (0.13)	0.03 (0.14)	−0.04 (0.2)	0.02 (0.13)	0.06 (0.14)	−0.01 (0.14)	0.06 (0.18)	−0.05 (0.13)	−0.06 (0.13)	0.02 (0.16)
Years since colonization	0.17*** (0.06)	0.17*** (0.06)	0.14** (0.06)	0.12** (0.06)	0.14** (0.06)	0.12* (0.06)	0.14** (0.07)	0.1 (0.07)	0.12* (0.06)	0.1 (0.06)	0.09 (0.07)
Additional control variable	0.01 (0.03)		−0.36** (0.16)		−0.04** (0.02)		−0.12 (0.27)		0.4** (0.18)		[0.533]
UK × Additional control		0.03 (0.05)		−0.73*** (0.23)		−0.06* (0.03)		−0.62** (0.3)		0.7*** (0.19)	
French × Additional control		−0.06 (0.04)		0.14 (0.26)		0.01 (0.03)		−0.65 (0.79)		−0.32 (0.42)	

(continued)

Table 5.4 (continued)

	Dependent variable is rule of law (WGI)										
	Control variables										
	Distance from metropolis		Landlocked		Distance from the coast		Altitude		Island		All controls together
	(1)	(2)	(3)	(4)	(5)	(6)	(7)	(8)	(9)	(10)	(11)
Spanish × Additional control		0.21* (0.12)		−0.35 (0.33)		−0.06 (0.05)		0.62* (0.34)		−0.39 (0.3)	
Portuguese × Additional control		−0.22** (0.1)		n.a.		−0.28*** (0.03)		−0.89*** (0.17)		1.46*** (0.16)	
Other empires × Additional control		−0.01 (0.04)		−0.05 (0.51)		−0.08*** (0.03)		−0.49 (0.33)		0.17 (0.23)	
Constant	−0.27 (0.26)	−0.46 (0.43)	−0.09 (0.19)	0.02 (0.21)	−0.03 (0.21)	0.06 (0.23)	−0.24 (0.33)	0.16 (0.35)	−0.21 (0.18)	−0.27 (0.18)	−0.4 (0.36)
R^2	0.50	0.55	0.52	0.54	0.52	0.56	0.46	0.53	0.53	0.59	0.48
Number of observations	102	102	102	102	102	102	86	86	102	102	86

Notes: Rule of law ranges from −2.5 to 2.5, where a higher value indicates better institutions. Its year of measurement is 2000. The endowments indicator is log population density in 1500, from Acemoglu et al. (2002). Variable descriptions are provided in Table A.1. The sample contains non-European countries colonized by Western powers (Table A.2). Robust standard errors are in parentheses. *, ** and *** denote statistical significance at the 10, 5 and 1% level, respectively. In the last column, we report the p-value of the joint significance test

export goods was profitable only close to the sea since transportation over land was very costly" (Bruhn and Gallego 2012, p. 443). In contrast, transportation costs and proximity to the sea did not matter much for the production of subsistence crops, such as wheat, which were consumed locally.[5] Altitude is another factor directly affecting transportation costs during colonial times. For many islands the cost of transportation to the metropolis would be lower since they normally have natural seaports (Acemoglu et al. 2002).[6] According to Congdon-Fors (2007), the transplantation of institutions from the metropolis to the colonies as well as their administration may be easier for islands due to their usually lower size and the fact that borders are not a point of contention. As expected, distance from the sea and landlockedness exert a statistically significant negative impact on institutional development, whereas island status is associated with better institutions. It is worth noting that the interaction of each individual control with colonial origin in addition to the inclusion of all these individual controls together (in column 11) do not cause any substantial change in our baseline findings.

Columns 1–8 of Table 5.5 control for other geographic variables that are commonly thought to affect institutional development: latitude, percentage of land in tropics, land quality, temperature and humidity, and regional dummies (Bloom and Sachs 1998; Acemoglu et al. 2001, 2002; Easterly and Levine 2003; Rodrik et al. 2004; Gallup et al. 2001). These factors are expected to affect institutional development in a number of ways. Theories linking climate and geography with institutions can be traced back to Baron de Montesquieu (1748)'s classic work "The Spirit of Laws". In general, tropical location is associated with poor land quality, high disease environments for both humans and crops, adverse weather conditions and low agricultural productivity. It is worth noting that the percentage of land in tropics presents a significantly negative coefficient, while latitude exhibits a significantly positive one. In addition, the sets of temperature and humidity indicators as well as of continental dummies appear jointly significant. Remarkably, the interaction of each individual control with colonizer identity as well as the inclusion of all these geographical factors together in column 9 do not overturn our baseline results. This supports the fact that our results are not due simply to a correlation between institutions and colonies concentrated in areas with certain geographic or climatic features.

Finally, one may wonder whether our interaction term for France, which appears positive (though in most regressions highly insignificant), is caused by a self-selection bias due to the possibility that the French settled in more prosperous

[5]A clear exception is the case of valuables such as gold and silver, for which colonizers usually engaged in mining even in places located far away from the sea (e.g., the silver mines in Potosí). As documented by Bruhn and Gallego (2012), Potosí is not only situated more than 400 miles away from the nearest natural seaport but has an elevation of about 4000 m. These factors did not prevent the transport of silver through the Andes from taking place. This transportation was conducted by means of mules, llamas and Indian carriers.

[6]As noted by Armstrong and Read (2003), in the case of island archipelagos, internal transportation costs may be higher.

areas (i.e., with higher precolonial population density) compared to the British. If we employ data from McEvedy and Jones (1978) to construct the average population density in 1900 for former British and French colonies in Africa, we obtain a value of population density of 10.5 persons per square kilometer for British colonies and 6.9 for French colonies. Therefore, French colonies in Africa do not appear to be initially more prosperous than the British at the time of the second wave of colonization. This appears in line with the historians' view supporting that, unlike British colonization of Africa that had mainly an economic motive, French interest in West Africa was mainly driven by political pressures (Fieldhouse 1966; Fage 2002). Indeed, "the areas Britain claimed were those in which her traders have been active, or saw future profit. Thus where with France, the flag tended to precede trade, with Britain trade preceded the flag, [...] with the result that Britain gained the smaller but richer part of West Africa" (Crowder 1968, p. 70).

Throughout Tables 4.1, 5.1, 5.2, 5.3, 5.4, and 5.5, we have checked that our main findings are not driven by differences in the timing and duration of colonization, sociological and anthropological factors, and geographical features of colonized territories. Our results show strong heterogeneity in the relationship among colonial empires, endowments and institutions. As mentioned above, this heterogeneity may be read from two sides: the impact of colonizer identity varies with the level of endowments and the relationship between endowments and institutions is very different across former colonial empires. The findings give support to our classification of Britain and France as 'economically-oriented' and 'politically-oriented' imperialisms, respectively, since for the former we consistently observe a negative relationship between endowments and current institutions, whereas for the latter no such relation is found. The results are also consistent with the consideration of the Spanish empire as a hybrid between these two styles. The coefficients on the interaction term for Spanish colonies are negative but smaller than those for the British and, in general, they are marginally significant or insignificant—reflecting that the *endowment view* is only partially applicable. Finally, concerning the Portuguese empire, its classification as 'economically-oriented' is congruent with the fact that the interaction term generally displays a negative and significant coefficient, though the small number of colonies included in this group drives the coefficient insignificant in some instances.

Table 5.5 Control variables IV: Geography and climate

	Dependent variable is rule of law (WGI)								
	Latitude		Land in geographical tropics (%)		Land quality		Temperature and humidity	Continental dummies	All controls together
	(1)	(2)	(3)	(4)	(5)	(6)	(7)	(8)	(9)
British colonies (Reference group)									
French colonies	−0.77*** (0.25)	−0.77** (0.33)	−0.71*** (0.21)	−0.62** (0.23)	−0.99*** (0.22)	−0.7** (0.28)	−0.81*** (0.3)	−0.65** (0.27)	−0.76*** (0.28)
Spanish colonies	−0.94*** (0.2)	−1.13*** (0.35)	−0.8*** (0.19)	−0.72 (0.45)	−1.04*** (0.2)	−0.67 (0.56)	−0.91*** (0.21)	−0.97*** (0.24)	−0.6* (0.34)
Portuguese colonies	−1.06*** (0.31)	−1.93 (1.3)	−1.14*** (0.29)	−3.02*** (0.48)	−1.5*** (0.25)	−4.83*** (0.7)	−1.22*** (0.36)	−0.85*** (0.3)	−1.02*** (0.22)
Other empires colonies	−0.91*** (0.33)	−0.93** (0.4)	−0.88** (0.39)	−1.52** (0.62)	−1.24*** (0.33)	−1.54** (0.58)	−1.07*** (0.35)	−1.23*** (0.27)	−0.88** (0.38)
UK × Endowments	−0.24*** (0.07)	−0.25*** (0.07)	−0.23*** (0.07)	−0.23*** (0.08)	−0.29*** (0.07)	−0.29*** (0.07)	−0.3*** (0.07)	−0.31*** (0.05)	−0.22*** (0.08)
French × Endowments	0.1 (0.13)	0.12 (0.15)	0.19 (0.12)	0.17 (0.11)	0.24* (0.14)	0.25* (0.14)	0.09 (0.18)	−0.02 (0.16)	0.11 (0.17)
Spanish × Endowments	−0.07 (0.14)	0.02 (0.17)	−0.14 (0.13)	−0.09 (0.14)	−0.25 (0.15)	−0.26 (0.17)	−0.16 (0.15)	−0.22 (0.13)	0.02 (0.18)
Portuguese × Endowments	−0.33** (0.16)	−0.37* (0.2)	−0.19 (0.16)	−0.19*** (0.04)	−0.18 (0.13)	−0.43*** (0.06)	−0.34* (0.18)	−0.24 (0.2)	−0.23* (0.13)
Other empires × Endowments	−0.04 (0.12)	−0.04 (0.13)	−0.04 (0.14)	0 (0.12)	−0.01 (0.13)	−0.03 (0.13)	−0.02 (0.14)	−0.02 (0.12)	0.03 (0.17)
Years since colonization	0.18*** (0.05)	0.17*** (0.06)	0.2*** (0.05)	0.22*** (0.05)	0.2*** (0.06)	0.19*** (0.06)	0.21*** (0.06)	0.13** (0.06)	0.09 (0.08)
Additional control variable	2.21*** (0.7)		−0.53*** (0.19)		−2.78 (2.72)		[0.059]	[0.001]	[0.003]

(continued)

Table 5.5 (continued)

	Dependent variable is rule of law (WGI)								
	Latitude		Land in geographical tropics (%)		Land quality		Temperature and humidity	Continental dummies	All controls together
	(1)	(2)	(3)	(4)	(5)	(6)	(7)	(8)	(9)
UK × Additional control		2.06** (0.96)		−0.62* (0.32)		−0.74 (3.51)			
French × Additional control		1.85 (1.34)		−0.72*** (0.22)		−8.23*** (3.01)			
Spanish × Additional control		3.28* (1.73)		−0.77 (0.53)		−6.74 (7.5)			
Portuguese × Additional control		7.77 (8.8)		1.93*** (0.44)		81.32*** (17.14)			
Other empires × Additional control		2.07 (1.35)		0.3 (0.65)		7.92 (11.26)			
Constant	−0.71*** (0.23)	−0.66** (0.27)	−0.24 (0.19)	−0.25 (0.21)	−0.17 (0.2)	−0.25 (0.24)	−1.24 (1.2)	0.09 (0.26)	−2.7** (1.26)
R^2	0.57	0.57	0.51	0.55	0.52	0.54	0.57	0.59	0.65
Number of observations	102	102	90	90	99	99	100	102	88

Notes: Rule of law ranges from −2.5 to 2.5, where a higher value indicates better institutions. Its year of measurement is 2000. The endowments indicator is log population density in 1500, from Acemoglu et al. (2002). Variable descriptions are provided in Table A.1. The sample contains non-European countries colonized by Western powers (Table A.2). Robust standard errors are in parentheses. *, ** and *** denote statistical significance at the 10, 5 and 1% level, respectively. In the last three columns, we report the p-value of the joint significance test

Chapter 6
Further Sensitivity Analyses

Abstract This chapter conducts a thorough sensitivity analysis that controls for the presence of outliers and sample selection, the use of alternative institutional indicators and different measures of endowments, and limiting the range in the distribution of endowments to French range. Among the alternative endowment variables considered, we use the level of population density before colonization, measures of land suitability for sugar versus wheat, and measures of mineral resources abundance. As with our baseline analysis, the evidence continues to reveal strong presence of heterogeneity in the relationship of colonial origin and endowments with current institutions.

Despite having discarded the possibility that our main results are driven by omitted factors potentially correlated with our independent variables and current institutions, this chapter describes the robustness of our main findings to several additional sensitivity analyses. These include sample selection and outliers, alternative institutional and endowment indicators, and limiting the range in the distribution of endowments to French range.

6.1 Robustness to Sample Selection and Outliers

This section explores the possibility that observations with extreme values in our main variables could be driving the results. The first column of Table 6.1 reproduces the reference estimation, while columns 2–10 evaluate the influence of outliers. We consider several statistical definitions of outliers such as leverage, standardized residuals, studentized residuals, Cook's distance, DFITS, Welsch distance and DF-Beta.[1] Once outliers are detected, we exclude these countries

[1]The cut-offs of the detection methods are the following: leverage, $2 \cdot k/n$; standardized residuals, |2|; studentized residuals, |2|; Cook's distance, $4/n$; DFITS, $|2 \cdot \sqrt{k/n}|$; Welsch distance, $|3 \cdot \sqrt{k}|$; DF-Beta, $|2/\sqrt{n}|$, where k is the number of parameters and n is the number of observations. DF-Beta is applied to the interaction terms 'UK colony × Pop. dens.' and 'FR colony × Pop. dens.' in columns 8 and 9, respectively (for outliers diagnostics and methods, see Belsley et al. 2004).

D. Oto-Peralías, D. Romero-Ávila, *Colonial Theories of Institutional Development*, Contributions to Economics, DOI 10.1007/978-3-319-54127-3_6

Table 6.1 Robustness checks: Outliers detection

Dependent variable is rule of law (WGI)	Basic regresion	Leverage	Standard. residuals	Student. residuals	Cook's distance	Dfits	Welsch distance	DF-Beta (UKxPOP)	DF-Beta (FRxPOP)	Median regression
	(1)	(2)	(3)	(4)	(5)	(6)	(7)	(8)	(9)	(10)
British colonies (Reference group)										
French colonies	−1*** (0.24)	−1*** (0.24)	−0.99*** (0.24)	−0.99*** (0.24)	−0.97*** (0.24)	−0.99*** (0.24)	−0.96*** (0.24)	−0.9*** (0.25)	−0.97*** (0.21)	−0.82** (0.35)
Spanish colonies	−1.02*** (0.2)	−1.12*** (0.23)	−1.2*** (0.17)	−1.2*** (0.17)	−1.08*** (0.21)	−1.29*** (0.16)	−1.1*** (0.21)	−1.07*** (0.19)	−1.08*** (0.2)	−1.15*** (0.3)
Portuguese colonies	−1.19*** (0.31)	n.a. n.a.	−1.26*** (0.3)	−1.26*** (0.3)	−1.46*** (0.17)	−1.57*** (0.15)	−0.48** (0.23)	−1.21*** (0.31)	−1.23*** (0.31)	−1.15*** (0.36)
Other empires colonies	−1.22*** (0.31)	−1.74*** (0.44)	−1.24*** (0.3)	−1.24*** (0.3)	−1.27*** (0.34)	−1.33*** (0.33)	−1.54*** (0.34)	−1.17*** (0.3)	−1.22*** (0.31)	−0.99** (0.39)
UK × Endowments	−0.3*** (0.07)	−0.3*** (0.06)	−0.36*** (0.05)	−0.36*** (0.05)	−0.35*** (0.05)	−0.37*** (0.05)	−0.35*** (0.05)	−0.35*** (0.04)	−0.29*** (0.07)	−0.32*** (0.07)
French × Endowments	0.21 (0.15)	0.21 (0.15)	0.21 (0.15)	0.21 (0.15)	0.21 (0.15)	0.21 (0.15)	0.21 (0.15)	0.21 (0.15)	0.18 (0.15)	0.21 (0.24)
Spanish × Endowments	−0.24* (0.14)	0.07 (0.22)	−0.23 (0.15)	−0.23 (0.15)	−0.08 (0.13)	−0.03 (0.15)	−0.08 (0.13)	−0.25* (0.14)	−0.25* (0.14)	−0.23 (0.2)
Portuguese × Endowments	−0.32* (0.16)	n.a. n.a.	−0.29* (0.16)	−0.29* (0.16)	n.a. n.a.	n.a. n.a.	−4.14*** (0.26)	−0.28* (0.16)	−0.3* (0.16)	−0.13 (0.13)
Other empires × Endowments	−0.02 (0.12)	0.44 (0.36)	−0.01 (0.12)	−0.01 (0.12)	0.05 (0.13)	0.06 (0.13)	0.15 (0.13)	−0.01 (0.12)	−0.01 (0.12)	−0.11 (0.19)
Years since colonization	0.17*** (0.06)	0.18*** (0.06)	0.21*** (0.05)	0.21*** (0.05)	0.19*** (0.06)	0.21*** (0.05)	0.2*** (0.06)	0.22*** (0.05)	0.2*** (0.06)	0.19** (0.08)

Constant	−0.23 (0.19)	−0.23 (0.2)	−0.28* (0.16)	−0.28* (0.16)	−0.27 (0.18)	−0.3 (0.18)	−0.3 (0.18)	−0.39** (0.18)	−0.29 (0.19)	−0.29 (0.23)
R^2	0.5	0.51	0.61	0.61	0.54	0.61	0.56	0.53	0.53	0.31
Number of observations	102	91	97	97	94	92	96	95	95	102

Notes: Rule of law ranges from −2.5 to 2.5, where a higher value indicates better institutions. Its year of measurement is 2000. Variable descriptions are provided in Table A.1. The sample contains non-European countries colonized by Western powers (Table A.2). Robust standard errors are in parentheses. *, ** and *** denote statistical significance at the 10, 5 and 1% level, respectively. Outliers in column 2 are Angola, Argentina, Burundi, Brazil, Cape Verde, Guinea-Bissau, Libya, Mozambique, Rwanda, Suriname and Uruguay. Outliers in column 3 are Chile, Egypt, Guyana, New Zealand and Zimbabwe. Outliers in column 4 are Chile, Egypt, Guyana, New Zealand and Zimbabwe. Outliers in column 5 are Angola, Brazil, Cape Verde, Egypt, Guinea-Bissau, Somalia, Suriname and Uruguay. Outliers in column 6 are Angola, Brazil, Chile, Cape Verde, Egypt, Guinea-Bissau, Guyana, Somalia, Suriname and Uruguay. Outliers in column 7 are Brazil, Cape Verde, Egypt, Guinea-Bissau, Suriname and Uruguay. Outliers in column 8 are Australia, Egypt, Guyana, India, New Zealand, Sudan and Singapore. Outliers in column 9 are Algeria, Haiti, Cambodia, Morocco, Madagascar, Mali and Tunisia and re-run the regressions. Moreover, column 10 presents the median regression, aimed at estimating the median of the dependent variable, which is less sensitive to outliers. It is remarkable that the results are highly robust to the presence of outliers. Throughout all these estimations, we find clear-cut evidence of heterogeneity in the relationship between endowments and institutions.

In columns 1–6 of Table 6.2, we verify that the results are not driven by specific regions or particular groups of countries. First, column 1 removes the colonies known as neo-Europes (USA, Canada, Australia and New Zealand), which are considered extreme cases of British colonialism, with initially low density of indigenous population and very good current institutions. The coefficient on the interaction term 'UK colony × Population density' remains negative and highly significant, although slightly lower compared to the baseline regression (−0.22 vs. −0.30). Columns 2–6 drop the regions of the Middle East and North Africa, South Asia, Latin America and the Caribbean, East Asia and Pacific, and sub-Saharan Africa, respectively. It is remarkable that the baseline results remain fairly unchanged, even when deleting the 42 sub-Saharan countries (though in this case, the relationship between endowments and institutions vanishes for the Spanish colonies).

For comparison purposes, in Table 6.3 we restrict the sample of former colonies to that analyzed by Acemoglu et al. (2001), which can be considered as the seminal article within the *endowment view*. Remarkably, the evidence in column 1 indicates that our baseline results completely hold. Whereas the interaction terms for the British, Spanish and Portuguese powers are significantly negative, as predicted by the *endowment view*, the interaction term for former French colonies appears highly insignificant, as suggested by the invariance of the French colonial strategy to the precolonial level of endowments. When we replace precolonial population density by potential settler mortality in column 2, the interaction terms are significantly negative for the British and Portuguese, whereas insignificant for the Spanish and French. When columns 3 and 4 replace rule of law with 'protection against expropiation risk', which is the institutional indicator employed in Acemoglu et al. (2001), the baseline results also remain unaltered.

6.2 Robustness to Institutional Indicators

We now proceed to check the robustness of our main findings to the use of a wide variety of alternative institutional indicators. These results are reported in detail in Tables 6.4 and 6.5. In columns 1–6 of Table 6.4 we use the six indicators from the World Bank Institute (Worldwide Governance Indicators). They are measured in 2000 and range from −2.5 to 2.5, with higher scores indicating better institutions. Each indicator measures a particular dimension of governance, understanding this concept broadly as "the traditions and institutions by which authority in a country is exercised" (Kaufmann et al. 2009). Column 1 reproduces the reference estimation, which uses *rule of law*. In column 2 the indicator is *voice and accountability*, which

Table 6.2 Robustness checks: Sample selection

Dependent variable is rule of law (WGI)						
	Drop neo-Europes	Drop Middle East and North Africa	Drop South Asia	Drop Latin Am. and Caribbean	Drop East Asia and Pacific	Drop Sub-Saharan Africa
	(1)	(2)	(3)	(4)	(5)	(6)
British colonies (Reference group)						
French colonies	−0.89*** (0.24)	−0.76*** (0.25)	−0.98*** (0.24)	−0.84*** (0.22)	−0.92*** (0.26)	−2.13*** (0.2)
Spanish colonies	−0.92*** (0.22)	−1.07*** (0.21)	−0.98*** (0.2)	−1.37*** (0.11)	−0.98*** (0.22)	−0.88*** (0.23)
Portuguese colonies	−1.08*** (0.32)	−1.2*** (0.32)	−1.15*** (0.31)	−1.02** (0.4)	−1.14*** (0.32)	n.a. n.a.
Other empires colonies	−1.11*** (0.32)	−1.15*** (0.29)	−1.19*** (0.32)	−1.54*** (0.35)	−1.27*** (0.45)	−1.07*** (0.16)
UK × Endowments	−0.22*** (0.08)	−0.33*** (0.06)	−0.33*** (0.08)	−0.31*** (0.07)	−0.23*** (0.07)	−0.31*** (0.06)
French × Endowments	0.21 (0.15)	0.08 (0.16)	0.21 (0.15)	0.15 (0.14)	0.24 (0.17)	0.5*** (0.15)
Spanish × Endowments	−0.24* (0.14)	−0.25* (0.15)	−0.24* (0.14)	n.a. n.a.	−0.24* (0.14)	−0.17 (0.12)
Portuguese × Endowments	−0.32* (0.16)	−0.26 (0.16)	−0.32* (0.16)	−0.63 (0.45)	−0.31* (0.16)	0.33*** (0.08)
Other empires × Endowments	−0.02 (0.12)	−0.05 (0.11)	−0.03 (0.12)	0.15 (0.14)	0.01 (0.16)	−0.19*** (0.05)
Years since colonization	0.17*** (0.06)	0.24*** (0.06)	0.17*** (0.06)	0.2*** (0.06)	0.19*** (0.06)	−0.05 (0.07)
Constant	−0.34* (0.18)	−0.48*** (0.18)	−0.23 (0.19)	−0.3 (0.2)	−0.34* (0.2)	0.7*** (0.26)

(continued)

Table 6.2 (continued)

Dependent variable is rule of law (WGI)						
	Drop neo-Europes	Drop Middle East and North Africa	Drop South Asia	Drop Latin Am. and Caribbean	Drop East Asia and Pacific	Drop Sub-Saharan Africa
	(1)	(2)	(3)	(4)	(5)	(6)
R^2	0.4	0.56	0.51	0.58	0.45	0.6
Number of observations	98	92	98	69	91	60

Notes: Rule of law ranges from −2.5 to 2.5, where a higher value indicates better institutions. Its year of measurement is 2000. Variable descriptions are provided in Table A.1. The sample contains non-European countries colonized by Western powers (Table A.2). Robust standard errors are in parentheses. *, ** and *** denote statistical significance at the 10, 5 and 1% level, respectively

Table 6.3 Sample restricted to that considered by Acemoglu et al. (2001)

	Dependent variable is rule of law (WGI)		Dependent variable is protection against expropriation risk	
	(1)	(2)	(3)	(4)
British colonies (Reference group)				
French colonies	−1.192*** (0.328)	−2.186** (1.049)	−2.457*** (0.673)	−1.815 (1.925)
Spanish colonies	−0.739*** (0.253)	−0.685 (2.032)	−1.166*** (0.419)	1.415 (2.404)
Portuguese colonies	−1.745*** (0.182)	1.924*** (0.563)	−1.710*** (0.314)	5.989*** (1.130)
Other empires colonies	−2.634*** (0.318)	13.246*** (4.241)	−5.414*** (0.537)	56.640*** (7.333)
UK × Pop. dens.	−0.318*** (0.068)		−0.507*** (0.119)	
French × Pop. dens.	0.249 (0.164)		0.851*** (0.300)	
Spanish × Pop. dens.	−0.231* (0.120)		−0.284 (0.194)	
Portuguese × Pop. dens.	−0.532*** (0.015)		−0.996*** (0.026)	
Other empires × Pop. dens.	1.033*** (0.227)		3.813*** (0.389)	
Years since colonization	0.042 (0.090)	0.044 (0.107)	0.035 (0.153)	0.055 (0.181)
UK × Settler mortality		−0.430*** (0.114)		−0.590*** (0.226)
French × Settler mortality		−0.069 (0.149)		−0.343 (0.281)
Spanish × Settler mortality		−0.383 (0.425)		−1.091** (0.468)
Portuguese × Settler mortality		−0.983*** (0.033)		−1.838*** (0.057)
Other empires × Settler mortality		−3.122*** (0.824)		−11.441*** (1.394)
Constant	0.160 (0.328)	1.808*** (0.675)	7.327*** (0.553)	9.499*** (1.171)
R^2	0.532	0.474	0.515	0.397
Number of observations	61	61	61	61

Notes: Variable descriptions are provided in Table A.1. The sample contains non-European countries colonized by Western powers (Table A.2). Robust standard errors are in parentheses. *, ** and *** denote statistical significance at the 10, 5 and 1% level, respectively. The difference in the number of countries with respect to the sample in Acemoglu et al. (2001) is due to the fact that we do not consider Hong Kong, Malta and Ethiopia

Table 6.4 Robustness checks: Institutional variables I

	Rule of law (WGI) (Reference model)	Voice and account. (WGI)	Political stability (WGI)	Control corruption (WGI)	Gover. effectiv. (WGI)	Regulatory quality (WGI)
	(1)	(2)	(3)	(4)	(5)	(6)
British colonies (Reference group)						
French colonies	−1*** (0.24)	−0.31 (0.26)	−0.49 (0.31)	−1.06*** (0.23)	−1.04*** (0.22)	−0.74*** (0.22)
Spanish colonies	−1.02*** (0.2)	−0.93*** (0.22)	−0.55** (0.23)	−0.95*** (0.22)	−0.95*** (0.2)	−0.74*** (0.23)
Portuguese colonies	−1.19*** (0.31)	−1.01*** (0.35)	−0.7 (0.48)	−1.1*** (0.27)	−1.13*** (0.23)	−1.23*** (0.32)
Other empires colonies	−1.22*** (0.31)	−0.66** (0.28)	−1.15** (0.46)	−1.04*** (0.35)	−1.11*** (0.31)	−1.3*** (0.34)
UK × Endowments	−0.3*** (0.07)	−0.29*** (0.06)	−0.33*** (0.07)	−0.37*** (0.06)	−0.33*** (0.07)	−0.28*** (0.06)
French × Endowments	0.21 (0.15)	−0.11 (0.16)	0.09 (0.21)	0.25* (0.13)	0.28* (0.15)	0.2 (0.12)
Spanish × Endowments	−0.24* (0.14)	−0.17 (0.21)	−0.17 (0.16)	−0.23 (0.16)	−0.17 (0.14)	−0.11 (0.17)
Portuguese × Endowments	−0.32* (0.16)	−0.12 (0.19)	−0.35 (0.23)	−0.29* (0.15)	−0.21* (0.11)	−0.35** (0.16)
Other empires × Endowments	−0.02 (0.12)	−0.17** (0.08)	−0.18 (0.19)	−0.07 (0.16)	0 (0.11)	0.04 (0.11)
Years since colonization	0.17*** (0.06)	0.35*** (0.06)	0.14** (0.06)	0.13** (0.06)	0.21*** (0.05)	0.23*** (0.06)
Constant	−0.23 (0.19)	−0.79*** (0.17)	−0.3 (0.21)	−0.05 (0.2)	−0.29 (0.18)	−0.34* (0.19)
R^2	0.5	0.53	0.37	0.51	0.55	0.51
Number of observations	102	102	101	102	102	102

Notes: The year of measurement of dependent variables is 2000. Variable descriptions are provided in Table A.1. The sample contains non-European countries colonized by Western powers (Table A.2). Robust standard errors are in parentheses. *, ** and *** denote statistical significance at the 10, 5 and 1% level, respectively

Table 6.5 Robustness checks: Institutional variables II

	Law and order (ICRG)	Democ. account. (ICRG)	Gover. stability (ICRG)	Corruption (ICRG)	Bureauc. quality (ICRG)	Investment profile (ICRG)	Legal struct. and prop. rights (FI)	Property rights (HF)	Executive constraints (Pol. IV)
	(1)	(2)	(3)	(4)	(5)	(6)	(7)	(8)	(9)
British colonies (Reference group)									
French colonies	−2.08*** (0.35)	0.24 (0.76)	−0.35 (0.29)	−0.59 (0.52)	−1.58*** (0.36)	−1.1 (0.9)	−2.23*** (0.4)	−27.7*** (7.33)	−0.42 (0.68)
Spanish colonies	−0.58 (0.38)	−0.4 (0.6)	−0.29 (0.23)	−0.32 (0.34)	−0.99*** (0.27)	−0.51 (0.83)	−1.77*** (0.34)	−24.59*** (6.49)	−0.12 (0.62)
Portuguese colonies	−1.64*** (0.57)	−1.05** (0.41)	−0.02 (0.39)	−0.96*** (0.28)	−1.75*** (0.45)	−2.91*** (1.06)	−2.22*** (0.18)	−28.7*** (7.27)	−0.81 (0.93)
Other empires colonies	−1.73*** (0.49)	−0.36 (0.66)	−1.63*** (0.48)	−0.92* (0.46)	−0.84** (0.41)	−2.43** (1.11)	−2.22*** (0.7)	−18.28*** (6.19)	1.3** (0.53)
UK × Endowments	−0.45*** (0.09)	−0.31** (0.15)	−0.15** (0.07)	−0.34*** (0.08)	−0.26*** (0.07)	−0.68*** (0.22)	−0.69*** (0.14)	−6.52*** (1.28)	−0.38** (0.15)
French × Endowments	1.01*** (0.32)	−0.54 (0.42)	0.25 (0.17)	0.18 (0.29)	0.49** (0.2)	0.28 (0.61)	0.44 (0.41)	1.2 (4.27)	−0.09 (0.36)
Spanish × Endowments	−0.42 (0.27)	0.1 (0.45)	−0.02 (0.11)	0.16 (0.17)	−0.09 (0.19)	0.21 (0.63)	−0.36** (0.18)	−4.49 (4.37)	−0.16 (0.41)
Portuguese × Endowments	−0.21 (0.36)	−0.22 (0.15)	−0.24 (0.24)	−0.15 (0.14)	−0.16 (0.25)	−0.3 (0.32)	−0.64*** (0.09)	−10.65** (4.13)	−0.02 (0.57)
Other empires × Endowments	0.17 (0.34)	−0.44** (0.2)	0.41*** (0.15)	0.31 (0.45)	0.06 (0.16)	0.8* (0.4)	−0.41 (0.29)	−9.01*** (2.32)	−0.91*** (0.27)
Years since colonization	−0.13 (0.1)	0.41** (0.16)	−0.01 (0.08)	0.21** (0.08)	0.25*** (0.08)	0.06 (0.22)	0.01 (0.1)	2.43 (1.8)	0.6*** (0.16)
Constant	4.38*** (0.32)	2.52*** (0.43)	10.23*** (0.23)	2.46*** (0.24)	1.8*** (0.24)	7.75*** (0.7)	6.17*** (0.36)	55.81*** (5.82)	3.06*** (0.45)
R^2	0.45	0.25	0.31	0.35	0.46	0.22	0.64	0.47	0.41
Number of observations	80	80	80	80	80	80	74	87	86

Notes: The year of measurement of dependent variables is 2000. Variable descriptions are provided in Table A.1. The sample contains non-European countries colonized by Western powers (Table A.2). Robust standard errors are in parentheses. *, ** and *** denote statistical significance at the 10, 5 and 1% level, respectively

captures perceptions of political rights and civil liberties. In column 3, *political stability* reflects perceptions about the likelihood of destabilization or subversion of government. Column 4 uses *control of corruption*, which reflects perceptions about the abuse of public power for private gain and the capture of the state by elites and private interests. In column 5 the indicator *government effectiveness* captures perceptions about the quality of public administration. Finally, column 6 introduces *regulatory quality*, which represents the level of friendly policies and norms for private sector development. Interestingly, for all the indicators we observe heterogeneity in the relationship between endowments and institutions. Thus, in the six dimensions of governance the coefficient on the interaction terms varies across former colonial empires, especially when one compares the British empire with the French.

The next block of institutional variables (shown in columns 1–6 of Table 6.5) corresponds to the International Country Risk Guide, a set of indicators widely used in the literature, which are provided by the international consulting firm Political Risk Services Group (see PRS Group 2011). They are based on subjective measures made by experts about different institutional dimensions related to the assessment of political risks. We focus on the indicators more closely associated with governance: *law and order* assesses the strength and impartiality of the legal system and the popular observance of the law; *democratic accountability* measures the responsiveness of government to people; *government stability* evaluates the government's ability to stay in office and implement its declared program; *corruption* measures how widespread corruption is in the political system; *bureaucracy quality* measures the institutional strength and quality of the public administration; *investment profile* assesses "factors affecting the risk to investment that are not covered by other political, economic and financial risk components".[2] Again, we find heterogeneity in the relationship between endowments and institutions. In this case, only former British colonies behave as predicted by the *endowment view*, since the coefficient on the interaction is always negative and significant. For the other groups of colonies, the relationship between endowments and institutions is either not significant or positive (except in column 2 for the 'other empires').

As further robustness checks, columns 7 and 8 introduce two additional indicators closely related to our main institutional indicator *rule of law*. *Legal structure and security of property rights*, provided by the Fraser Institute, comprises judicial independence, trusted legal framework for private businesses activity, military interference, protection of intellectual property and integrity of the legal system (Gwartney and Lawson 2006). *Property rights* is an indicator provided by the Heritage Foundation which measures the degree of protection of property rights by laws and the government, the independence of the judiciary and the enforcement of contracts (Heritage Foundation 2012). Finally, the last column employs the

[2]The scale ranges from 0 to 12 for government stability and investment profile, from 0 to 6 for law and order, democratic accountability and corruption, and from 0 to 4 for bureaucracy quality. In all cases a higher value indicates better institutions.

indicator *executive constraints (decision rules)*, from the Polity IV project, which is an objective indicator that measures the "checks and balances between the various parts of the decision-making process" (Marshall et al. 2010).[3] In the three cases, the results indicate the existence of heterogeneity in the relationship between endowments and institutions across the former colonial empires.

6.3 Robustness to Endowment Indicators

Skeptics could still be concerned with the particular indicator of endowments employed. Although we previously argued that population density in 1500 is the best available indicator of endowments, this chapter introduces several alternative indicators of initial conditions. Initial conditions in the colonies (i.e., endowments) can be classified into two types: those related to the colonial powers' ability to extract wealth by exploiting indigenous resources, and those related to the feasibility of settlements by Europeans. The first type comprises human resources and natural resources, which are divided into minerals and non-minerals. The second type entails the disease environment and the density of indigenous population. In both cases a higher level of these initial conditions is associated with worse institutions, because they either increase the potential to extract rents or reduce the attractiveness for settlement. Figure 6.1 presents our classification of endowments and the respective indicators.

Population density in 1500 is included in the two categories, since it is an obstacle to settlement and also represents a measure of the human resources exploitable by Europeans. In columns 1 and 2 of Table 6.6, we employ population density before colonization as a more accurate measure of precolonial conditions at a country's specific time of colonization.[4] Given the relatively high correlation between this measure and the one employed in our baseline analysis (with a correlation coefficient equal to 63.14%), it is not surprising that our results remain fairly unchanged. Like population density measures, the rate of precolonial urbanization is known to be an obstacle to settlement and also represents a measure of human resources exploitable by Europeans. This indicator is also used in Acemoglu et al. (2002) as a proxy for precolonial wealth. In the additive model (column 3), we observe a negative relation between the rate of precolonial urbanization and institutions.[5] The

[3]The scale for the property rights indicators goes from 0 to 10 and 0 to 100, respectively, with higher scores implying better protection of property rights. The scale for *executive constraints* ranges from 1 to 7, where a higher score means more constraints on the executive.

[4]Since this variable has not been constructed and used previously in the colonialism literature, we were required to compute it on the basis of historical population estimates from Goldewijk et al. (2010) and the use of geospatial software (ArcGIS) to impute each country's value.

[5]In this case, the coefficient on former French colonies can be differentiated only marginally from the British coefficient. This may stem from the fact that data on urbanization rates in 1500 are missing for sub-Saharan Africa.

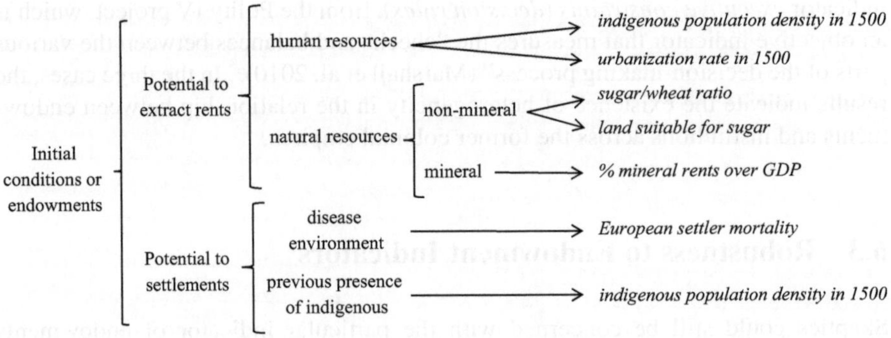

Fig. 6.1 Classification of endowments

interaction model in column 4 provides evidence that only in the case of British colonies, more developed territories before colonization have worse institutions today.

Another popular indicator of endowments—often used as an instrument for institutions—is the potential mortality rate of European settlers, which reflects an initial condition related to the feasibility of settlement (Acemoglu et al. 2001). The additive model in column 5 reflects the expected negative relation between potential settler mortality and current institutions. It is also interesting to note that former French colonies do not have worse institutions than the British once potential settler mortality is controlled for. However, the interaction model in column 6 again reveals significant heterogeneity in the relationship between endowments and institutions across colonial empires.

In columns 7–10 we focus on the feasibility of introducing the system of plantation crops. According to Engerman and Sokoloff (1997, 2000) the plantation system in the New World led to highly unequal societies that favored institutions built to benefit the elites. Sugarcane was a widespread crop in plantation systems, while wheat was not advantageous in large-scale cultivation. Column 7 introduces the suitability of land for sugarcane relative to wheat, which enters with a significantly negative coefficient. However, in the interaction model (column 8) we see that the negative relationship between the "sugar/wheat ratio" and institutions is driven only by former British and Spanish colonies. The next two columns show a similar pattern when the other proxy for suitability for sugarcane crops is used.[6] We

[6]This indicator measures the percentage of land suitable for sugarcane crops. It is based on own calculations, from FAO/IIASA (2002) data. It differs from the Easterly indicator in that the land suitable for sugarcane is measured regardless of the land suitable for wheat. One might argue that what really matters is the possibility of establishing the plantation system *in absolute terms*, rather than *the ratio* with respect to wheat crops. Moreover, this indicator has the advantage of being available for a larger sample of countries. A much less accurate measure such as a country dummy for being a sugar producer also renders a highly significant negative coefficient on the interaction term for British colonies. To conserve space, the results with this simple measure are unreported and available from the authors upon request.

Table 6.6 Robustness checks: Alternative indicators of endowments

Dependent variable is rule of law (WGI)	Population density before colonization		Urbanization in 1500		European settler mortality		Sugar/wheat ratio		Land suitable for sugar		Mineral resources		Log State Antiquity Index (at time of colonization)	
	(1)	(2)	(3)	(4)	(5)	(6)	(7)	(8)	(9)	(10)	(11)	(12)	(13)	(14)
Endowments	−0.11**		−0.06*		−0.33***		−2.53***		−3.65**		0.00		−0.08*	
	(0.04)		(0.03)		(0.09)		(0.48)		(1.58)		(0.03)		(0.04)	
British colonies (Reference group)														
French colonies	−0.65***	−0.95***	−0.91*	−2.75***	−0.2	−2.08*	−0.1	−0.14	−0.44**	−0.54**	−0.68***	−0.76***	−0.35	−1.3**
	(0.19)	(0.24)	(0.5)	(0.47)	(0.24)	(1.04)	(0.21)	(0.22)	(0.2)	(0.23)	(0.19)	(0.2)	(0.22)	(0.58)
Spanish colonies	−0.99***	−0.97***	−0.44	−1.06*	−0.64**	−0.5	−0.76***	−0.7***	−0.52*	−0.53	−0.95***	−1.19***	−0.8***	−0.99*
	(0.23)	(0.25)	(0.3)	(0.57)	(0.26)	(2.02)	(0.22)	(0.23)	(0.3)	(0.4)	(0.24)	(0.24)	(0.29)	(0.5)
Portuguese colonies	−1.25***	−1.38***	−0.7**	−1.2**	−1.01***	1.83***	−0.61***	−0.66***	−1.15***	−1.63***	−1.08***	−1.24***	−0.89*	0.34
	(0.28)	(0.27)	(0.35)	(0.46)	(0.26)	(0.59)	(0.19)	(0.2)	(0.31)	(0.34)	(0.35)	(0.43)	(0.46)	(0.87)
Other empires colonies	−1.16***	−1.16***	−1.16***	−1.72**	−0.8***	−0.15	−0.43*	−0.68***	−0.89***	−1.16***	−1.17***	−1.39***	−0.97***	−1.03**
	(0.21)	(0.24)	(0.32)	(0.66)	(0.22)	(0.69)	(0.23)	(0.22)	(0.25)	(0.28)	(0.23)	(0.25)	(0.22)	(0.43)
UK × Endowments		−0.13**		−0.15***		−0.39***		−3.43***		−12.69**		−0.07**		−0.13*
		(0.06)		(0.05)		(0.11)		(0.89)		(5.24)		(0.03)		(0.07)
French × Endowments		0.1		0.07**		−0.04		−0.39		−2.76		0.01		0.06
		(0.11)		(0.03)		(0.15)		(2.06)		(2.74)		(0.04)		(0.07)
Spanish × Endowments		−0.07		−0.04		−0.42		−2.3***		−4.5**		0.2***		−0.07
		(0.11)		(0.04)		(0.42)		(0.52)		(2.12)		(0.06)		(0.07)
Portuguese × Endowments		−0.29***		n.a.		−0.95***		n.a.		25.86**		0.6		−0.48***
		(0.07)		n.a.		(0.07)		n.a.		(10.89)		(0.72)		(0.17)
Other empires × Endowments		−0.14**		−0.05		−0.51***		0.92		1.89		0.04**		−0.11**
		(0.07)		(0.07)		(0.13)		(1.7)		(5.1)		(0.02)		(0.05)
Years since colonization	0.17***	0.15**	−0.13	−0.14	0.13	0.12	0.31***	0.29***	0.17**	0.16**	0.19***	0.19***	0.19**	0.17**
	(0.06)	(0.06)	(0.13)	(0.13)	(0.08)	(0.09)	(0.07)	(0.07)	(0.07)	(0.07)	(0.06)	(0.06)	(0.08)	(0.09)
Constant	−0.22	−0.15	1.04*	1.57***	1.16*	1.42**	−0.97***	−0.95***	−0.44**	−0.35	−0.35	−0.27	−0.22	0.01
	(0.22)	(0.22)	(0.57)	(0.54)	(0.59)	(0.65)	(0.24)	(0.25)	(0.21)	(0.23)	(0.22)	(0.23)	(0.36)	(0.49)
R^2	0.37	0.40	0.33	0.48	0.43	0.46	0.39	0.42	0.27	0.31	0.33	0.38	0.30	0.34
Number of observations	102	102	43	43	74	74	67	67	88	88	101	101	84	84

Notes: Rule of law ranges from −2.5 to 2.5, where a higher value indicates better institutions. Its year of measurement is 2000. Variable descriptions are provided in Table A.1. The sample contains non-European countries colonized by Western powers (Table A.2). Robust standard errors are in parentheses. *, ** and *** denote statistical significance at the 10, 5 and 1% level, respectively

also employ an indicator of mineral natural resources endowments, which is constructed as the average of mineral rents over GDP during the period 1960–2000. Engerman and Sokoloff (1997, 2000) and Lange et al. (2006) emphasize the important role played by mineral resources in accounting for the type of institutions and policies implanted in the colonies. While the additive model (column 11) does not report any relationship between endowments and institutions, the interaction model (column 12) shows evidence of heterogeneity in this relationship. For former British colonies the relationship with endowments is significantly negative, which contrasts with that observed for the remaining groups.[7]

Finally, as an additional endowment variable we employ the natural log of the state antiquity index in the first year of colonization, proposed by Bockstette et al. (2002). Arguably, countries with a long tradition of statehood can be thought of as more attractive for a potential colonizer since they are expected to have well-articulated hierarchical societies with well-developed indigenous systems of tribute and coercive labor that can be exploited to extract resources from the colonies (e.g., in the Inca and Aztec empires). Indeed, the additive model (column 13) indicates that greater state antiquity is associated with worse institutions, whereas the interaction model (column 14) shows that this statistically significant negative relation between a country's tradition of statehood and institutional quality holds for former British, Portuguese and Other Empires' colonies.

To summarize, this subsection has shown that for several indicators of endowments there is high heterogeneity across former colonial empires in the relationship between endowments and current institutions. These results call into question the universal validity of the *endowment view* and warn that the potential effect of colonizer identity depends on the level of endowments.

6.4 Limiting the Range in the Distribution of Endowments to French Range

One possible weakness of the main empirical analysis is that the range in the distribution of endowments differs across colonial powers. When comparing the two largest colonial empires, the range of variation of population density in 1500 for former British colonies is considerably higher than that for French colonies. To shed some further light on this issue, we restrict the analysis to those colonies with precolonial population density within the French range [0, 2.5].[8] When we re-estimate all the specifications shown in Tables 4.1, 5.1, 5.2, 5.3, 5.4, and 5.5,

[7]The striking positive coefficient for the interaction term of Spanish colonies is due to the extreme value of Chile. Once it is excluded, the coefficient becomes negative (but far from being statistically significant).

[8]Note that this problem is partially mitigated by using other endowments indicators such as potential settler mortality rate, for which differences in range across colonial powers are relatively lower.

we again obtain consistent evidence of a highly significant negative coefficient on 'UK colony × Pop. dens.', as predicted by the *endowment view*, whereas the coefficient on 'French colony × Pop. dens.' appears positive but in most cases insignificant.[9] These results are presented in Tables 6.7, 6.8, 6.9, and 6.10. As with the analysis for the whole sample of colonies, when we restrict the sample of colonies within the French range of endowments, the heterogeneity in the relationship of endowments and colonizer identity with institutions appears highly robust to controlling for (1) several variables accounting for the duration of colonization and the time variation in the colonial strategies of colonial powers within the two main waves of colonialism, (2) sociological and anthropological factors that include religion, and the degree of ethnolinguistic fractionalization and precolonial centralization, and (3) several measures of the distance to the metropolis of European colonial powers in order to account for the differences in transportation costs from the metropolis to the colonies and the associated geographic cost of controlling colonial dominions.

Based on our basic specification, Fig. 6.2 depicts the predicted values of *rule of law* for British and French colonies along with 95% confidence intervals for the restricted range. By doing so, we can make one interesting point even clearer than above. For values of the log of precolonial population density between 0 and about 1, the effect of British colonization on institutions is higher than that of French colonization; and for values between 1 and about 1.6 there are no statistical differences in institutional levels between British and French colonies. However, for values within the interval [1.6, 2.5], French colonies exceed the British in terms of institutional scores. This supports the claim by Acemoglu et al. (2001, p. 1388) that "researchers are [probably] overestimating how *bad* French institutions are".

In conclusion, the evidence provided so far reveals strong presence of heterogeneity in the relationship of colonial origin and endowments with current institutions. On the one hand, the impact of colonizer identity varies with the level of endowments; on the other hand, the relationship between endowments and institutions is very different across the former colonial empires. These findings have two major implications. First, the *endowment view* is not universally applicable, since it does not fit the experience of former French colonies and 'Other Empires' colonies. Second, former British colonies are not always associated with better institutions and, in fact, former French colonies at least equal the British when the level of endowments is high. This evidence is robust to the inclusion of a wide array of control variables, the presence of outliers and sample selection, the use of alterna-

[9] Wald tests always reject the equality of coefficients between the interaction terms of British and French colonies at the highest significance level (except in one specification where the sample only contains 29 observations).

Table 6.7 Reference model and control variables I (The timing of colonization). Population density limited to the range of values of French colonies

Dependent variable is rule of law (WGI)												
			Additional control variables									
	Additive model	Reference model	Years since colonization	Years since independence		Duration of colonization		Colonization after 1850		Gap between first sighted and colonized		All controls together
	(1)	(2)	(3)	(4)	(5)	(6)	(7)	(8)	(9)	(10)	(11)	(12)
Endowments	−0.24* (0.14)											
British colonies (Reference group)												
French colonies	−0.5** (0.22)	−1.6*** (0.24)	−1.32*** (0.34)	−1.54*** (0.22)	−1.22*** (0.34)	−1.54*** (0.22)	−1.38*** (0.26)	−1.6*** (0.24)	−1.91*** (0.39)	−1.53*** (0.24)	−1.79*** (0.34)	−1.43*** (0.23)
Spanish colonies	−1*** (0.21)	−1.71*** (0.35)	−2.52*** (0.31)	−1.59*** (0.51)	−2.01*** (0.27)	−1.59*** (0.51)	−4.32*** (0.78)	−1.72*** (0.34)	−1.73*** (0.37)	−1.66*** (0.36)	−2.16*** (0.31)	−1.47*** (0.44)
Portuguese colonies	−1.47*** (0.29)	−2.31*** (0.43)	−21.62*** (0.14)	−2.34*** (0.43)	−130.88*** (1.83)	−2.34*** (0.43)	−20.93*** (0.15)	−2.34*** (0.41)	−0.87*** (0.28)	−2.28*** (0.45)	−2.12*** (0.24)	−2.36*** (0.44)
Other empires colonies	−1.31*** (0.3)	−2.34*** (0.46)	−2.58*** (0.56)	−2.3*** (0.47)	−2.59*** (0.83)	−2.3*** (0.47)	−2.53*** (0.49)	−2.39*** (0.47)	−1.63*** (0.35)	−2.4*** (0.48)	−1.37*** (0.24)	−2.41*** (0.51)
UK × Endowments		−1.01*** (0.14)	−1.01*** (0.14)	−1*** (0.14)	−1.04*** (0.17)	−1*** (0.14)	−0.97*** (0.14)	−1*** (0.13)	−1.01*** (0.14)	−1.01*** (0.14)	−1.02*** (0.14)	−0.97*** (0.14)
French × Endowments		0.22 (0.15)	0.23* (0.14)	0.2 (0.15)	0.17 (0.15)	0.2 (0.15)	0.18 (0.15)	0.22 (0.15)	0.23 (0.14)	0.15 (0.16)	0.08 (0.17)	0.13 (0.16)
Spanish × Endowments		0.18 (0.39)	0.09 (0.42)	0.22 (0.41)	0.09 (0.44)	0.22 (0.41)	0.26 (0.33)	0.15 (0.38)	0.18 (0.41)	0.18 (0.38)	0.61* (0.33)	0.19 (0.4)
Portuguese × Endowments		0.2 (0.3)	10.72*** (0)	0.24 (0.3)	−4.39*** (0.23)	0.24 (0.3)	10.84*** (0.01)	0.19 (0.29)	−4.38*** (0.39)	0.22 (0.31)	1.37*** (0.17)	0.27 (0.3)
Other empires × Endowments		0.52 (0.37)	0.06 (0.21)	0.51 (0.38)	0.45 (0.33)	0.51 (0.38)	−0.36* (0.2)	0.57 (0.38)	−0.02 (0.29)	0.58 (0.39)	−0.02 (0.16)	0.65 (0.42)
Years since colonization	0.17*** (0.06)	0.14*** (0.05)		0.15*** (0.05)	0.14** (0.05)	0.03 (0.31)	−0.42** (0.18)	0.2** (0.08)	0.14 (0.09)	0.16*** (0.06)	0.11* (0.06)	0.1 (0.24)
Additional control variable				−0.12 (0.32)		0.12 (0.32)		0.22 (0.22)		0.0 (0.00)		[0.469]

UK × Additional control			0.13** (0.05)		0.27 (0.91)		0.54*** (0.18)		−0.03 (0.29)		0.0 (0.00)	
French × Additional control			−0.07 (0.21)		−0.54*** (0.17)		0.46 (0.33)		0.38 (0.28)		0.0 (0.00)	
Spanish × Additional control			0.32*** (0.1)		0.25 (0.16)		1.69*** (0.53)		n.a. n.a.		0.02 (0.02)	
Portuguese × Additional control			3.59*** (0)		520.41*** (7.97)		4.03*** (0.18)		5.2*** (0.14)		−0.01*** (0)	
Other empires × Additional control			0.36*** (0.13)		0.66 (0.88)		1.02*** (0.25)		−0.67 (0.55)		0** (0)	
Constant	−0.24 (0.25)	0.41*** (0.15)	0.43*** (0.14)	0.41*** (0.15)	0.35 (0.27)	0.41*** (0.15)	0.58*** (0.15)	0.15 (0.28)	0.42 (0.35)	0.24 (0.21)	0.49 (0.32)	−0.16 (0.35)
R^2	0.45	0.68	0.71	0.68	0.71	0.68	0.73	0.69	0.71	0.69	0.73	0.7
Number of observations	68	68	68	68	68	68	68	68	68	68	68	68

Notes: Rule of law ranges from −2.5 to 2.5, where a higher value indicates better institutions. Its year of measurement is 2000. The endowments indicator is log population density in 1500, from Acemoglu et al. (2002). Variable descriptions are provided in Table A.1. The sample contains non-European countries colonized by Western powers (Table A.2). Robust standard errors are in parentheses. The last column reports the p-value of the joint significance test of all the additional controls. *, ** and *** denote statistical significance at the 10, 5 and 1% level, respectively. In the last column, we report the p-value of the joint significance test

Table 6.8 Control variables II: Sociological and anthropological factors. Population density limited to the range of values of French colonies

Dependent variable is rule of law (WGI)											
	Additional control variables										
	Religion		Ethnic fractionalization		Several precolonial cultures		Precolonial centralization		Indigenous mortality		All controls together
	(1)	(2)	(3)	(4)	(5)	(6)	(7)	(8)	(9)	(10)	(11)
British colonies (Reference group)											
French colonies	−1.57*** (0.23)	−1.4*** (0.23)	−1.53*** (0.29)	−2.41*** (0.44)	−1.41** (0.54)	−1.94*** (0.61)	−1.6*** (0.25)	−1.87*** (0.28)	−1.56*** (0.26)	−1.41*** (0.22)	−1.47*** (0.51)
Spanish colonies	−1.52*** (0.39)	−1.41 (1.65)	−1.72*** (0.35)	−1.81*** (0.58)	−1.49** (0.58)	−1.7*** (0.45)	−1.73*** (0.35)	−1.81*** (0.3)	−1.69*** (0.35)	−1.91*** (0.24)	−1.2* (0.64)
Portuguese colonies	−2.23*** (0.43)	−1.36*** (0.33)	−2.17*** (0.44)	4.11*** (0.28)	−2.16*** (0.27)	−2.57*** (0.4)	−2.26*** (0.49)	−25.54*** (0.21)	−2.13*** (0.5)	−2.26*** (0.53)	−1.73*** (0.55)
Other empires colonies	−2.35*** (0.53)	−2.89*** (0.38)	−2.35*** (0.42)	−1.64*** (0.23)	−1.89** (0.78)	−2.46** (0.91)	−2.36*** (0.46)	−1.95*** (0.14)	−2.35*** (0.45)	−2.54*** (0.42)	−1.97** (0.83)
UK × Endowments	−1.01*** (0.16)	−1.02*** (0.15)	−0.94*** (0.15)	−0.87*** (0.15)	−0.8*** (0.29)	−0.94*** (0.28)	−1*** (0.15)	−0.98*** (0.17)	−0.98*** (0.14)	−0.98*** (0.15)	−0.89*** (0.31)
French × Endowments	0.21 (0.15)	0.11 (0.14)	0.17 (0.17)	0.33* (0.16)	0.25 (0.17)	0.36* (0.18)	0.25 (0.15)	0.09 (0.13)	0.23 (0.15)	0.16 (0.15)	0.01 (0.2)
Spanish × Endowments	0.22 (0.39)	0.22 (0.37)	0.29 (0.38)	0.39 (0.36)	0.48 (0.58)	0.43* (0.24)	0.24 (0.42)	0.48** (0.24)	0.15 (0.39)	0.08 (0.44)	0.67 (0.56)
Portuguese × Endowments	0.17 (0.3)	−0.33* (0.19)	0.15 (0.3)	0.66*** (0.14)	n.a. n.a.	n.a. n.a.	0.15 (0.34)	12.14*** (0.02)	0.11 (0.34)	0.22 (0.35)	n.a. n.a.
Other empires × Endowments	0.52 (0.48)	0.75*** (0.27)	0.59* (0.35)	0.8*** (0.14)	0.41 (0.49)	0.5 (0.5)	0.55 (0.38)	0.91*** (0.15)	0.61 (0.4)	0.68* (0.34)	0.38 (0.57)
Years since colonization	0.14** (0.06)	0.15** (0.06)	0.12** (0.05)	0.08* (0.05)	0.08 (0.08)	0.05 (0.09)	0.13** (0.06)	0.12** (0.05)	0.11 (0.07)	0.15* (0.08)	0.02 (0.09)
Additional control	[0.69]		−0.25 (0.35)		−0.17 (0.25)		−0.04 (0.19)		0.15 (0.23)		[0.596]
UK × Additional control		0 (0)		−0.7* (0.39)		−0.62* (0.33)		−0.16 (0.27)		0.11 (0.24)	

French × Additional control		−0.01 (0.01)		0.56 (0.43)		0.47 (0.31)		0.64** (0.28)		−1.01*** (0.22)	
Spanish × Additional control		0 (0.02)		−0.45 (1.09)		−0.15 (0.3)		−0.24 (0.25)		0.34 (0.27)	
Portuguese × Additional control		−0.02*** (0)		−9.18*** (0.13)		n.a. n.a.		22.99*** (0.34)		n.a. n.a.	
Other empires × Additional control		0.01*** (0)		−2.02*** (0.2)		n.a. n.a.		−1.26*** (0.11)		0.88*** (0.28)	
Constant	0.81 (0.55)	0.45*** (0.14)	0.57** (0.24)	0.85*** (0.29)	0.34 (0.6)	0.75 (0.64)	0.45*** (0.17)	0.49*** (0.17)	0.4** (0.17)	0.32** (0.16)	1.2 (1.2)
R^2	0.69	0.72	0.68	0.75	0.48	0.54	0.69	0.76	0.69	0.72	0.56
Number of observations	67	68	67	67	44	44	66	66	68	68	44

Notes: Rule of law ranges from −2.5 to 2.5, where a higher value indicates better institutions. Its year of measurement is 2000. The endowments indicator is log population density in 1500, from Acemoglu et al. (2002). Variable descriptions are provided in Table A.1. The sample contains non-European countries colonized by Western powers (Table A.2). Robust standard errors are in parentheses. *, ** and *** denote statistical significance at the 10, 5 and 1% level, respectively. In column 1 and 11, we report the p-value of the joint significance test. In column 2, colonial origin dummies are interacted with the percentage of catholics

Table 6.9 Control variables III: Transportation costs. Population density limited to the range of values of French colonies

Dependent variable is rule of law (WGI)											
	Control variables										
	Distance from metropolis		Landlocked		Distance from the coast		Altitude		Island		All controls together
	(1)	(2)	(3)	(4)	(5)	(6)	(7)	(8)	(9)	(10)	(11)
British colonies (Reference group)											
French colonies	−1.58*** (0.24)	−1.82*** (0.43)	−1.76*** (0.32)	−1.71*** (0.33)	−1.53*** (0.35)	−1.71*** (0.41)	−1.33*** (0.29)	−1.19** (0.53)	−1.59*** (0.25)	−1.42*** (0.21)	−1.3*** (0.35)
Spanish colonies	−1.75*** (0.36)	−2.67*** (0.4)	−1.75*** (0.35)	−1.78*** (0.35)	−1.71*** (0.36)	−1.75*** (0.36)	−1.38*** (0.44)	−1.41*** (0.48)	−1.7*** (0.36)	−1.46*** (0.43)	−1.46*** (0.5)
Portuguese colonies	−2.32*** (0.46)	−6.06*** (0.45)	−2.36*** (0.43)	−2.4*** (0.44)	−2.26*** (0.44)	−1.35*** (0.25)	−1.73*** (0.43)	−0.97*** (0.3)	−2.28*** (0.48)	−1.98*** (0.47)	−1.77*** (0.46)
Other empires colonies	−2.36*** (0.48)	−3*** (0.79)	−2.34*** (0.46)	−2.36*** (0.46)	−2.31*** (0.49)	−1.96*** (0.57)	−2.07*** (0.53)	−1.47 (1.11)	−2.32*** (0.49)	−4.19*** (0.32)	−2.01*** (0.56)
UK × Endowments	−1.01*** (0.14)	−1.02*** (0.14)	−1.05*** (0.12)	−1.11*** (0.13)	−0.99*** (0.15)	−0.99*** (0.2)	−0.81*** (0.2)	−0.81*** (0.21)	−1.01*** (0.14)	−0.95*** (0.14)	−0.82*** (0.19)
French × Endowments	0.19 (0.14)	0.18 (0.13)	0.3 (0.18)	0.26 (0.19)	0.19 (0.18)	0.26 (0.21)	0.22 (0.15)	0.2 (0.18)	0.22 (0.15)	0.19 (0.14)	0.2 (0.16)
Spanish × Endowments	0.27 (0.4)	0.05 (0.51)	0.18 (0.39)	0.17 (0.39)	0.22 (0.41)	0.55 (0.49)	0.45 (0.47)	0.15 (0.47)	0.2 (0.41)	0.22 (0.49)	0.5 (0.57)
Portuguese × Endowments	0.14 (0.34)	1.66*** (0.14)	0.24 (0.3)	0.25 (0.31)	0.16 (0.31)	−0.42** (0.19)	−0.11 (0.35)	−0.58** (0.25)	0.19 (0.32)	0.04 (0.33)	−0.15 (0.36)
Other empires × Endowments	0.64 (0.42)	0.38 (0.43)	0.49 (0.37)	0.48 (0.38)	0.5 (0.39)	0.29 (0.46)	0.56 (0.41)	0.4 (0.6)	0.5 (0.4)	5.61*** (0.87)	0.68 (0.63)
Years since colonization	0.17*** (0.05)	0.16*** (0.05)	0.15*** (0.05)	0.16*** (0.05)	0.13** (0.05)	0.13** (0.06)	0.09 (0.07)	0.07 (0.08)	0.14** (0.06)	0.09 (0.06)	0.13 (0.08)
Additional control variable	−0.04 (0.03)		0.28 (0.25)		−0.01 (0.03)		−0.33 (0.27)		0.03 (0.2)		[0.00]
UK × Additional control		−0.09 (0.06)		0.79*** (0.23)		−0.01 (0.08)		−0.35 (0.5)		0.32* (0.19)	

French × Additional control		−0.06 (0.05)		0.16 (0.27)		0.01 (0.03)		−0.7 (0.85)		−0.31 (0.43)	
Spanish × Additional control		0.05 (0.06)		n.a. n.a.		−0.1 (0.1)		0.05 (0.24)		0.03 (0.23)	
Portuguese × Additional control		0.37*** (0.01)		n.a. n.a.		−0.29*** (0)		−1.15*** (0.03)		n.a. n.a.	
Other empires × Additional control		0.02 (0.08)		n.a. n.a.		−0.08** (0.04)		−1.5 (1.28)		−5.49*** (0.95)	
Constant	0.58** (0.25)	0.96*** (0.32)	0.39** (0.15)	0.41*** (0.14)	0.43*** (0.15)	0.44*** (0.16)	0.36 (0.32)	0.42 (0.37)	0.41** (0.16)	0.38** (0.16)	0.52 (0.34)
R^2	0.69	0.71	0.69	0.7	0.68	0.7	0.53	0.55	0.68	0.72	0.56
Number of observations	68	68	68	68	68	68	54	54	68	68	54

Notes: Rule of law ranges from −2.5 to 2.5, where a higher value indicates better institutions. Its year of measurement is 2000. The endowments indicator is log population density in 1500, from Acemoglu et al. (2002). Variable descriptions are provided in Table A.1. The sample contains non-European countries colonized by Western powers (Table A.2). Robust standard errors are in parentheses. *, ** and *** denote statistical significance at the 10, 5 and 1% level, respectively. In the last column, we report the p-value of the joint significance test

Table 6.10 Control variables IV: Geography and climate. Population density limited to the range of values of French colonies

Dependent variable is rule of law (WGI)	Latitude		Land in geographical tropics (%)		Land quality		Temperature and humidity	Continental dummies	All controls together
	(1)	(2)	(3)	(4)	(5)	(6)	(7)	(8)	(9)
British colonies (Reference group)									
French colonies	−1.43*** (0.26)	−1.41*** (0.35)	−1.32*** (0.23)	−1.06*** (0.25)	−1.59*** (0.24)	−1.22*** (0.25)	−1.67*** (0.37)	−1.42*** (0.37)	−1.38*** (0.32)
Spanish colonies	−1.54*** (0.35)	−1.34*** (0.43)	−1.25*** (0.38)	−3.05*** (1.04)	−1.73*** (0.35)	−1.38** (0.64)	−1.81*** (0.45)	−1.64*** (0.36)	−1.59*** (0.55)
Portuguese colonies	−2.29*** (0.38)	−4.27*** (0.22)	−2.13*** (0.47)	−3.88*** (0.35)	−2.38*** (0.47)	−4.73*** (0.3)	−2.29*** (0.43)	−2.17*** (0.54)	−2.01*** (0.59)
Other empires colonies	−2.14*** (0.46)	−2.3*** (0.49)	−2.1*** (0.56)	−2.68*** (0.27)	−2.35*** (0.48)	−3.07*** (0.3)	−2.11*** (0.5)	−2.2*** (0.49)	−1.6*** (0.52)
UK × Endowments	−0.91*** (0.15)	−0.9*** (0.15)	−0.83*** (0.16)	−0.86*** (0.16)	−1.01*** (0.14)	−1.02*** (0.15)	−0.97*** (0.22)	−0.93*** (0.18)	−0.76** (0.28)
French × Endowments	0.13 (0.14)	0.12 (0.16)	0.21 (0.13)	0.18 (0.11)	0.24 (0.15)	0.25* (0.14)	0.29 (0.19)	0.15 (0.16)	0.23 (0.21)
Spanish × Endowments	0.05 (0.37)	0.18 (0.39)	−0.17 (0.45)	1.46* (0.86)	0.16 (0.41)	0.16 (0.48)	0.39 (0.64)	0.15 (0.4)	1.13 (0.85)
Portuguese × Endowments	0.28 (0.28)	0.7*** (0.17)	0.35 (0.35)	−1.24*** (0.24)	0.25 (0.33)	−0.27 (0.2)	0.16 (0.3)	0.21 (0.34)	0.05 (0.41)
Other empires × Endowments	0.54 (0.38)	0.58 (0.38)	0.6 (0.45)	0.18 (0.37)	0.5 (0.39)	0.26 (0.16)	0.38 (0.37)	0.45 (0.39)	0.04 (0.41)
Years since colonization	0.15*** (0.05)	0.15** (0.06)	0.15*** (0.06)	0.14* (0.07)	0.16** (0.06)	0.11* (0.06)	0.19*** (0.05)	0.14** (0.07)	0.17** (0.07)
Additional control variable	1.72** (0.71)		−0.3 (0.19)		−1.02 (2.77)		[0.44]	[0.820]	[0.00]
UK × Additional control		1.85* (1.01)		−0.17 (0.34)		2.5 (2.74)			

French × Additional control		1.84 (1.39)		−0.69*** (0.22)		−7.29** (3)			
Spanish × Additional control		−0.03 (1.21)		1.12 (0.84)		−2.09 (4.41)			
Portuguese × Additional control		12.6*** (0.22)		3.82*** (0.08)		68.09*** (1.23)			
Other empires × Additional control		3.94 (3.22)		0.97* (0.5)		28.82*** (4.97)			
Constant	0.05 (0.23)	0.01 (0.3)	0.3 (0.19)	0.29 (0.21)	0.43** (0.17)	0.34* (0.19)	−1.71 (1.8)	0.34 (0.29)	−4.44** (1.63)
R^2	0.71	0.72	0.59	0.68	0.68	0.74	0.72	0.69	0.72
Number of observations	68	68	58	58	66	66	67	68	57

Notes: Rule of law ranges from −2.5 to 2.5, where a higher value indicates better institutions. Its year of measurement is 2000. The endowments indicator is log population density in 1500, from Acemoglu et al. (2002). Variable descriptions are provided in Table A.1. The sample contains non-European countries colonized by Western powers (Table A.2). Robust standard errors are in parentheses. *, ** and *** denote statistical significance at the 10, 5 and 1% level, respectively. In the last three columns, we report the p-value of the joint significance test

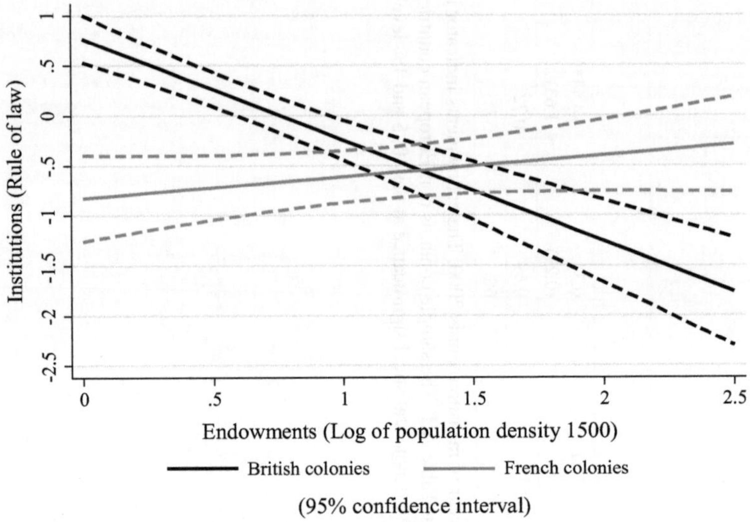

Fig. 6.2 Predicted values of rule of law by the level of population density for British and French colonies, with population density limited to the range of French colonies

tive institutional indicators and different measures of endowments, and limiting the range in the distribution of endowments to French range. The next chapter investigates the main mechanism through which the independent variables of our model affect current institutions.

Chapter 7
Exploring the Mechanism of Colonial Rule

Abstract Our model predicts that domestic conditions in the metropolis determined the style of imperialism, which affected the choice of colonial policy (that could be responsive or not to colonies' initial conditions and endowments), and in turn postcolonial institutional development. This chapter tries to trace the link of colonies' initial endowments and their interaction with the domestic conditions in the metropolis to current institutions through their effect on the colonial strategy adopted. As argued above, the British colonial strategy varied according to local conditions and in large parts of Africa was based on indirect rule. In contrast, the French colonial policy was more uniform and based on direct rule. The empirical strategy is operationalized through the use of a suitable measure of the choice of colonial policy such as the number of Africans per European administrator, with a higher value implying a more indirect form of rule. The empirical strategy builds on a Two-stage Least Squares framework. In a first stage, the colonial strategy is explained on the basis of colonies' initial endowments and their interaction with domestic conditions in the metropolis, whereas in a second stage, rule of law is regressed on the extent of indirect rule. The form of colonial rule is clearly found to mediate between colonies' initial endowments and their interaction with metropolis' domestic conditions and current institutional levels.

7.1 Introduction

Our model predicts that domestic conditions in the metropolis determined the style of imperialism. This affected the choice of colonial policy, which could be responsive or not to colonies' initial conditions and endowments, and in turn postcolonial institutional development. Table 7.1 estimates the reduced-form effect of colonies' initial endowments and their interaction with metropolis' domestic conditions on current institutions. This is a way to test whether, consistent with our model, the effect of endowments on institutional development is conditional on metropolis' domestic conditions. It is remarkable that the three domestic conditions considered (i.e., continental character of the metropolis measured by its surface area, openness of the political regime in the nineteenth century and demographic pressure for resources in the nineteenth century measured by population density) interact significantly with colonies' endowments in the expected direction. That is, domestic

D. Oto-Peralías, D. Romero-Ávila, *Colonial Theories of Institutional Development*, Contributions to Economics, DOI 10.1007/978-3-319-54127-3_7

Table 7.1 Exploring the mechanism of colonial rule: Reduced-form relationship

	Dependent variable is rule of law (WGI)		
	(1)	(2)	(3)
Endowments	−0.40*** (0.10)	0.18 (0.19)	0.06 (0.16)
Colonial power surface area	−0.0003** (0.00)		
Endowments × Colonial power surface area	0.0006** (0.00)		
Colonial power *Polity2* (nineteenth century)		0.26*** (0.07)	
Endowments × Colonial power *Polity2* (nineteenth century)		−0.08** (0.04)	
Colonial power population density (nineteenth century)			0.01*** (0.00)
Endowments × Colonial power population density (nineteenth century)			−0.003** (0.00)
Years since colonization	0.08 (0.05)	0.15*** (0.05)	0.18*** (0.04)
Constant	−0.33* (0.17)	−1.91*** (0.42)	−1.54*** (0.24)
R^2	0.24	0.35	0.38
Number of observations	102	102	102

Notes: Rule of law ranges from −2.5 to 2.5, where a higher value indicates better institutions. Its year of measurement is 2000. The endowments indicator is log population density in 1500, from Acemoglu et al. (2002). Variable descriptions are provided in Table A.1. The sample contains non-European countries colonized by Western powers (Table A.2). Robust standard errors are in parentheses. *, ** and *** denote statistical significance at the 10, 5 and 1% level, respectively

conditions conducive to an 'economically-oriented' style of imperialism interact negatively with colonies' initial endowments, while those related to a 'politically-oriented' style interact positively.

In what follows, we describe the main features of colonial policy of the British and French empires, with a particular focus on Africa, and then we move to the empirical analysis of the mechanism associated with colonial rule. The reason for focusing the description and analysis to these empires within Africa is simply because the proxy for colonial rule used (i.e., the number of Africans per European administrator as a measure of the extent of direct/indirect rule) is only available for 33 sub-Saharan former colonies (Richens 2009). Notwithstanding, in order to highlight the variability of British colonial rule to local conditions, we will also comment on other British colonies than those in Africa.

7.2 Colonial Rule in the British and French Empires

In the preceding chapters we have provided consistent evidence that the level of endowments is negatively associated with current institutional development in former British colonies, whereas they are found to be unrelated in former French colonies. Since former British colonies in sub-Saharan Africa are generally characterized by adverse endowments (i.e., high precolonial population density and high potential mortality rates of European settlers), full application of direct rule in this context was rare, with Mauritius being perhaps the closest colony in British Africa to this colonial policy paradigm.[1]

It is well-documented the fact that direct rule in extreme form was implemented in the settler colonies of North America and Australasia, which received a massive inflow of white immigrants from the metropolis who established representative constitutional systems. Direct rule was also applied in strategically oriented colonies such as Hong Kong, Singapore and Ceylon (Sri Lanka), as well as in the plantation colonies of the West Indies. None of these colonies received a large inflow of white settlers. At the other extreme of the spectrum, indirect rule was widespread among extractive colonies, particularly in sub-Saharan Africa and some parts of Asia. As pointed out by Lange (2004), indirect rule was implemented in different degrees depending on colonies' initial endowments. In general, adverse endowments, as given by high precolonial population density and a high tropical disease environment, were associated with more extent of indirect rule. Examples of the latter are Nigeria, Sierra Leone and Uganda. Between the extremes of direct and indirect rule, there is a hybrid form of colonialism that was implemented in such sub-Saharan African colonies as Kenya, South Africa, Zambia and Zimbabwe, as well as in India (Lange et al. 2006).

According to Fieldhouse (1966), the existence of this broad spectrum of institutional arrangements in the British Empire rests on the fact that the British opted for a flexible colonial administration system, which was responsive to local conditions and initial colonial endowments, granted a high degree of local autonomy, and in many parts of the empire took the form of indirect rule. Regarding the implementation of indirect rule, Zweigert and Kötz (1998, p. 113) argue that "English colonial administrators relied as much as possible on existing native rules, kept the local courts decentralized, and left mature native law almost intact".

As emphasized by Lange (2009, p. 28) in the context of British colonialism, while indirect rule implies "domination via collaborative relations between a dominant colonial center and several regionally based indigenous institutions", direct rule "entails the construction of a complete system of colonial domination in which both local and central institutions are well integrated and governed by the same authority and organization principles". The former led to a bifurcated form of rule: one dominated by local chiefs that ruled the countryside, and another controlled by the tiny colonial administration that normally lacked state capacity to rule

[1]Note that this colony was largely uninhabited at the time of colonization.

beyond the colonial capital city. In contrast, in directly ruled areas, the colonial legal-administrative apparatus was more centralized and bureaucratized, and could broadcast power throughout an entire territory (system of "integrated domination" versus that of "dispersed domination" in indirectly ruled areas,—see Migdal 1994; Lange 2009).

Indirect rule thus led to the strengthening of the position of traditional chiefs as administrators of customary law, which was molded to the chief's benefit. They also held legislative, executive and judicial powers as a means of controlling social relations in their chiefdoms, thereby being only accountable to British officials rather than being subjected to traditional checks and balances by the native population as in precolonial times (Lange 2004). In the cases in which the British failed to identify the traditional indigenous rulers, in many instances because they did not exist (like in South Nigeria or Kenya), they appointed local headmen as "warrant" chiefs vested with authority over the native population, but with no claim to legitimacy on the basis of their lineage (Daniels et al. 2011; Crowder and Ikime 1970; Afigbo 1972, 1985; Wylie 1977; Migdal 1988).[2]

In addition, in indirectly ruled areas the British established a parallel jurisdictional model in which, on the one hand, colonial courts dealt only with disputes involving Europeans and, on the other, native courts dealt only with disputes involving indigenous people. This dual court system entailed hardly any contact of the native population with the common law, in addition to many inconsistencies and high uncertainty in the parallel legal system. All this can account for the negative effects—intended or not—derived from a colonial administration based

[2]Richens (2009) finds evidence that indirect rule had worse consequences in the context of fragmented precolonial societies than in politically organized ones. Botswana is a case in point. Precolonial sociopolitical structures and systems of representation of the Tswana chiefdoms could be maintained to a greater extent than in other indirectly ruled colonies because Tswana chiefs, despite collaborating with the British over the whole colonial period, firmly opposed increased colonial control of domestic matters. As a result, institutional constraints to legitimate chiefs were not dismantled, and the tribal assembly could continue to exercise the legislative, executive and judicial powers of the tribe (Lange 2009). This institutional inheritance in the postcolonial period was central for developing checks and balances on political leaders that continued to be accountable to their people, as in precolonial times (Acemoglu and Robinson 2010). Somehow related, Acemoglu et al. (2014a) and Heldring and Robinson (2014) hypothesize that the effect of indirect rule is less pervasive in politically centralized societies. Accordingly, the greater power of traditional elites in precolonial politically centralized states, such as the Asante in Ghana and the Buganda in Uganda, led post-independence leaders to fully dismantle the organizational structures created by indirect rule and marginalize traditional elites—because of the expected difficulty for the former to control such powerful traditional elites. In contrast, in countries lacking centralized polities prior to colonization, whereby chiefs were usually created by the British, chiefs were not abolished and their powers were further institutionalized during the post-independence period. This generated a more intense form of indirect rule, a system of local despotism which effectively impeded state governance and broad-based development (Mamdani 1996). A clear example of the latter is Sierra Leone in which the British, upon their arrival, dismantled the hierarchical structure of the existing indigenous federated states. They were replaced by newly created chiefdoms as a way to weaken any opposition and local resistance via the application of a divide-and-rule policy (Lange 2009).

on a system of indirect rule. In short, indirect rule promoted decentralized despotism and total absence of centralized control. This rendered an ineffective central administration lacking infrastructural power and bureaucratization, which were incapable of protecting rights and enforcing law and order (Mamdani 1996).[3]

In contrast, in the British settler colonies of North America and Australasia that applied an extreme form of direct rule, social and society-state relations were regulated countrywide by the same set of rules, which were enforced by courts presided over by British officials, which only used British colonial law rather than customary rules. Another characteristic was the presence of large police forces that were monopolized by Europeans. Thus, settler colonies under direct rule could build legal-administrative capacity through centralization, bureaucratic organization and inclusiveness, conducive to an effective state able to provide basic public goods and maintain law and order throughout the territory (Lange 2009).

Within Africa, Mauritius is an example of a directly ruled British colony with a considerable legal-administrative apparatus able to exert control over the entire colony. This contrasts with most other British sub-Saharan African colonies either ruled through indirect or hybrid colonialism, whose minuscule colonial administration dependent on indigenous chiefs encountered great difficulties in reaching effectively rural populations. However, a main difference between the full-blown directly ruled settler colonies of North America and Australasia, relative to other directly ruled areas in sub-Saharan Africa like Mauritius and more generally other British African colonies, is that the former "quickly featured more representative political institutions and property rights and so the colonial powers were unable to extract resources from them in the same way they could in non-settler colonies" (Robinson 2012, pp. 514–515).[4]

Concerning the colonial policy implemented by France, the ultimate goal of integrating the colonies into *La Plus Grande France* was to assimilate indigenous institutions and culture to those of the mother country (Fieldhouse 1966). Thus, they abolished indigenous institutions and imposed French beliefs and practices outright (Firmin-Sellers 2000). French colonial rule was closer to the paradigm of direct rule, with clear rules and chain of command, and a centralized bureaucratic system of colonial control centered on Paris. This colonial philosophy implied centralism, lack of local autonomy and uniformity in the way French colonies

[3]Acemoglu et al. (2014a) argue that indirect rule strengthened local elites, who were largely unaccountable to their people, and undermined the colonial and postcolonial central state that was non-bureaucratized, lacked a monopoly of violence and a well-functioning fiscal system, thus failing to provide even the most basic public goods. Acemoglu et al. (2014b) provide evidence consistent with these claims for Sierra Leone.

[4]As Lange (2009) points out, an important differentiation within the group of British settler colonies is also in order. Unlike the full-blown settler colonies of North America and Australasia, the settler colonies in sub-Saharan Africa (i.e., Zimbabwe, Kenya and South Africa, and to a lesser extent Swaziland, Botswana and Zambia) featured a much smaller number of European settlers and a much larger number of indigenous people. In these settler colonies that lacked large populations of white settlers, highly extractive labor and land market institutions were established.

were ruled, irrespective of their particular features. All these characteristics make French colonial rule largely invariant to initial conditions. This should be reflected in a homogeneous effect of colonial policy on current institutional quality, irrespective of the level of endowments.

The different colonial strategies of France and Britain are reflected in the unequal presence of colonial officials in the colonies. For instance, this presence was much larger in French West Africa than in British Nigeria. In the 1930s, the ratio of colonial officials per thousand population was 24/100 for the former, whereas 7/100 for the latter (see Kirk-Greene 1980).[5]

Regarding the differences between the French and British systems of colonial administration in Africa, Crowder (1964) points out that "even if both make use of chiefs, it is not possible to place the French system of native administration in the same category as British Indirect Rule". The ideals inspiring the government system were very different in both cases. The British followed the principle of "separate development" of colonies, while the French "were inspired by the concept of assimilation even after its formal abandonment as official policy in favour of a *politique d'association*". The status and power of the chiefs also strongly differed. In the British system, the relationship with the colonial officer was advisory, with the native chief being the head of "a local government unit" that corresponded to a pre-colonial reality. In contrast, in French Africa the chief was completely subordinate to the colonial officer and was not the head of a local government unit. Besides, the French system "deliberately sapped the traditional powers of the chiefs in the interest of uniformity of administrative system" [...] and "individual territories were not considered as having special characters, so that the same administrative organization was imposed on them all". "In conclusion, the differences between the French and the British systems of administration in Africa were not only differences in degree but in kind. Both may have used chiefs, but the position of the chief in each system was radically different" (Crowder 1964, pp. 197–205).

French colonies, like British settler colonies, can be thought to have been directly ruled. However, there is a crucial difference between the two. The former incorporated chiefs into the overall system of colonial administration, admittedly only in a subordinate manner but still occupying an intermediate position between the colonial administration and the native population. Like in indirectly ruled British colonies, this colonial dependence on chiefs gave the latter direct access to valuable information and resources that could be used for their own benefit. In

[5]Comparing French West Africa with British Africa, Whittlesey (1936/1937, p. 367) notes that "[t]he total white population of the British colonies is about 11,000, that of the French about 31,000. The proportion of traders is notably higher in the British territory because the British employ approximately twice as large a personnel to manage a store as do the French. The ratio of missionaries is probably about the same. The proportion of functionaries is therefore much higher in the French possessions. Obviously more political officers are needed for direct than for indirect government."

addition, chiefs were generally unaccountable to their people, which allowed them to extract rents and under-provide public goods.[6]

Hence, it is not surprising to find studies with evidence showing no significant differences between the adverse effect on past and contemporary developmental outcomes of French direct colonialism and that of British indirect colonialism in the African continent. For instance, Dupraz (2016) exploits the partition of German Kamerun after World War I into the Anglophone and Francophone Cameroons. He finds no border discontinuity in primary education, but a positive British effect in secondary school completion, which tends to fade away in the late colonial period due to greater education investment efforts of the French after World War II. Even though significant differences in education did not persist, the effect on religion is found to be strongly persistent due to the higher role of missions in British Cameroon.[7] Lee and Schultz (2012) also exploit the geographic discontinuity between French and British Cameroon, finding that rural areas on the British side have higher levels of wealth and a locally provided public good such as piped water. However, for centrally provided public goods such as education, there are no statistically significant differences between both sides of the discontinuity, whereas the provision of roads was greater on the French side.

Along similar lines, Cogneau et al. (2016) use historical archives data to investigate the patterns of public expenditures in nine French and four British colonies of West Africa from 1900 to independence. The overall patterns of public spending in French and British West Africa do not exhibit significant differences. It is only when the most populous country, Nigeria (with a population of 24.5 million in 1930 and the lowest level of expenditure per capita in every decade except the 1920s) is compared with French colonies, that the latter outperform the former. According to the authors, this can be explained by the application of an extreme form of indirect rule in Nigeria and the difficulty in administering such a populated territory. Focusing on the border between Côte d'Ivoire and Ghana, Bubb (2013) finds no statistically significant differences in the management of property rights on land across the border. Finally, using data of recruits to the Ghanaian colonial army between 1908 and 1955, Cogneau and Moradi (2014) find evidence of the presence of a discontinuity in education and religion between the two parts of German

[6]According to Miles (1987), when the French selected chiefs, the ability to speak French or prior service to the colonial administration prevailed over traditional forms of chiefs' legitimacy to their people. Indeed, progressive erosion of chief's traditional authority, combined with his unpopular tasks of taxation and recruitment of forced labor and troops, converted him "into an agent of the most hated aspects of French colonial rule" (Crowder 1968, p. 193).

[7]As described by Cogneau and Moradi (2014), while the British entrusted religious missions with education, the French set a network of publicly provided non-religious schools as key to converting Africans into Frenchmen. In French colonies, government-certified teachers were employed, and instruction of government curriculum was conducted only in French. In contrast, missions in British Africa had freedom to run their schools, recruit teachers who could teach in local vernacular languages and adjust the content of the curriculum to local circumstances. In other words, this education system can be thought of as decentralized, whereas the one in French Africa was centralized.

Togoland in which it was divided at the end of World War I. The British side that corresponds to Ghana exhibits higher education and religiosity levels than the French side (Togo) in the South, whereas there are no statistical differences in the North. This is due to the strong educational and evangelization efforts made by Christian missions in southern Ghana.[8] Cogneau and Moradi (2014) also document higher educational levels in southern Ghana relative to southern Côte d'Ivoire in the 1930s, with the differences completely vanishing in the 1940s.

At the end, the result was that the implementation of indirect rule to a different degree in the colonies of British Africa led to similarly low developmental outcomes to those derived from the more uniform but rigid French system of colonial rule that attempted to replace indigenous institutions and customs with French traditions, beliefs and practices. Something similar can be told if we were to focus on one of the features of colonial rule: the transplantation of European law into African colonial dominions. As shown by Oto-Peralías and Romero-Ávila (2014b), not only the superficial implantation of the British common law that failed to integrate with local laws and indigenous customs, but also the more rigid transplantation of the French civil law that abolished native rules, equally led to unreceptive transplants.

In sum, in the words of Lange (2005, p. 135), "although French colonies appear more direct, French colonialism had similar, if not more pronounced, effects on state governance and development". Indeed, Lange (2005) refers to a particular study (that of Firmin-Sellers 2000), focusing on two neighboring regions in Côte d'Ivoire and Ghana sharing similar precolonial political institutions, which shows that chiefs in the former French colony had greater control over land and fewer checks on the execution of their powers than in the neighboring region of Ghana.

Having said that, it is important to stress a key difference between British and French styles of imperialism. The British followed a colonial strategy highly responsive to the endowments found in the colonies. Those initially sparsely populated territories with favorable disease conditions due to a temperate climate received large European settlements favoring "institutions of private property"—as in the settler colonies of North America and Australasia—whereas in those places where European settlement was discouraged by high tropical disease or where the extraction of indigenous resources was favored by the existence of a dense (and relatively prosperous) native population, extractive institutions were established—as in indirectly ruled colonies in British Africa.[9] In contrast, the French

[8]Gallego and Woodberry (2010) assign a key role to competition among missions in accounting for the superior educational outcomes in British Africa.

[9]For instance, if we compare Botswana with Nigeria we can see clearly how endowments determined the extent of indirect rule applied to them. Botswana was relatively sparsely populated compared to Nigeria, with a population density before colonization of 0.28 vs. 23.38. Not surprisingly, the extent of indirect rule was much higher in Nigeria. The number of Africans per European administrator was 56,428 in Nigeria, while 13,193 in Botswana (Richens 2009). If the extent of indirect rule is measured as the ratio of colonially recognized customary court cases over the total number of court cases in 1955, with the latter comprising both customary court cases

implemented a uniform colonial strategy aimed at assimilating the native population. This led to a more centralized system of government and a more homogeneous colonial administration across the Empire, which was largely invariant to the initial conditions encountered in the colonies upon their arrival (Fieldhouse 1966).

7.3 Empirical Analysis of the Colonial Rule Mechanism

Having described the main features of colonial rule in the British and French empires, we next try to trace the link of colonies' initial endowments and their interaction with the domestic conditions in the metropolis to current institutions through their effect on the colonial strategy adopted. As argued above, the British colonial strategy varied according to local conditions and in large parts of Africa was based on indirect rule. In contrast, the French colonial policy was more uniform and based on direct rule. To operationalize the identification strategy, we need a suitable measure of the choice of colonial policy. For that purpose, we use the number of Africans per European administrator, as a measure of the extent of direct/indirect rule, with a higher value implying a more indirect form of rule. This variable is taken from Richens (2009) and is available for 33 sub-Saharan former colonies. Our identification strategy based on a Two-stage Least Squares (2SLS) framework is simple. In a first stage, we try to explain the colonial strategy on the basis of colonies' initial endowments and their interaction with domestic conditions in the metropolis, also controlling for years since colonization:

$$colonial\_policy_i = \gamma_0 + \gamma_1 \cdot endow_i + \gamma_2 \cdot endow_i \times dom\_cond_i + \gamma_3 \cdot year\_colon_i + \varepsilon_i \tag{7.1}$$

where $colonial\_policy_i$ stands for the extent of direct/indirect rule, $endow_i$ represents precolonial population density, dom_cond_i reflects the domestic conditions in the metropolis and $year\_colon_i$ stands for years since colonization. In a second stage, we regress rule of law on the extent of indirect rule and years since colonization[10]:

$$institutions_i = \delta_0 + \delta_1 \cdot colonial\_policy_i + \delta_2 \cdot year\_colon_i + \nu_i \tag{7.2}$$

The exclusion restriction—which is tested with an overidentification test—entails that, conditional on the controls included in the regression, colonies' initial endowments and their interaction with domestic conditions in the metropolis do not

heard by native chiefs and magistrate court cases handled by British officials (Lange 2004), the extent of indirect rule is 93.4 in Nigeria vs. 42.5 in Botswana.

[10]The small number of observations prevented us from including more variables in the exogenous control set.

Table 7.2 Exploring the mechanism of colonial rule: 2SLS results

Dependent variable is rule of law (WGI)			
	(1)	(2)	(3)
Panel A: Second stage results			
Colonial policy: Africans per European administrator	−0.029***	−0.03***	−0.029***
95% Wald confidence set	[−0.049, −0.009]	[−0.050, −0.010]	[−0.049, −0.009]
95% CLR confidence set	[−0.055, −0.016]	[−0.056, −0.016]	[−0.055, −0.016]
95% LM K confidence set	[−0.054, −0.016]	[−0.060, −0.016]	[−0.055, −0.016]
95% AR confidence set	[−0.063, −0.013]	[−∞, −0.013]	[−0.065, −0.013]
Years since colonization	0.051 (0.21)	0.047 (0.21)	0.051 (0.21)
Panel B: First stage results			
Endowments	11.247*** (2.502)	−29.156 (27.24)	−9.687 (12.743)
Endowments × Colonial power surface area	−0.022 (0.014)		
Endowments × Colonial power *Polity2* (nineteenth century)		6.036 (4.219)	
Endowments × Colonial power population density (nineteenth century)			0.127 (0.081)
Years since colonization	−5.89 (5.844)	−6.246 (5.627)	−5.925 (5.802)
F-statistic	10.10	9.96	10.18
R^2	0.09	0.10	0.09
Number of observations	33	33	33
Panel C: Overidentification test			
P-value	0.42	0.51	0.44

Notes: Rule of law ranges from −2.5 to 2.5, where a higher value indicates better institutions. Its year of measurement is 2000. The endowments indicator is log population density in 1500, from Acemoglu et al. (2002). Variable descriptions are provided in Table A.1. The sample only contains former African colonies for which data on the endogenous variable are available. The estimations include a constant term, which is omitted for space considerations. Robust standard errors are in parentheses. Small sample adjustments are used. *, ** and *** denote statistical significance at the 10, 5 and 1% level, respectively

affect current institutions directly, but through their impact on the colonial strategy. In other words, our instruments must be uncorrelated with any other determinants of current institutions as follows: $corr(Z_i, \nu_i) = 0$, where Z_i are the instruments.

Panels A and B of Table 7.2 present the results for the second and first stages and Panel C reports the *p-value* associated with the over-identification test. Given the limited number of observations, this analysis employs robust standard errors corrected for small-sample bias. As shown in Panel B, the instruments generally enter with the expected sign but are found individually insignificant. However, the first-stage F-statistic points to the joint significance of both instruments. The fact that this statistic is above 10 in two specifications and about 10 in another indicates that the weak instrument problem may not be a cause for concern here (Staiger and Stock 1997). The results show that domestic conditions conducive to an 'economically-oriented' style of imperialism interact positively with higher values of colonies' precolonial population density, thus favoring the system of indirect rule—with negative repercussions on postcolonial institutional development.

For robustness purposes, besides the standard Wald confidence set, Panel A of Table 7.2 reports a series of 95% confidence intervals for the relevant structural parameter of the second-stage (δ_1), which are obtained by grid search and are robust to the weak instrument problem, thereby providing correct inference.[11] Remarkably, the 2SLS estimate of the effect of the extent of indirect rule on current institutions appears highly significant and operates in the expected direction in all cases. It is also reassuring that the 95% confidence intervals are generally precisely estimated (as given by a tightly bounded confidence set) and always exclude zero. This enables us to strongly reject the proposition that colonial policy did not affect current institutions. The *p-value* from the χ^2 over-identification test favors our identification strategy, as we fail to reject the null hypothesis even at the 10% level irrespective of the domestic condition considered. This suggests that colonies' initial endowments and their interaction with metropolis' domestic conditions may affect current institutions via the form of colonial rule.[12]

Not surprisingly, a simple exercise interacting colonizer identity with colonies' precolonial population density to explain colonial policy only renders a significantly positive coefficient on the interaction term for the "economically-oriented" colonial powers, whereas insignificant for the "politically-oriented" ones. This is shown in column 1 of Table 7.3. In addition, columns 2 and 3 of Table 7.3 provide some preliminary evidence that early European settlement (as measured by Easterly and Levine 2016) and the quality of colonial administration (measured through log governors' salary in 1913 as in Jones 2013) in the British colonies were affected by the level of endowments. The estimates indicate that densely populated British colonies attracted less European settlement and were characterized by lower colonies' institutional quality, as given by the lower salaries colonial governors received. This again supports the fact that the British responded differently, depending on the level of endowments found in the colonies upon their arrival in many relevant dimensions related to colonial administration, which in turn would

---

[11]These are calculated on the basis of the Anderson and Rubin—AR—(1949) test, the conditional likelihood ratio (CLR) of Moreira (2003) and the Lagrange Multiplier K test of Kleibergen (2005).

[12]Nevertheless, we would like to emphasize that it is impossible to rule out the possibility that the exclusion restriction is violated, particularly in a cross-country regression analysis like the one conducted here. Therefore, the evidence of this 2SLS exercise should be taken as suggestive. In addition, a word of caution about the external validity of this analysis focusing on African colonies is in place. Even though we consider that the evidence observed in Africa reflects a general pattern, more empirical work is needed to validate this hypothesis.

Table 7.3 Exploring the mechanism of colonial rule

	Dependent variable is		
	Number of Africans per European administrator	European share in colonial times	Log governors' salaries
	(1)	(2)	(3)
British colonies (Reference group)			
French colonies	21.37 (31.52)	−0.11*** (0.03)	−0.85*** (0.24)
Spanish colonies	n.a.	−0.11* (0.06)	n.a.
Portuguese colonies	n.a.	−0.19*** (0.05)	−0.69*** (0.19)
Other empires colonies	−21.42*** (4.43)	−0.14*** (0.04)	−0.29* (0.17)
UK × Endowments	7.89** (3.36)	−0.07*** (0.02)	−0.13+ (0.08)
French × Endowments	−15.87 (26.02)	0.01 (0.01)	0.02 (0.12)
Spanish × Endowments	n.a.	−0.06 (0.05)	n.a.
Portuguese × Endowments	n.a.	0.01 (0.03)	0.11* (0.06)
Other empires × Endowments	18.02*** (0.3)	0.01 (0.01)	0 (0.01)
Years since colonization	−4.58 (4.44)	0.04** (0.01)	0.13* (0.07)
Constant	34.47*** (7.29)	0.05 (0.04)	7.75*** (0.23)
R^2	0.15	0.39	0.5
Number of observations	33	98	61

Notes: Rule of law ranges from −2.5 to 2.5, where a higher value indicates better institutions. Its year of measurement is 2000. The endowments indicator is log population density in 1500, from Acemoglu et al. (2002). Variable descriptions are provided in Table A.1. The sample contains non-European countries colonized by Western powers (Table A.2). Robust standard errors are in parentheses. +, *, ** and *** denote statistical significance at the 11, 10, 5 and 1% level, respectively

affect postcolonial institutional development. This contrasts with the French empire which appears insensitive to initial endowments, thus failing to provide any statistically significant evidence of an effect of the level of endowments on early European settlement or the quality of colonial administration.

Chapter 8
The Legacy of European Colonialism on Relevant Determinants of Institutional Development

Abstract This chapter investigates the effect of European colonialism (measured through colonizer identity and its interaction with endowments) on important determinants of institutional development. The goal of this analysis is to help us understand why the legacy of colonialism has been so pervasive for institutional and economic development, and which factors may potentially act as channels. The percentage of European settlers is thought to be a key determinant of current institutions. Other factors such as early institutions, political instability in the early years of independence, cultural influence, human capital, inequality and social conflict may also be important channels from colonial policies to current institutions. The picture we find is complex. Today's institutions are not simply the consequence of the persistence of institutions introduced by Europeans in the colonial era. Current institutions are rather the result of processes set in motion or intensified by European colonizers. Our evidence suggests that processes such as inequality, education and to a lower extent social conflict continue to influence the institutions of former colonies today.

The evidence of heterogeneity in the relationship among colonial origin, endowments and institutions is empirically convincing, as shown in the preceding pages. We end this study by exploring the legacy of European colonialism on several relevant determinants of institutional development. This may help us understand why the effects of colonial policies were so pervasive. In addition, it constitutes a way to shed light on factors that may have played a role in shaping national institutions today. So far, we have argued that the British colonial strategy is consistent with the *endowment view*. Thus, in densely populated and high-disease environments they implemented worse policies and implanted malfunctioning institutions, and vice versa. This explanation is consistent with the fact that in the British empire there were many systems of colonial administration, such as self-government, direct rule and indirect rule (Fieldhouse 1966; Lange 2004). In contrast, France undertook a more uniform colonial policy throughout its empire and applied a more homogeneous system of administration. Arguably, this is explained by the French colonial philosophy, which conceives the colonial empire as an intrinsic part of the Republic and pursues the ideal of *assimilation*. This greater homogeneity is consistent with the lack of applicability of the *endowment view*.

D. Oto-Peralías, D. Romero-Ávila, *Colonial Theories of Institutional Development*, Contributions to Economics, DOI 10.1007/978-3-319-54127-3_8

Before presenting the empirical analysis, we first outline our conception about the institutional development in former colonies as follows. Countries' current institutions are the result of a long and complex social process. Many factors in this process had their origin or were intensified during the colonial era. That is why colonialism must be regarded as a critical event in the history of former colonies. The impact of colonial policies was crucial in areas such as inequality, economic activity, social and ethnic conflicts, immigration, education, culture and economic and political institutions. These and other factors have shaped the institutions of colonies after independence.

In the previous section we showed that endowments and their interaction with colonial origin determined the form of colonial rule. We now conjecture that the form of colonial rule, in turn, may have affected a wide array of factors shaping current institutions. Table 8.1 is a preliminary attempt to empirically investigate the relevance of these factors that can be considered as determinants of current institutions while—at the same time—were also affected by the process of European colonialism. Therefore, these factors can be understood as channels or intermediate variables. Panel A shows the bivariate relationship between each potential channel and current institutions, and Panel B reports how colonizer identity and endowments affect each factor. We consider the variables included in Table 8.1 to have played a relevant role in explaining the effect of our colonial variables on current institutions if: (1) the variable is significantly correlated with institutions in the expected direction in Panel A, and (2) there is the same pattern of heterogeneity between endowments and each variable in Panel B as between endowments and rule of law in our baseline model.[1]

The percentage of European settlers in colonial times is a basic candidate for a channel, as recognized by many scholars. However, there is controversy between those who claim that this factor mainly affected the formation of early institutions (Acemoglu et al. 2001) and those who see the influence of European settlers in many other areas such as culture, human capital, inequality or elite formation (Landes 1998; Easterly and Levine 2016; Angeles 2007; or Angeles and Neanidis 2009, 2015). Column 1 shows that this factor is positively correlated with current institutions, accounting for 30% of the variation. Panel B considers European settlers as the dependent variable and shows heterogeneity in the impact of endowments across different colonizers. This again implies that the negative relationship between endowments and settlers is only found for former British colonies. Thus, European settlement can be considered as a relevant channel in our framework.[2]

Column 2 introduces a determinant of current institutions that is probably considered to be essential: the early postcolonial institutions. It has been argued

[1]Before describing the results reported in Table 8.1, we point out that the variables investigated are interconnected and some are placed in a higher position in the causal chain than others. The most obvious case is European settlers, which can influence other factors such as culture, human capital, inequality, etc. This point must also be considered when interpreting the results. Investigating these interrelationships across channels is beyond the scope of this study.

[2]Note that the results reported in column 1 (Panel B) were anticipated in Table 7.3.

Table 8.1 Heterogeneity in the effect of endowments on several determinants of modern day institutions

Determinants of modern day institutions →	European settlers	Executive constraints in the first year of indep.	Institutional instability after indep.	Education	European languages	Index of power resources	Internal conflict
	(1)	(2)	(3)	(4)	(5)	(6)	(7)
Panel A: Bivariate model	Dependent variable is rule of law (WGI)						
Determinant of current institutions	2.65*** (0.50)	0.09* (0.05)	−0.22** (0.09)	0.26*** (0.03)	0.99*** (0.2)	0.06*** (0.01)	0.28*** (0.04)
R^2	0.30	0.1	0.08	0.45	0.23	0.49	0.45
Number of observations	98	91	91	82	95	97	80
Panel B: Interaction model	Dependent variable is determinant of modern day institutions						
British colonies (Reference group)							
French colonies	−0.11*** (0.03)	−2*** (0.66)	−0.39* (0.23)	−2.09*** (0.47)	−0.2*** (0.06)	−7.79*** (2.1)	−1.49* (0.79)
Spanish colonies	−0.11* (0.06)	−3.69*** (0.89)	−0.21 (0.22)	−1.82*** (0.65)	0.08 (0.13)	−7.89** (3.02)	−1.07 (0.73)
Portuguese colonies	−0.19*** (0.05)	−3.04*** (0.59)	−0.31* (0.17)	−4.26*** (0.65)	−0.28 (0.17)	−11.84*** (3.02)	−2.63*** (0.94)
Other empires colonies	−0.14*** (0.04)	−1.14 (1.52)	0.21 (0.65)	−1.78*** (0.54)	−0.37*** (0.09)	−6.37*** (2.07)	−2.41** (0.94)
UK × Endowments	−0.07*** (0.02)	0.06 (0.19)	0.27*** (0.08)	−0.82*** (0.18)	−0.08*** (0.02)	−3.98*** (1.26)	−0.87*** (0.16)
French × Endowments	0.01 (0.01)	−0.23 (0.33)	0.07 (0.12)	0.47 (0.34)	−0.02 (0.02)	0.49 (0.62)	0.47 (0.46)
Spanish × Endowments	−0.06 (0.05)	0.55*** (0.17)	0.16* (0.09)	−0.97*** (0.18)	−0.06 (0.07)	−3.67*** (1.19)	−0.71* (0.39)
Portuguese × Endowments	0.01 (0.03)	0.92*** (0.29)	0.02 (0.07)	−0.59*** (0.02)	−0.21* (0.11)	0.03 (1.49)	−1.01* (0.54)

(continued)

Table 8.1 (continued)

Determinants of modern day institutions →	European settlers	Executive constraints in the first year of indep.	Institutional instability after indep.	Education	European languages	Index of power resources	Internal conflict
	(1)	(2)	(3)	(4)	(5)	(6)	(7)
Other empires × Endowments	0.01	−0.33	−0.11	−0.04	0.05**	−0.21	0.19
	(0.01)	(0.68)	(0.28)	(0.15)	(0.02)	(0.43)	(0.42)
Years since colonization	0.04**	0.18	−0.15*	0.71***	0.14***	2.09**	0.03
	(0.01)	(0.26)	(0.08)	(0.19)	(0.04)	(0.8)	(0.18)
Constant	0.05	4.36***	0.86***	1.47***	0.02	6.35**	8.47***
	(0.04)	(0.63)	(0.22)	(0.52)	(0.08)	(2.43)	(0.44)
R^2	0.39	0.37	0.28	0.6	0.61	0.47	0.43
Number of observations	98	91	91	82	95	97	80

Notes: Rule of law ranges from −2.5 to 2.5, where a higher value indicates better institutions. Its year of measurement is 2000. The endowments indicator is log population density in 1500, from Acemoglu et al. (2002). Variable descriptions are provided in Table A.1. The sample contains non-European countries colonized by Western powers (Table A.2). Robust standard errors are in parentheses. *, ** and *** denote statistical significance at the 10, 5 and 1% level, respectively. In columns 2 and 3 we also include the variable years since independence

that early institutions introduced by colonial powers influenced institutions of the newly independent countries, which endured over time (Acemoglu et al. 2001). Arguably, institutions in the first year of independence can be considered to be those associated with the last colonial phase (Olsson 2009). Panel A shows that institutions (*executive constraints*) in the first year of independence has some explanatory power on current institutions, once we control for years since independence.[3] However, the goodness of fit is significantly lower than in column 1 (0.10 vs. 0.30). Panel B shows marked differences across colonial powers with respect to initial post-colonial institutions, but interestingly the different impact of endowments between France and Britain disappears.

From column 2 an interesting question arises: why are institutions in the first year of independence not affected by endowments in British colonies and therefore unlikely to be a valid intermediate variable? The answer is that institutions at that time, in reality, are not closely related to current institutions, even after controlling for years since independence.[4] Though many former colonies became independent with open political systems following the model of the metropolis, they would soon end up in dictatorship and chaos (Fieldhouse 1966).[5] A clear involution is observed in many ex-colonies after independence (Huntington 1991). As a matter of fact, 23 of the 41 sub-Saharan countries from the sample in column 2 saw a reduction in their democracy score (*polity2*) 10 years after independence relative to the year of independence. Thus, one important factor to consider is institutional instability in the years following independence, which is measured through the standard deviation of *executive constraints* during the 10 years after independence. Column 3 (Panel A) shows a negative relationship between political instability after independence and current institutions. Panel B reports a highly significant positive effect of endowments on institutional instability only in former British colonies, which accords with the previous findings by Lange (2004) pointing to the pervasive effects on political institutions that resulted from indirect rule.

Human capital is thought to be a crucial factor in the formation of sound institutions, since it is necessary for society to be aware of its political and legal rules. Besides, colonial educational policy may differ from one empire to another, as reviewed in Chap. 7. Proponents of the *colonial origin view* such as Grier (1999)

---

[3]For variables referring to the time of independence, we always include as control ‘years since independence’.

[4]In fact, in Panel A (column 2) the significantly positive coefficient on this variable is driven by the four neo-Europes.

[5]The experience of Nigeria is a case in point. In 1960 the former colony gained independence from Great Britain. The constitution established a federal system with an elected prime minister. However, ethnic and territorial tensions led to coups, military rule and civil war (Britannica Encyclopaedia 2012). In this respect, Samuel P. Huntington—commenting on “the second reverse wave of democratization”—states that, in addition to the case of Nigeria (already mentioned) and Botswana (the only one that maintained democratic practices), the other 33 African countries that obtained the independence between 1956 and 1970 became authoritarian. “The colonization of Africa led to the largest multiplication of independent authoritarian governments in history” (Huntington 1991, p. 139).

suggest that the British introduced a more effective education system than the French, adjusting to local culture and tradition and reaching better educational outcomes in indigenous populations. However, authors like Lange (2004) notes that the widespread introduction of indirect rule in British colonies did not necessarily rendered good outcomes in the provision of public goods for the indigenous population. Galor et al. (2009) associate lower land inequality in North America versus Latin America at the time of colonization with the emergence of early "human-capital promoting institutions" in the former (see also Engerman and Sokoloff 2000). Glaeser et al. (2004) find that human capital explains future institutions, which is consistent with the Lipset hypothesis. They also argue that human capital is a very important channel of European influence, finding that settler mortality and European settlers appear more correlated with education than with institutions.[6]

In column 4 we use the average years of schooling in 1960 (from Barro and Lee 2010) as an indicator of education level. This variable has a large positive impact on current institutions and high explanatory power, with an R^2 of 0.45. Placing education as the dependent variable (Panel B), we find that former French colonies have worse educational scores than former British colonies at low levels of endowments, but not when endowments are high.

Culture is considered a prominent channel of European influence (Landes 1998). Colonialism spread around the world many aspects of European culture such as traditions, religion, political and philosophical ideas, etc. In this sense, Western European culture, especially from the eighteenth and nineteenth centuries, was imbued with rationalistic and individualistic elements.[7] Institutions such as the separation of powers and representative democracy or the process of codification and systematization of the legal system are related to modern European culture. A central element that Europeans also exported was their languages. European languages, besides being an intrinsic part of Western culture, served as an important vehicle of cultural transmission. Hence, we use the percentage of people speaking European languages as a proxy for European cultural influence. Column 5 in Panel A shows that the language indicator has a positive and highly significant effect on current institutions. Placing the language indicator as the dependent variable in Panel B, we observe similar patterns of heterogeneity to those found previously.

Undoubtedly, another important factor when explaining the impact of colonialism on institutions is inequality. Angeles (2007, p. 1173) states that "different

[6]They state that Europeans "brought with them themselves, and therefore their know-how and human capital" (Glaeser et al. 2004, p. 289). Even they believe that human capital and institutions were not the only baggage that European settlers carried with them, but there were many channels that worked. This view fits with the multichannel approach presented in this chapter. Using a wide sample of colonies and non-colonies, Gennaioli et al. (2013, 2014) find evidence of the central role of human capital in driving regional growth around the world.

[7]According to Max Weber, the modern Western culture "is characterized by rationalization and intellectualization and, above all, by the disenchantment of the world" (Science as a Vocation, several editions).

experiences during the colonial period are a major explanation behind today's differences in inequality across countries". Inequality is thought to exhibit strong persistence over time. As Engerman and Sokoloff (1997) point out, inequality and institutions biased toward the dominant elites are mutually supportive. We use as indicator of inequality the Vanhanen Index of Power Resources, which measures the level of dispersion of economic, intellectual and organization resources in society (Vanhanen 2003a, b).[8] Column 6 shows that inequality is strongly related to institutions and accounts for nearly 50% of the variance. Panel B provides evidence of heterogeneity in the relationship between inequality and endowments across former colonies. In former British and Spanish colonies, the larger the endowments the higher the inequality, while in French colonies the opposite pattern is observed (though the coefficient does not enter significantly).

The last column deals with social conflict as a relevant determinant of institutions. Economic, political and ethnic conflicts undermine many of the necessary conditions for the development of quality institutions. For example, they create government instability, lack of legitimacy, legal uncertainties, lack of law compliance, erosion of social trust or inefficient institutions.[9] We use internal conflict from ICRG as indicator of this factor.[10] Panel A shows that lower internal conflict leads to better institutions, with an R^2 of 45%. When social conflict enters as the dependent variable in Panel B, we find the expected pattern: former British colonies enjoy more social peace than the French for low levels of endowments, but not for high levels.[11]

This result deserves some further comment. The negative relationship between endowments and social conflict in former British colonies may be induced by the application of indirect rule. In principle, this limited form of colonialism was intended to facilitate administrative work and benefit indigenous peoples (Fieldhouse 1966). However, the long-term consequences of empowering local

[8]The scale ranges from 0 to 100, with a higher value implying a more equal distribution of power resources and lower inequality. We compute the average over the period 1963–2000 to obtain a measure of structural inequality.

[9]In the view of Acemoglu (2003), social conflict theories constitute an appropriate analytical framework for the persistence of inefficient institutions. From this perspective, social groups in power favor certain institutions that serve their interests despite being inefficient and detrimental to society as a whole.

[10]Internal conflict measures the political violence in a country and the current or possible impact on governance. A higher score means a lower level of conflict (PRS Group 2011). We take a long-period average (1980–2000) in order to reflect the structural nature of social conflict.

[11]We have found similar results using ethnic tension (also from ICRG), instead of internal conflict, as an alternative proxy for social conflict.

elites and chiefs were detrimental to the future capacity and unity of the state by encouraging local despotism and territorial fragmentation. The system of indirect rule was established to a greater extent in areas with fewer Europeans settlements, larger indigenous population and a worse disease environment (Lange 2004).[12] Therefore, indirect rule may help explain the relation between endowments and social conflict in former British colonies. Social conflict can thus be considered a channel through which indirect rule adversely affects institutions.[13] Altogether, these results accord with the previous findings by Lange and Dawson (2009) suggesting that British colonialism brought subsequent inter-communal violence and civil conflict.[14]

To summarize, the evidence provided in this chapter shows that European colonialism has affected a number of relevant determinants of current institutions. Interestingly, the heterogeneity observed in the coefficient on endowments in our baseline model is also observed when the indicator of institutions (i.e., *rule of law*) is replaced by determinants of current institutions such as European settlers, education, inequality, and social conflict. In conclusion, many factors were affected by European colonialism, which help explain countries' current institutions.

[12]Literally, Lange (2004, p. 917) notes that "the disease environment and the presence of precolonial populations not only influenced European settlement [...] but also directly affected the extent of indirect rule and thereby indirectly shaped postcolonial state governance among non-settler colonies".

[13]We have deepened the analysis of this issue through another interesting variable, which fits well with the effects of dispersion of power attributed to indirect rule. It is *polity fragmentation*, which refers to the existence of separate polities within the borders of the state and over which the official polity exercises no effective authority (Marshall et al. 2010). Results with this indicator are entirely consistent with our line of argument. Thus, only for former British colonies larger endowments are associated with greater political fragmentation (which, in turn, leads to worse institutions).

[14]Limiting ourselves to former British colonies, let us consider three simple models to analyze the relationship between indirect rule, social conflict and current institutions (the indirect rule indicator comes from Lange 2004). First, $\textit{rule of law} = \alpha + \beta \cdot \textit{indirect rule}$, with $\beta = -0.02$ ($S.E. = 0.004$, $N = 25$, $R^2 = 0.49$), which reflects a negative effect of indirect rule on current institutions as in Lange (2004). We also consider a second model, $\textit{internal conflict} = \alpha + \beta \cdot \textit{indirect rule}$, with $\beta = -0.03$ ($S.E. = 0.01$, $N = 25$, $R^2 = 0.17$), which supports our hypothesis that indirect rule fostered internal conflict. Finally, a third model shows that internal conflict intervenes in the effect of indirect rule on institutions, but it is not the only channel through which the effect occurs. This model is as follows: $\textit{rule of law} = \alpha + \beta_1 \cdot \textit{internal conflict} + \beta_2 \cdot \textit{indirect rule}$, with $\beta_1 = -0.14$ ($S.E. = 0.05$) and $\beta_2 = -0.01$ ($S.E. = 0.003$), $N = 25$, $R^2 = 0.63$.

Chapter 9
Conclusions

Abstract This chapter provides some concluding remarks on the analysis of the interaction between initial endowments and colonial origin in the explanation of institutional development in former colonies. This study has proposed a model of two styles of imperialism that integrates the *colonial origin* and the *endowment views* explaining current institutions. Our results uncover remarkable heterogeneity that can be read in two ways: the impact of colonizer identity varies with the level of endowments, and the relationship between endowments and institutions is very different across former colonial powers. A couple of important consequences can be derived from this finding. First, the *endowment view* is not universally applicable. Negative effects of endowments on institutions are only observed for former British colonies and to a lower extent for Spanish and Portuguese colonies, but not for the rest. Second, former British colonies are not always associated with better institutions since former French colonies at least equal the British when the level of endowments is sufficiently high. Our analysis also shows that the form of colonial rule is a key factor to explain current institutional development. In addition, we provide evidence suggesting that European colonialism affected many relevant determinants of current institutions. Factors such as inequality, education and social conflict continue to influence the institutions of former colonies today.

Nowadays there is widespread consensus on the importance of institutions for economic progress. Many social scientists have seen the imprint of colonial past in countries' current institutions. Some scholars focus on the identity of the colonizing nation, considering that Britain implemented better policies and institutions in their colonies than the other European powers. Others emphasize the initial conditions encountered by Europeans, arguing that colonial policies implemented in environments with large endowments or high potential settler mortality led to pernicious institutions. A third group advocates that both factors are relevant for the institutional development of former colonies.

We stick to this last view. A model of two styles of imperialism is presented that integrates both explanations of current institutions. We argue that Britain and Portugal adopted an 'economically-oriented' style, which was pragmatic and sensitive to initial conditions. Indeed, in the British empire many systems of colonial administration were in place. There were settlement colonies with political regimes similar to that in the metropolis, whereas particularly in extractive colonies a

D. Oto-Peralías, D. Romero-Ávila, *Colonial Theories of Institutional Development*, Contributions to Economics, DOI 10.1007/978-3-319-54127-3_9

system of indirect rule was established—which ultimately seems to have exerted a negative impact on postcolonial institutions (Lange 2004). For this style of imperialism the *endowment view* is applicable, because in territories with large endowments European powers established extractive institutions, with negative consequences for subsequent institutional development. In contrast, France followed a 'politically-oriented' style of imperialism, in which ideological and political motivations were more present. This led to a uniform colonial policy largely independent of initial endowments. Arguably, this is explained by the French colonial philosophy, which conceives the colonial empire as an intrinsic part of the Republic and pursues the ideal of *assimilation*. The Spanish case is a hybrid between both models. Formally Spain implanted the same institutions across the New World colonies, but in practice, due to the limited resources of the metropolis, the intensity of colonial penetration varied depending on the possibilities to extract rents.

Our theoretical framework, along with the historical revision made, has enabled us to raise testable hypotheses about the relationship between precolonial endowments and current institutions. We expect to find a negative relationship between both variables for British and Portuguese colonies, no such relationship for French colonies, and mixed results for the Spanish empire. For testing these theory-based hypotheses, we use an interaction model that allows for the possibility of heterogeneity in the effect of endowments on current institutions across colonial empires. The results strongly support our predictions regarding the British and French empires. For the Spanish empire we find evidence congruent with our classification as a hybrid style of imperialism. In the case of Portugal, the results also suggest a pattern consistent with our prediction, though they must be only taken as suggestive given the small number of Portuguese colonies in our sample. An important consequence of our findings is that the *endowment view* is not universally applicable. In this regard, we hold that the applicability of the endowments theory depends on the style of imperialism adopted by the colonial power. Another interesting observation can be made: former British colonies are not always associated with better institutions, since former French colonies equal the British when the level of endowments is sufficiently high.

The last part of this study analyzes whether the heterogeneity found in the relationship between endowments and institutions across colonial empires also holds for several relevant determinants of current institutions such as social conflict, inequality, and human capital. We find this to be the case. Endowments are negatively related to these factors for British colonies, but not for French colonies.[1] Therefore, the legacy of European colonial policies appears to affect current institutions through a variety of variables.

To conclude, the picture we find is complex. Today's institutions are not simply the consequence of the persistence of institutions introduced by Europeans in the

[1]Note that a higher value of the social conflict and inequality measures is associated with lower social conflict and a more equal distribution of power in society.

colonial era. Current institutions are rather the result of processes set in motion or intensified by European colonizers. Our evidence suggests that processes such as inequality, education and to a lower extent social conflict continue to influence the institutions of former colonies. So, our study not only has historical interest, but also analyzes factors and social processes that are still present today. Although this is already a mature literature, more research on this field is warranted. It is important to uncover specific mechanisms helping explain why colonial powers reacted differently to the level of endowments, and why factors such as political instability after independence, education, inequality and internal conflict exhibit also high heterogeneity in their links with endowments across colonial powers, which can be traced through to their current state of institutions. Further work on these issues at a more disaggregated level of analysis (regional and local levels) will be welcome by the academic community and interested readers.

Appendix: Tables and Figures

Table A.1 Description of variables

Variable	Description	Source
Africans per European administrator	Number of Africans (in thousands) per European administrator. There are only data for 33 sub-Saharan countries	Richens (2009)
Altitude	Mean elevation of each country, measured in kilometers	Michalopoulos (2012)
Bureaucracy quality	Measure of the institutional strength and quality of public administration. Year 2000. The scale ranges from 0 to 4, where a higher value indicates better institutions	ICRG (PRS Group, 2011)
Colonial origin	Colonial origin variable: French, British, Spanish, Portuguese and others. We include the British settler colonies (the US, Canada, Australia and New Zealand). In the event that a particular colony was colonized by several colonial powers, the last one that occupied the territory is considered, provided that the domain lasts for a period of no less than 10 years	Teorell and Hadenius (2005), from Teorell et al. (2011)
Colonial power Polity2 (nineteenth century)	Average value of the *polity2* indicator of the colonial power during the nineteenth century. The indicator is rescaled, taking values from 0 (strongly autocratic) to 10 (strongly democratic)	Marshall et al. (2010)

(continued)

D. Oto-Peralías, D. Romero-Ávila, *Colonial Theories of Institutional Development*, Contributions to Economics, DOI 10.1007/978-3-319-54127-3

Table A.1 (continued)

Variable	Description	Source
Colonial power population density (nineteenth century)	Average population density of the colonial power during the nineteenth century (from 1820 to 1900)	Maddison (2010)
Colonial power surface area	Surface area (in 1000 km^2) of the colonial power. For the case of Germany, it is considered the German Empire that lasted from 1871 to 1914 (data obtained from Encyclopedia Britannica)	World Bank (2011)
Colonization after 1850	Dummy variable indicating whether the country has been colonized after the year 1850	Olsson (2009)
Control of corruption	Indicator that reflects perceptions about the abuse of public power for private gain and the capture of the state by elites and private interests. Year 2000. The scale ranges from −2.5 to 2.5, where a higher value indicates better institutions	Kaufmann et al. (2009), from Teorell et al. (2011)
Corruption	Indicator that measures how widespread corruption is in the political system. Year 2000. The scale ranges from 0 to 6, where a higher value indicates better institutions	ICRG (PRS Group, 2011)
Democratic accountability	It measures the responsiveness of government to people. Year 2000. The scale ranges from 0 to 6, where a higher value indicates better institutions	ICRG (PRS Group, 2011)
Distance from metropolis	The distance between former colonies and their colonizer countries in thousands of kilometers calculated following the great circle formula, which uses latitude and longitude of the most important city (in terms of population)	Mayer and Zignago (2011)
Distance from the coast	Distance in hundreds of kilometers from the centroid of the country to the nearest coast	Own elaboration using ArcGIS
Duration of colonization	Year of colonization minus year of independence (in hundreds of years)	Olsson (2009)
Education	Average years of school of population aged 25 and over, in 1960	Barro and Lee (2010; new version 1.2)
Ethnic fractionalization	Probability that two randomly selected individuals from a given country do not belong to the same ethnolinguistic group	Alesina et al. (2003), from Teorell et al. (2011)

(continued)

Table A.1 (continued)

Variable	Description	Source
European languages	Fraction of population speaking one of the five primary Western European languages as a mother tongue: English, French, German, Portuguese and Spanish	Hall and Jones (1999)
European share in colonial times	European share of the population in each country during the period of colonization	Easterly and Levine (2016)
Executive constraints	Objective indicator that measures "checks and balances between the various parts of the decision-making process". Year 2000. The scale ranges from 1 to 7, where a higher score means higher constraints on the executive	Marshall et al. (2010), from Teorell et al. (2011)
Executive constraints in the first year of indep.	The extent of institutionalized constraints on the decision-making powers of chief executives. The scale ranges from 1 to 7, where a higher score means higher constraints. We select the value of this indicator in the first year of independence [using Olsson (2009)'s indicator of year of independence]	Marshall et al. (2010), from Teorell et al. (2011)
Gap between first sighted and colonized	Number of years between when a territory was first sighted by Western Europeans and when it was first colonized by a European power	Woodberry (2004, 2012)
Government effectiveness	Indicator reflecting perceptions about the quality of public administration. Year 2000. The scale ranges from −2.5 to 2.5, where a higher value indicates better institutions	Kaufmann et al. (2009), from Teorell et al. (2011)
Government stability	Indicator that evaluates the government's ability to stay in office and implement its declared program. Year 2000. The scale ranges from 0 to 12, where a higher value indicates better institutions	ICRG (PRS Group, 2011)
Humidity	Humidity comprises the variables morning minimum, morning maximum, afternoon minimum and afternoon maximum (in percent)	Acemoglu et al. (2002)
Index of Power Resources	Level of dispersion of power resources (economic, intellectual, and organizational resources) in society. The scale ranges from 0 (low) to 100 (high distribution of	Vanhanen (2003a, b), from Teorell et al. (2011)

(continued)

Table A.1 (continued)

Variable	Description	Source
	power resources). It is calculated by multiplicative aggregation. Average 1960–1999	
Indigenous mortality	Dummy variable indicating whether the country belongs to the New World (North America, the Caribbean and Latin America) or Oceania, which were the territories where the contact with European colonizers caused a more dramatic decline in native population due to vulnerability to European diseases	Own elaboration according to Easterly and Levine (2016)'s methodology
Institutional instability after indep.	Standard deviation of executive constraints in the 10 years after independence [using Olsson (2009)'s indicator of year of independence]	Marshall et al. (2010), from Teorell et al. (2011)
Internal conflict	Political violence in a country and the current or possible impact on governance. The scale ranges from 0 to 12, where a higher score means a lower level of conflict. Average 1984–2000	ICRG -PRS Group (2011)
Investment profile	Indicator that assesses "factors affecting the risk to investment that are not covered by other political, economic and financial risk components". Year 2000. The scale ranges from 0 to 12, where a higher value indicates better institutions	ICRG (PRS Group, 2011)
Island	Dummy variable indicating whether the country is an island	Acemoglu et al. (2002)
Land in geographical tropics (%)	Percentage of land in geographical tropics, from the Center of International Development (Geographic datasets)	Gallup et al. (2001)
Land quality	Measure of land suitability for agriculture. It is calculated as the amount of land suitable for cultivation over total land area	Global Land Use Database (SAGE) (Ramankutty et al. 2002)
Land suitable for sugar	Logarithm of one plus the percentage of land very suitable and suitable for sugarcane, at low inputs levels. Own elaboration from FAO data	FAO/IIASA (2002)
Landlockedness	Dummy variable taking a value of one for countries with no direct access to the sea	Own elaboration using ArcGIS

(continued)

Table A.1 (continued)

Variable	Description	Source
Latitude	The absolute value of the latitude of the capital city divided by 90	La Porta et al. (1999), from Teorell et al. (2011)
Law and order	Indicator that assesses the strength and impartiality of the legal system and the popular observance of the law. Year 2000. The scale ranges from 0 to 6, where a higher value indicates better institutions	ICRG (PRS Group, 2011)
Legal structure and security of property rights	Indicator that comprises judicial independence, trusted legal framework for private businesses activity, military interference, protection of intellectual property and integrity of the legal system. Year 2000. The scale ranges from 0 to 10, with higher scores implying better protection of property rights	Gwartney and Lawson (2006), from Teorell et al. (2011)
Log governors' salaries	Logarithm of the colonial governor's salary (consisting of base salary plus allowances) of each colony, denominated in British pounds sterling, as measured in 1913	Jones (2013)
Log State Antiquity Index (in the first year of colonization)	Logarithm of the State Antiquity Index in the first year of colonization. Following Bockstette et al. (2002), a discount rate of 5% is used	Bockstette et al. (2002)
Mineral resources	Average of mineral rents over GDP during the period 1960–2000	World Bank (2011)
Political stability	Indicator measuring perceptions about the likelihood of destabilization or subversion of government. Year 2000. The scale ranges from −2.5 to 2.5, where a higher value indicates better institutions	Kaufmann et al. (2009), from Teorell et al. (2011)
Polity fragmentation	Existence of separate polities within the borders of the state and over which the official polity exercises no effective authority. The scale ranges from 0 ("no overt fragmentation") to 3 ("serious fragmentation"). Year 2000 (the first year available)	Marshall et al. (2010), from Teorell et al. (2011)
Population density in 1500	Logarithm of population density in 1500, using as denominator total arable land	Acemoglu et al. (2002)

(continued)

Table A.1 (continued)

Variable	Description	Source
Population density before colonization	Logarithm of population density at the beginning of the century in which the country was colonized, in inhabitants/km^2	Own elaboration using ArcGIS and data from Goldewijk et al. (2010)
Precolonial centralization	A country's percentage of population that belonged to centralized ethnic groups, computed as in Gennaioli and Rainer (2007)	Gennaioli and Rainer (2007), Atlas Narodov Mira (1964) and Ethnographic Atlas of Murdock (1967)
Property rights	Indicator that measures the degree of protection of property rights by laws and the government, the independence of the judiciary and the enforcement of contracts. Year 2000. The scale ranges from 0 to 100, with higher scores implying better protection of property rights	Heritage Foundation, from Teorell et al. (2011)
Region dummies	World Bank geographical classification	World Development Indicators (World Bank, 2011)
Regulatory quality	Indicator measuring the level of friendly policies and norms for private sector development. Year 2000. The scale ranges from −2.5 to 2.5, where a higher value indicates better institutions	Kaufmann et al. (2009), from Teorell et al. (2011)
Religion	Protestants, Catholics, Muslims and others as a percentage of population in 1985–1995	La Porta et al. (1999), from Teorell et al. (2011)
Rule of law	Confidence in and compliance with the rules of society. It comes from the Worldwide Governance Indicators (WGI) project. Year 2000. The scale ranges from −2.5 to 2.5, where a higher value indicates better institutions	Kaufmann et al. (2009), from Teorell et al. (2011)
Settler mortality	Logarithm of potential European settler mortality, measured in terms of deaths per annum per 1000	Acemoglu et al. (2001)
Several precolonial cultures	Dummy variable taking a value of 1 if there was more than one pre-colonial indigenous culture and 0 otherwise. Gallego (2010) uses this variable as a proxy for the number of pre-colonial ethnic groups. The ultimate source is Murdock and White (1969)	Gallego (2010)
Sugar/Wheat ratio	The indicator is calculated as: log [(1 + share of arable land suitable for sugarcane)/(1 + share of arable	Easterly (2007)

(continued)

Table A.1 (continued)

Variable	Description	Source
	land suitable for wheat)]. It is derived from the "Wheat/Sugar ratio" indicator of Easterly	
Temperature	Temperature includes the variables average temperature, minimum and maximum monthly high, and minimum and maximum monthly low. The variables are measured in degrees centigrade	Acemoglu et al. (2002)
Urbanization in 1500	Percent of population living in urban areas with at least 5000 inhabitants, in 1500. Data for sub-Saharan Africa are not available	Acemoglu et al. (2002)
Voice and accountability	Indicator measuring perceptions on political rights and civil liberties. Year 2000. The scale ranges from −2.5 to 2.5, where a higher value indicates better institutions	Kaufmann et al. (2009), from Teorell et al. (2011)
Years since colonization	2000 minus year of colonization (in hundreds of years)	Olsson (2009)
Years since independence	2000 minus year of independence (in hundreds of years)	Olsson (2009)

Table A.2 List of former colonies

British colonies		French colonies	Spanish colonies	Portuguese colonies
Antigua and Barbuda	Myanmar	Algeria	Argentina	Angola
Australia	Namibia	Benin	Bolivia	Brazil
Bahamas, The	New Zealand	Burkina Faso	Chile	Cape Verde
Bahrain	Nigeria	Cambodia	Colombia	Guinea-Bissau
Bangladesh	Pakistan	Cameroon	Costa Rica	Mozambique
Barbados	Qatar	Central African Rep.	Cuba	
Belize	Sierra Leone	Chad	Dominican Republic	
Botswana	Singapore	Comoros	Ecuador	
Canada	South Africa	Congo, Rep.	El Salvador	Others empires colonies:
Dominica	Sri Lanka	Côte d'Ivoire	Equatorial Guinea	
Egypt, Arab Rep.	St. Kitts and Nevis	Gabon	Guatemala	Burundi

(continued)

Table A.2 (continued)

British colonies		French colonies	Spanish colonies	Other empires colonies
Eritrea	St. Lucia	Guinea	Honduras	Congo, Dem. Rep.
Gambia, The	St. Vincent and the G.	Haiti	Mexico	Indonesia
Ghana	Sudan	Lao PDR	Nicaragua	Libya
Grenada	Swaziland	Madagascar	Panama	Papua New Guinea
Guyana	Tanzania	Mali	Paraguay	Philippines
India	Trinidad and Tobago	Mauritania	Peru	Rwanda
Jamaica	Uganda	Morocco	Uruguay	Somalia
Kenya	United Arab Emirates	Niger	Venezuela, RB	Suriname
Kuwait	United States	Senegal		
Lesotho	Yemen, Rep.	Togo		
Malawi	Zambia	Tunisia		
Malaysia	Zimbabwe	Vietnam		

Table A.3 Descriptive statistics

Variable	Obs	Mean	Std. Dev.	Min	Max
Dependent variables					
Rule of law	102	−0.35	0.86	−2.27	1.76
Voice and accountability	102	−0.30	0.90	−2.07	1.74
Political stability	101	−0.34	0.97	−2.79	1.29
Control of corruption	102	−0.26	0.88	−1.77	2.18
Government effectiveness	102	−0.27	0.84	−2.25	2.26
Regulatory quality	102	−0.20	0.85	−2.50	1.96
Law and order	80	3.40	1.32	1.00	6.00
Democratic accountability	80	3.30	1.65	0.00	6.00
Government stability	80	9.99	0.83	6.58	11.17
Corruption	80	2.70	1.04	1.00	6.00
Bureaucracy quality	80	1.85	1.02	0.00	4.00
Investment profile	80	7.20	2.51	1.00	11.00
Legal structure and security of property rights	74	5.02	1.67	1.98	9.49
Property rights	87	46.78	22.80	10.00	90.00
Executive constraints	86	4.28	1.91	1.00	7.00
Endowments indicators					
Log of population density in 1500	102	0.49	1.45	−3.83	4.61
Log of population density before colonization	102	0.86	1.88	−4.61	4.70
Urbanization in 1500	43	6.49	4.86	0.00	17.79
Settler mortality	74	4.79	1.16	2.15	7.99

(continued)

Table A.3 (continued)

Variable	Obs	Mean	Std. Dev.	Min	Max
Sugar/Wheat ratio	67	0.01	0.15	−0.58	0.39
Mineral resources	101	1.20	2.91	0.00	15.57
Ln State Antiquity Index (at time of colonization)	84	4.20	2.27	0.00	6.64
Land suitable for sugar	88	0.03	0.04	0.00	0.23
Colonial policy indicators and European share					
Africans per European administrator	33	35.50	35.46	5.84	203.08
Log governors' salaries	61	7.69	0.72	6.42	9.24
European share in colonial times	98	0.08	0.18	0.00	0.91
Control variables					
Years since colonization	102	2.62	1.57	0.78	5.38
Years since independence	102	0.69	0.60	0.07	2.24
Duration of colonization	102	1.94	1.31	0.38	5.13
Colonization after 1850	102	0.42	0.50	0.00	1.00
Gap between first sighted and colonized	102	179.87	159.13	1.00	477.00
Catholics	102	35.16	35.37	0.00	96.60
Muslims	102	24.81	36.35	0.00	99.80
Other religions or beliefs	101	27.32	26.00	0.10	98.00
Ethnic Fractionalization	101	0.52	0.25	0.00	0.93
Several precolonial cultures	68	0.34	0.48	0.00	1.00
Precolonial centralization	97	0.47	0.42	0.00	1.00
Indigenous mortality	102	0.37	0.49	0.00	1.00
Distance from metropolis	102	7.00	2.82	1.02	19.15
Landlockedness	102	0.17	0.37	0.00	1.00
Distance from the coast	102	3.15	3.44	0.00	14.38
Altitude	86	0.55	0.41	0.03	1.89
Island	102	0.21	0.41	0.00	1.00
Latitude	102	0.18	0.11	0.00	0.67
Land in geographical tropics (%)	90	0.50	0.42	0.00	1.00
Land quality	99	0.05	0.03	0.00	0.13
Temperature variable 1	100	22.57	6.08	4.00	31.00
Temperature variable 2	100	28.46	6.59	10.00	40.00
Temperature variable 3	100	37.54	6.11	24.00	48.00
Temperature variable 4	100	6.18	10.38	−37.00	20.00
Temperature variable 5	100	15.62	7.06	−1.00	26.00
Humidity variable 1	100	69.58	17.51	18.00	97.00
Humidity variable 2	100	86.05	8.04	54.00	98.00
Humidity variable 3	100	51.98	17.88	10.00	86.00
Humidity variable 4	100	72.25	10.58	35.00	92.00
Colonial power Polity2 (nineteenth century)	102	4.99	1.33	2.59	9.37
Colonial power population density (nineteenth century)	102	87.12	41.24	0.19	159.14

(continued)

Table A.3 (continued)

Variable	Obs	Mean	Std. Dev.	Min	Max
Colonial power surface area	102	510.23	1181.08	30.53	9632.03
Determinants of modern day institutions (Table 8.1)					
Executive constraints in the first year of indep.	91	3.51	2.18	1.00	7.00
Institutional instability after indep.	91	0.49	0.82	0.00	3.13
Education	82	2.28	2.16	0.00	9.76
European languages	95	0.31	0.42	0.00	1.06
Index of Power Resources	97	6.73	9.43	0.30	53.35
Internal conflict	80	7.64	2.12	1.97	12.00
Polity fragmentation	91	0.24	0.75	0.00	3.00

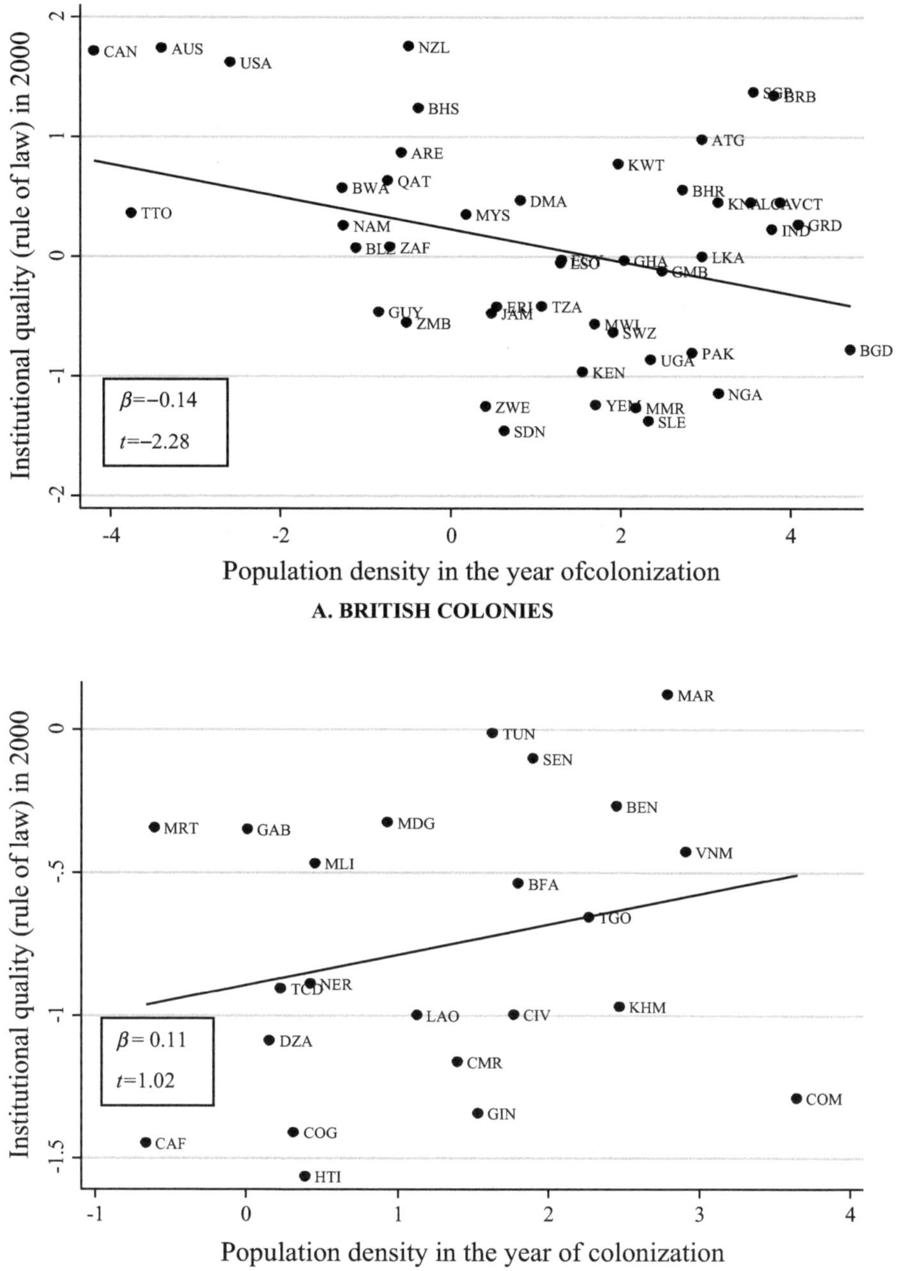

A. BRITISH COLONIES

B. FRENCH COLONIES

Fig. A.1 The relationship between log of population density in the year of colonization (x-axis) and rule of law in 2000 (y-axis)

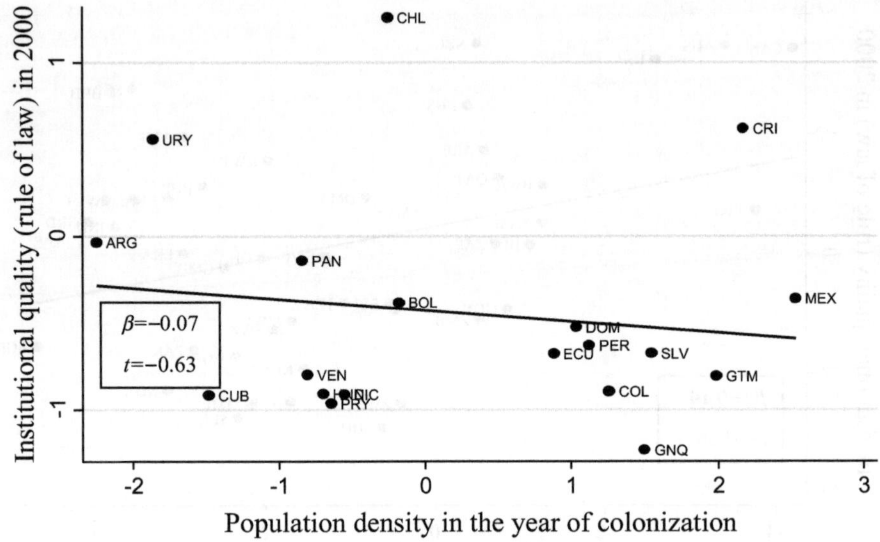

C. SPANISH COLONIES

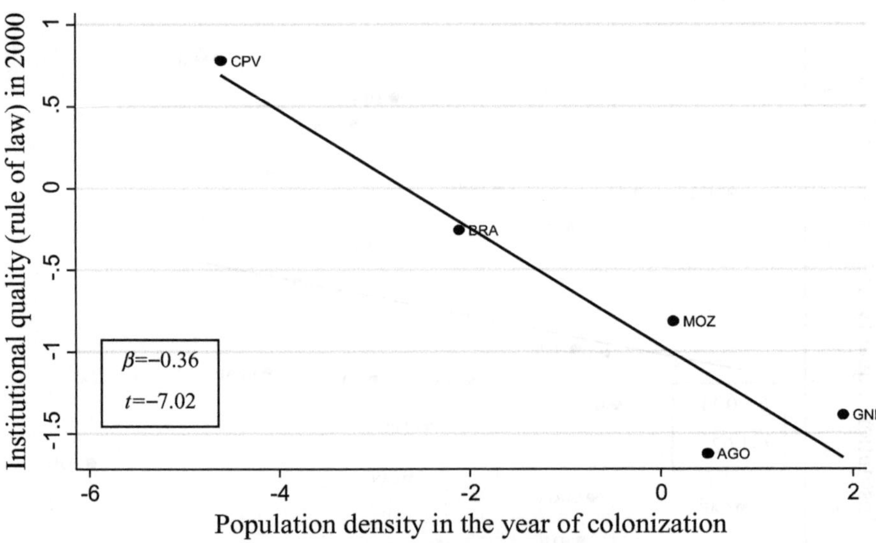

D. PORTUGUESE COLONIES

Fig. A.1 (continued)

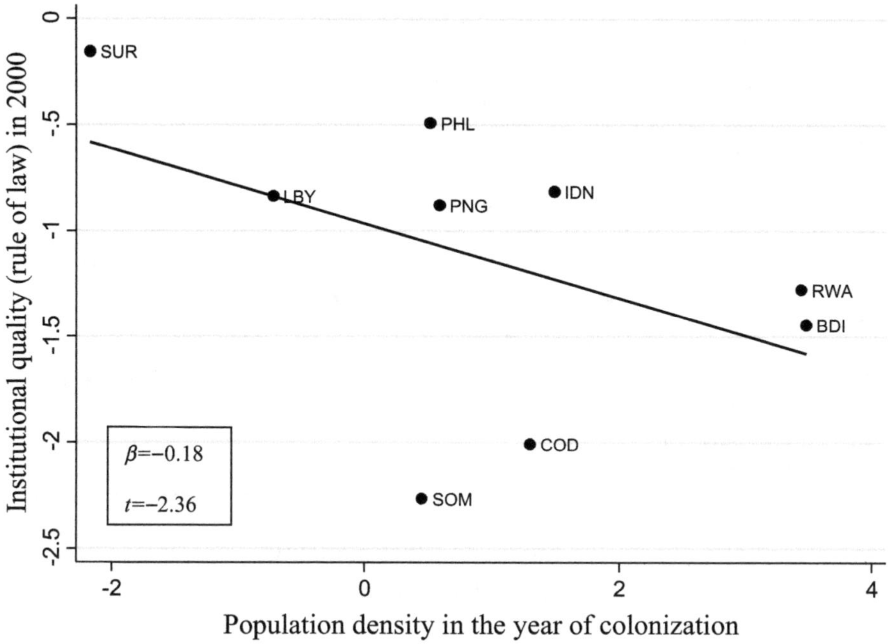

E. OTHER COLONIES

Fig. A.1 (continued)

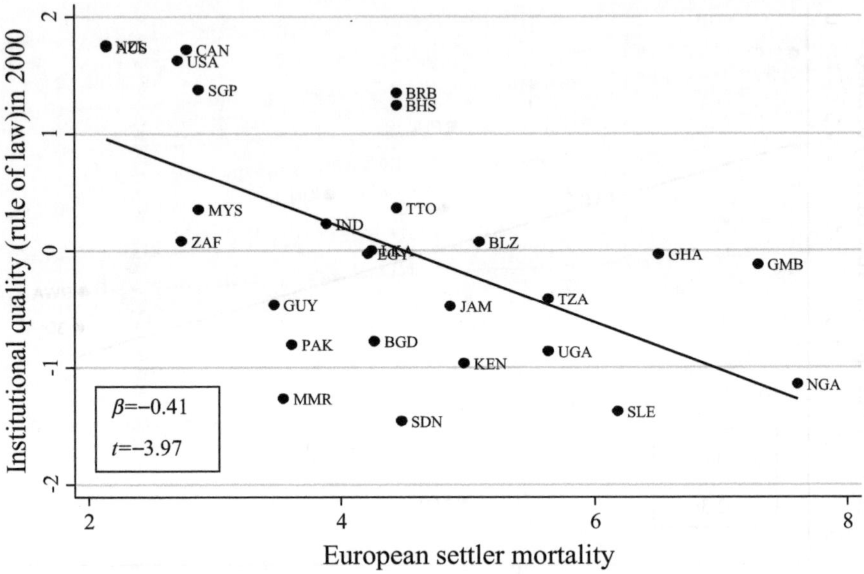

A. BRITISH COLONIES

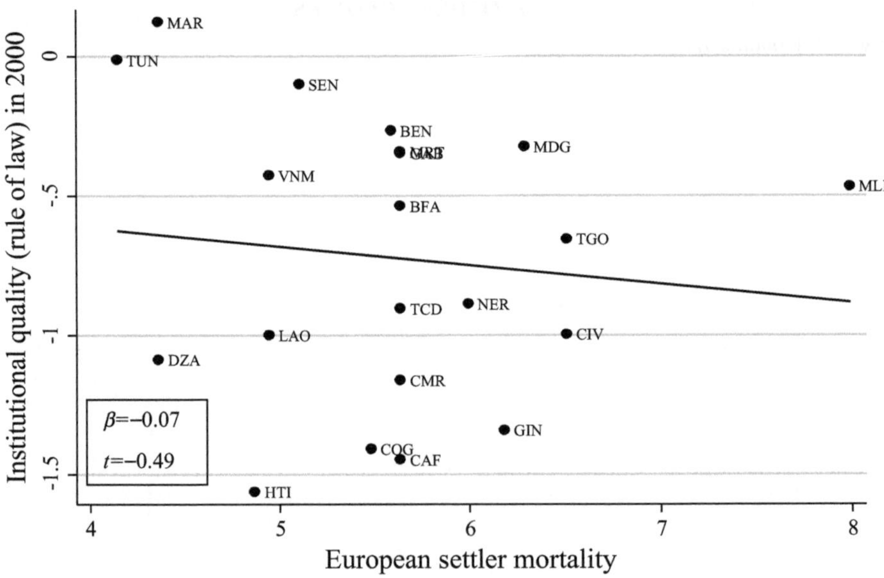

B. FRENCH COLONIES

Fig. A.2 The relationship between the European settler mortality rate (x-axis) and rule of law in 2000 (y-axis)

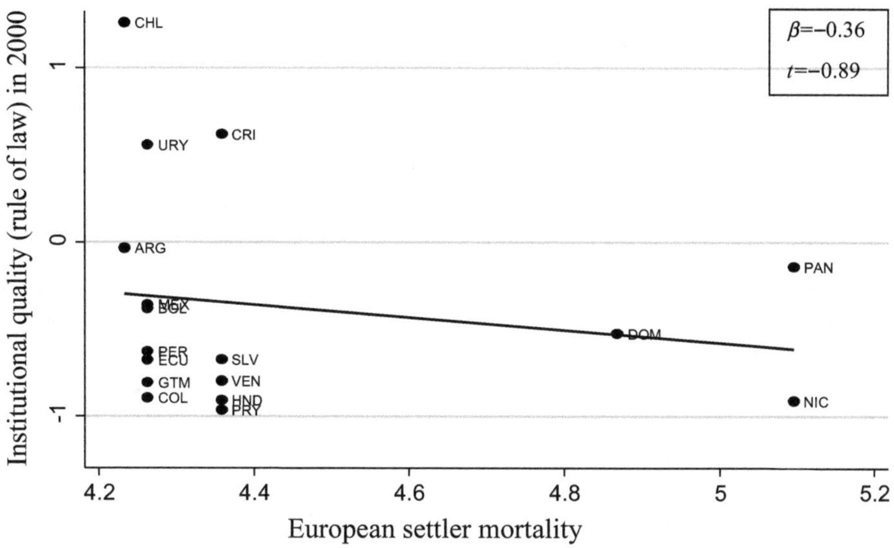

C. SPANISH COLONIES

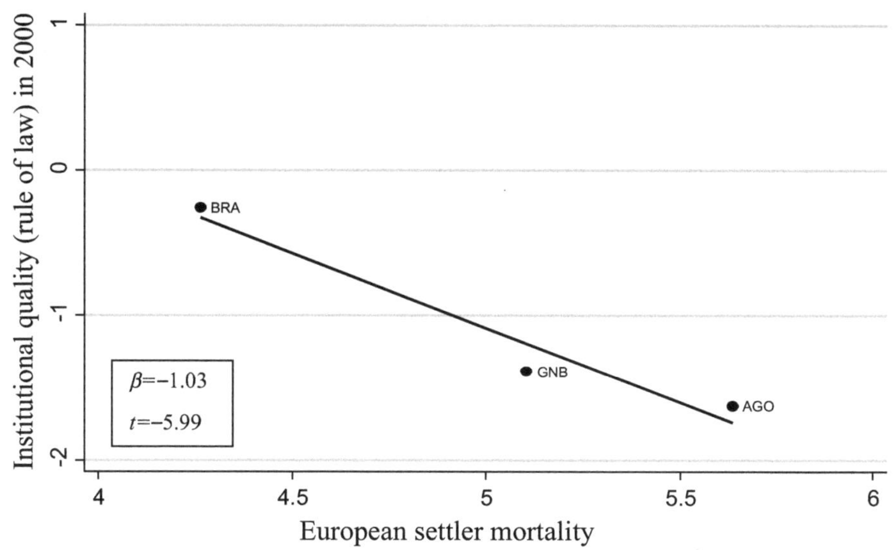

D. PORTUGUESE COLONIES

Fig. A.2 (continued)

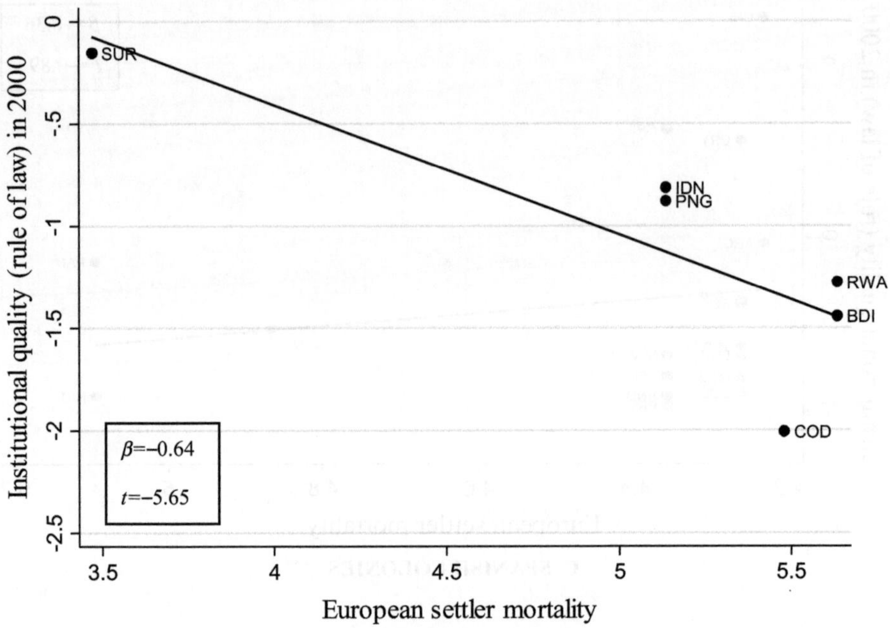

E. OTHER COLONIES

Fig. A.2 (continued)

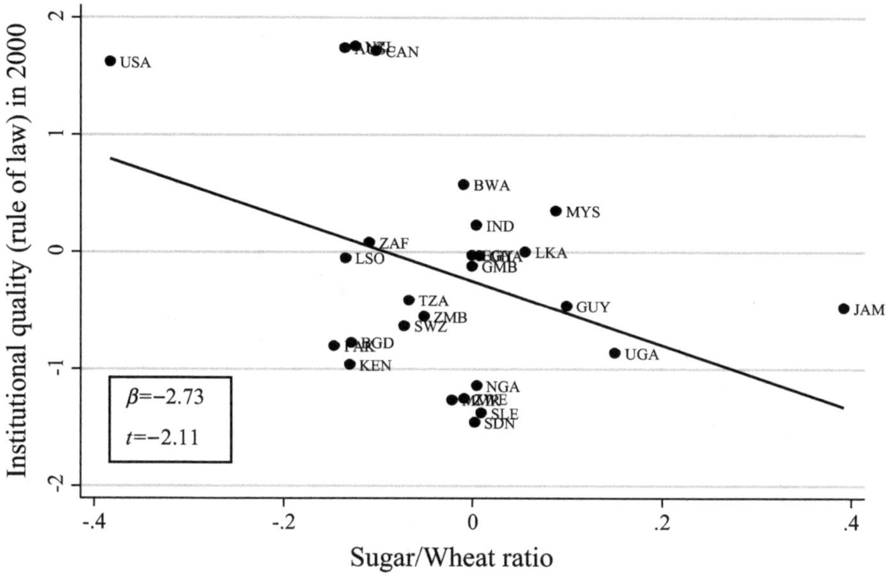

A. BRITISH COLONIES

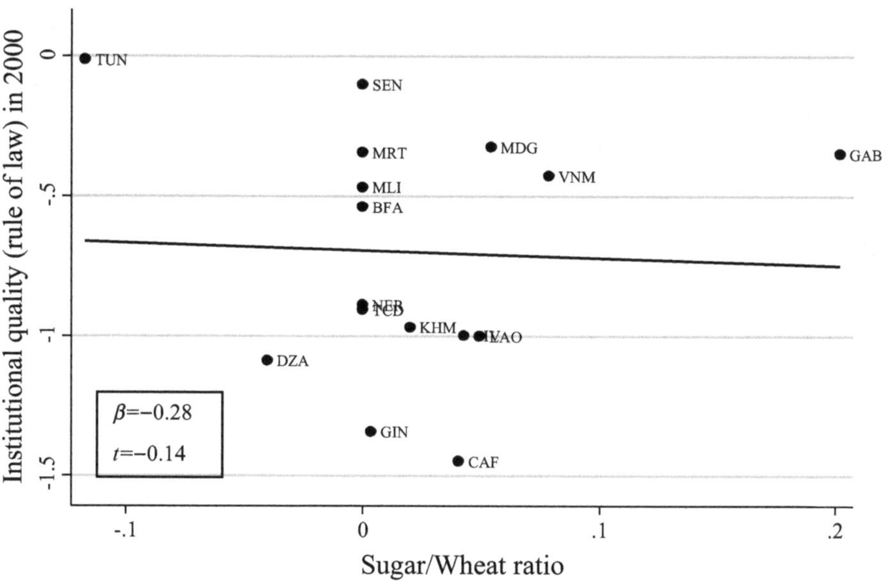

B. FRENCH COLONIES

Fig. A.3 The relationship between the sugar/wheat ratio (x-axis) and rule of law in 2000 (y-axis)

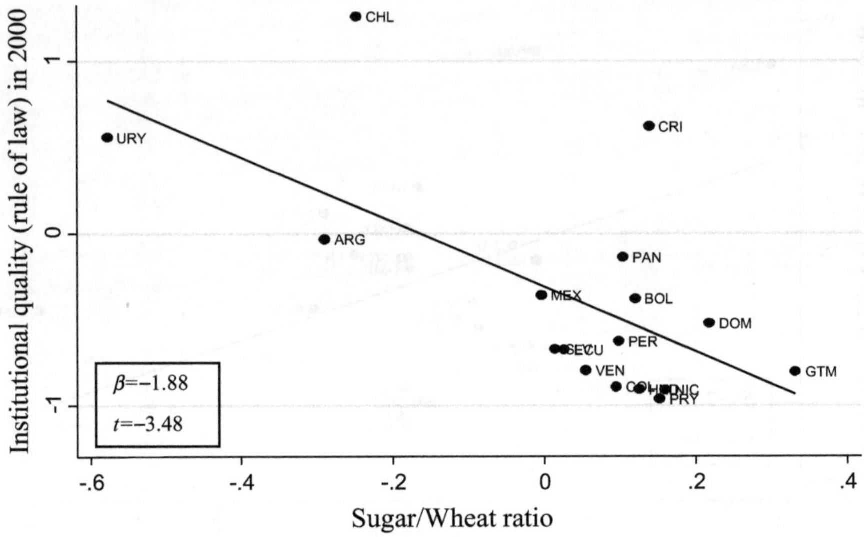

C. SPANISH COLONIES

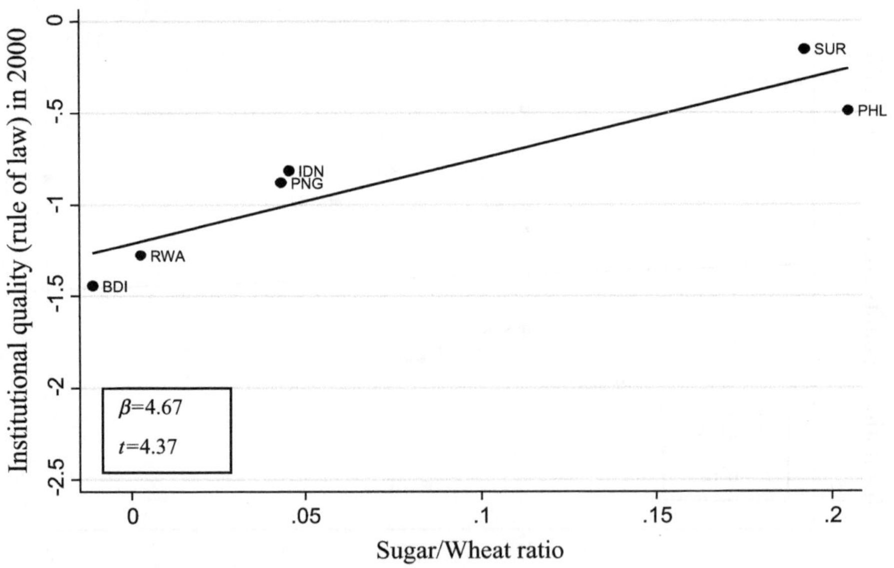

D. OTHER COLONIES

Fig. A.3 (continued)

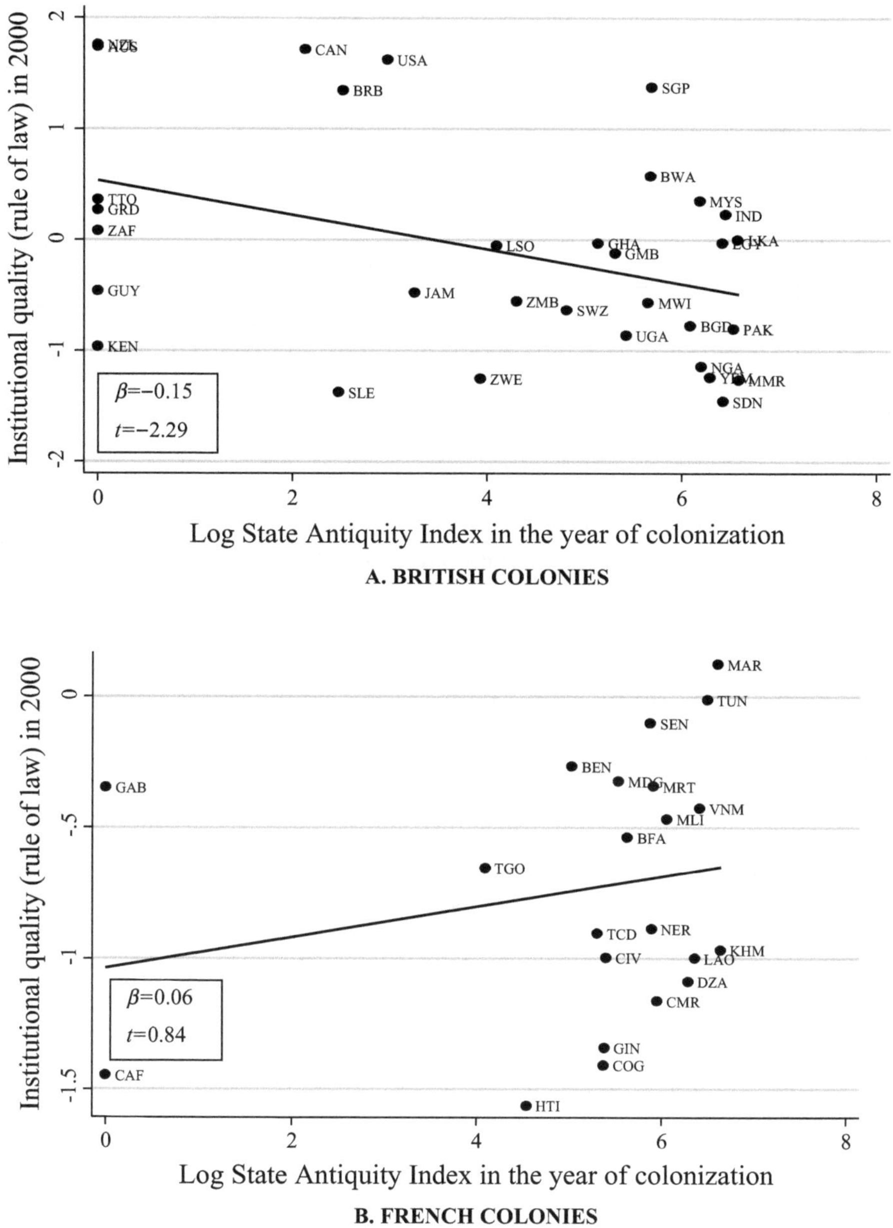

Fig. A.4 The relationship between the log state antiquity index (x-axis) and rule of law in 2000 (y-axis)

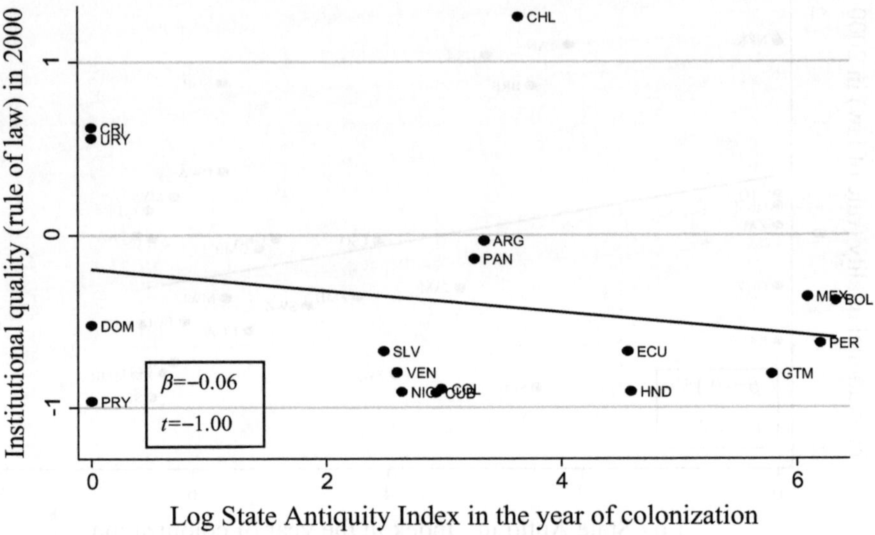

C. SPANISH COLONIES

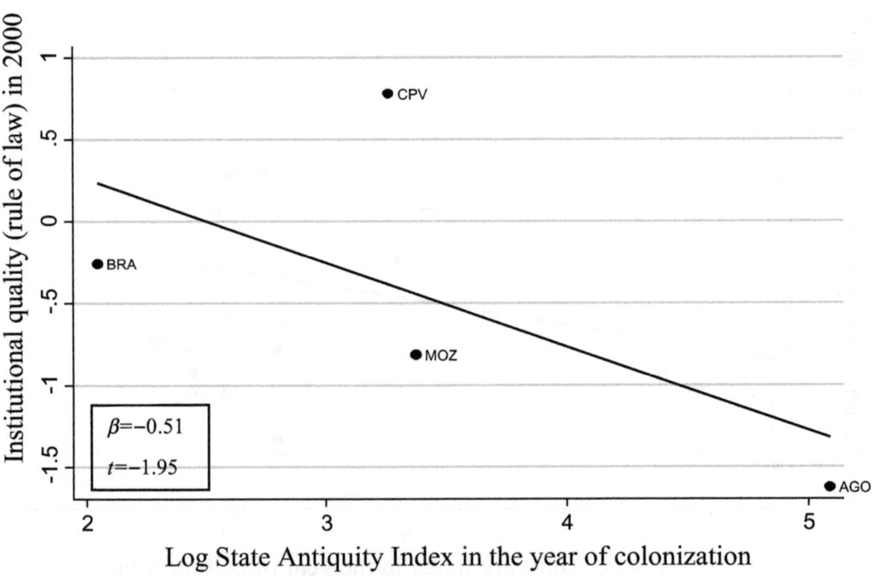

D. PORTUGUESE COLONIES

Fig. A.4 (continued)

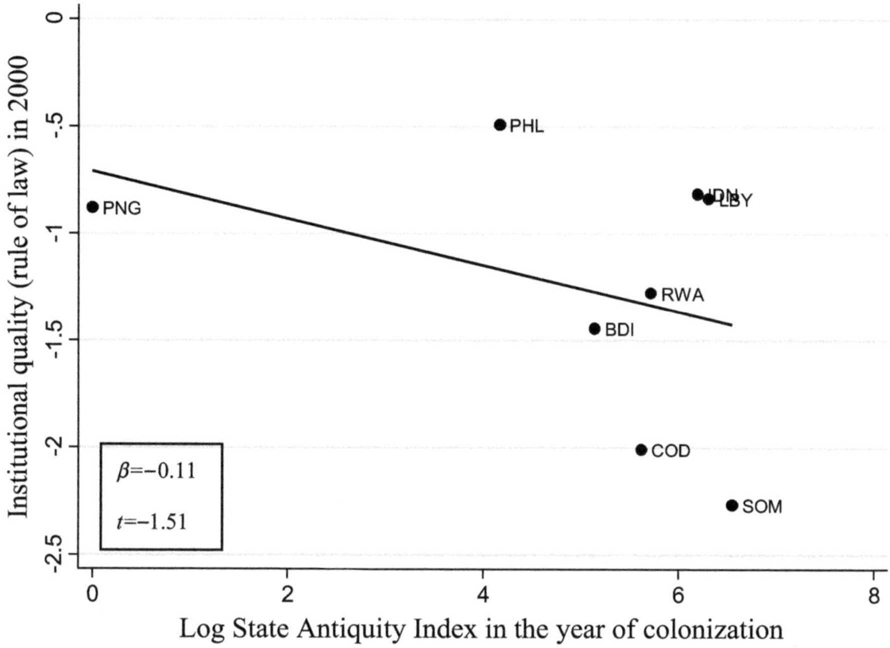

E. OTHER COLONIES

Fig. A.4 (continued)

References

Acemoglu D (2003) Why not a political Coase theorem? Social conflict, commitment, and politics. J Comp Econ 31:620–652
Acemoglu D, Dell M (2010) Productivity differences between and within countries. Am Econ J Macroecon 2(1):169–188
Acemoglu D, Johnson S (2005) Unbundling institutions. J Polit Econ 113(5):949–995
Acemoglu D, Robinson JA (2010) Why is Africa poor? Econ Hist Dev Reg 25:21–50
Acemoglu D, Robinson JA (2012) Why nations fail: the origins of power, prosperity, and poverty. Crown Publishers, New York
Acemoglu D, Johnson S, Robinson JA (2001) The colonial origins of comparative development: an empirical investigation. Am Econ Rev 91(5):1369–1401
Acemoglu D, Johnson S, Robinson JA (2002) Reversal of fortune: geography and institutions in the making of the modern world income distribution. Q J Econ 117(4):1231–1294
Acemoglu D, Johnson S, Robinson JA (2005) The rise of Europe: Atlantic trade, institutional change and economic growth. Am Econ Rev 95(3):546–579
Acemoglu D, Bautista MA, Querubín P, Robinson JA (2008) Economic and political inequality in development: the case of Cundinamarca, Colombia. In: Helpman E (ed) Institutions and economic performance. Harvard University Press, Cambridge, MA, pp 181–245
Acemoglu D, Cantoni D, Johnson S, Robinson JA (2011a) The consequences of radical reform: the French Revolution. Am Econ Rev 101:3286–3307
Acemoglu D, Hassan TA, Robinson JA (2011b) Social structure and development: a legacy of the Holocaust in Russia. Q J Econ 126:895–946
Acemoglu D, Chaves IN, Osafo-Kwaako P, Robinson JA (2014a) Indirect rule and state weakness in Africa: Sierra Leone in comparative perspective. In: Edwards S, Johnson S, Weil D (eds) African economic successes. University of Chicago Press, Chicago
Acemoglu D, Reed T, Robinson JA (2014b) Chiefs: elite control of civil society and economic development in Sierra Leone. J Polit Econ 122(2):319–368
Afigbo AE (1972) The warrant chiefs: indirect rule in Southeastern Nigeria 1891-1929. Longman, London
Afigbo AE (1985) The social repercussions of colonial rule: the new social structures, Chapter 19. In: Adu Boahen A (ed) General history of Africa VII: Africa under colonial domination 1880-1935. University of California Press, Berkeley, pp 487–507
Ahlerup P, Olsson O (2012) The roots of ethnic diversity. J Econ Growth 17(2):71–102
Alesina A, Baqir R, Easterly W (1999) Public goods and ethnic divisions. Q J Econ 114:1243–1284
Alesina A, Devleeschauwer A, Easterly W, Kurlat S, Wacziarg R (2003) Fractionalization. J Econ Growth 8:155–194

D. Oto-Peralías, D. Romero-Ávila, *Colonial Theories of Institutional Development*, Contributions to Economics, DOI 10.1007/978-3-319-54127-3

Alesina A, Giuliano P, Nunn N (2013) On the origins of gender roles: women and the plough. Q J Econ 128(2):469–530

Alsan M (2015) The effect of the TseTse Fly on African development. Am Econ Rev 105 (1):382–410

Andersen TB, Bentzen J, Dalgaard C-J, Sharp P (2017a) Pre-reformation roots of the protestant ethic. Econ J 1–53. doi:10.1111/ecoj.12367

Andersen TB, Jensen PS, Skovsgaard CS (2017b) The heavy plow and the agricultural revolution in Medieval Europe. J Dev Econ 118:133–149

Anderson TW, Rubin H (1949) Estimation of the parameters of a single equation in a complete system of stochastic equations. Ann Math Stat 20(1):46–63

Angeles L (2007) Income inequality and colonialism. Eur Econ Rev 51(5):1155–1176

Angeles L, Elizalde A (2017) Pre-colonial institutions and socioeconomic development: the case of Latin America. J Dev Econ 124:22–40

Angeles L, Neanidis KC (2009) Aid effectiveness: the role of the local elite. J Dev Econ 90:120–134

Angeles L, Neanidis KC (2015) The persistent effect of colonialism on corruption. Economica 82:319–349

Arias LM, Girod DM (2014) Indigenous origins of colonial institutions. Q J Polit Sci 9(3):371–406

Armstrong HW, Read R (2003) Microstates and subnational regions: mutual industrial policy lessons. Int Reg Sci Rev 26(1):117–141

Arndt C, Oman C (2006) Uses and abuses of governance indicators. OECD Development Centre Studies, Paris

Atlas Narodov Mira (1964) Atlas of the peoples of the world. Moscow, Glavnoe Upravlenie Geodezii i Kartografii

Austin G (2008) The 'reversal of fortune' thesis and the compression of history: perspectives from African and comparative economic history. J Int Dev 20:996–1027

Bai Y, Kung J K-s (2011) Climate shocks and Sino-nomadic conflict. Rev Econ Stat 93 (3):970–981

Bai Y, Kung J K-s (2015) Diffusing knowledge while spreading God's message: protestantism and economic prosperity in China, 1840-1920. J Eur Econ Assoc 13(4):669–698

Balas A, La Porta R, Lopez-de-Silanes F, Shleifer A (2009) The divergence of legal procedures. Am Econ J Econ Policy 1:138–162

Banerjee A, Iyer L (2005) History, institutions, and economic performance: the legacy of colonial land tenure systems in India. Am Econ Rev 95(4):1190–1213

Bardhan P (2005) Institutions matter, but which ones? Econ Transit 13(3):499–532

Barro R, Lee J-W (2010) A new data set of educational attainment in the world, 1950-2010. NBER working paper no. 15902

Baten J, van Zanden JL (2008) Book production and the onset of modern economic growth. J Econ Growth 13:217–235

Beck T, Levine R (2005) Legal institutions and financial development. In: Menard C, Shirley MM (eds) Handbook for new institutional economics. Kluwer Academic Publishers, Norwell, MA

Beck T, Demirgüç-Kunt A, Levine R (2003a) Law, endowments, and finance. J Financ Econ 70:137–181

Beck T, Demirgüç-Kunt A, Levine R (2003b) Law and finance: why does legal origin matter? J Comp Econ 31:653–675

Becker SO, Woessmann L (2009) Was Weber wrong? A human capital theory of Protestant economic history. Q J Econ 124(2):531–596

Becker SO, Boeckh K, Hainz C, Woessmann L (2016) The empire is dead, long live the empire! Long-run persistence of trust and corruption in the bureaucracy. Econ J 126(590):40–74

Belsley D, Kuh E, Welsch R (2004) Regression diagnostics. Identifying influential data and sources of collinearity. Wiley, Hoboken, NJ

Bertocchi G, Canova F (2002) Did colonization matter for growth? An empirical exploration into the historical causes of Africa's underdevelopment. Eur Econ Rev 46:1851–1871

Betts RF (1985) Methods and institutions of European domination, Chapter 13. In: Adu Boahen A (ed) General History of Africa VII: Africa under colonial domination 1880-1935. University of California Press, Berkeley, pp 312–331
Blanton R, Mason D, Athow B (2001) Colonial style and post-colonial ethnic conflict in Africa. J Peace Res 38(4):473–491
Bloom DE, Sachs JD (1998) Geography, demography, and economic growth in Africa. Brook Pap Econ Act 2:207–273
Bockstette V, Chanda A, Putterman L (2002) States and markets: the advantage of an early start. J Econ Growth 7:347–369
Botero JC, Djankov S, La Porta R, Lopez-de-Silanes F, Shleifer A (2004) The regulation of labor. Q J Econ 119:1339–1382
Botticini M, Eckstein Z (2005) Jewish occupational selection: education, restrictions, or minorities? J Econ Hist 65(4):922–948
Botticini M, Eckstein Z (2007) From farmers to merchants, voluntary conversions and diaspora: a human capital interpretation of Jewish history. J Eur Econ Assoc 5(5):885–926
Britannica Encyclopaedia (2012) Encyclopedia Britannica 2012 ultimate edition. Encyclopedia Britannica, London
Broms R (2017) Colonial revenue extraction and modern day government quality in the British Empire. World Dev 90:269–280. doi:10.1016/j.worlddev.2016.10.003
Bruhn M, Gallego FA (2012) Good, bad, and ugly colonial activities: do they matter for economic development? Rev Econ Stat 94(2):433–461
Bubb R (2013) The evolution of property rights: state law or informal norms? J Law Econ 56:555–594
Cain PJ, Hopkins AG (1980) The political economy of British expansion overseas, 1750-1914. Econ Hist Rev 33(4):463–490
Cantoni D (2015) The economic effects of the Protestant reformation: testing the Weber hypothesis in the German lands. J Eur Econ Assoc 13(4):561–598
Chaney E (2008) Ethnic cleansing and the long-term persistence of extractive institutions: evidence from the expulsion of the *Moriscos*. Harvard University working paper, Harvard University, Cambridge
Chaney E (2013) Revolt on the Nile: economic shocks, religion, and political power. Econometrica 81(5):2033–2053
Chaney E, Hornbeck R (2016) Economic dynamics in the Malthusian era: evidence from the 1609 Spanish expulsion of the *Moriscos*. Econ J 126(594):1404–1440
Clarence-Smith G (1985) The third Portuguese Empire, 1825-1975. A study in economic imperialism. Manchester University Press, Manchester
Cogneau D, Moradi A (2014) Borders that divide: education and religion in Ghana and Togo since colonial times. J Econ Hist 74(3):694–729
Cogneau D, Yannick D, Sandrine M-S (2016) African states and development in historical perspective: colonial public finances in British and French West Africa. Paris School of Economics working paper, Paris
Congdon-Fors H (2007) Islands status, country size and institutional quality in former colonies. Göteborg University working paper no. 257
Crowder M (1964) Indirect rule—French and British style. J Int Afr Inst 34(3):197–205
Crowder M (1968) West Africa under colonial rule. Northwestern University Press, Evanston, IL
Crowder M, Ikime O (eds) (1970) West African Chiefs: their changing status under colonial rule and independence. Africana Publishing Corporation, New York
Daniels RJ, Trebilcock MJ, Carson LD (2011) The legacy of the empire: the common law inheritance and commitments to legality in former British colonies. Am J Comp Law 59:111–178
de Montesquieu B (1748) The complete works of M. de Montesquieu, The spirit of laws, vol 1. T. Evans, London
de Sousa J, Lochard J (2012) Trade and colonial status. J Afr Econ 21(3):409–439

de Sousa Ferreira E (1974) Portuguese colonialism in Africa: the end of an era. The effects of Portuguese colonialism on education, science, culture and information. The Unesco Press, Paris
Dell M (2010) The persistent effects of Peru's mining Mita. Econometrica 78(6):1863–1903
Dell M (2012) Path dependence in development: evidence from the Mexican revolution. Massachusetts Institute of Technology working paper, MIT, Cambridge, MA
Dittmar JE (2011) Information technology and economic change: the impact of the printing press. Q J Econ 126(3):1133–1172
Djankov S, La Porta R, Lopez-de-Silanes F, Shleifer A (2002) The regulation of entry. Q J Econ 117:1–37
Djankov S, La Porta R, Lopez-de-Silanes F, Shleifer A (2003) Courts. Q J Econ 118:453–517
Djankov S, McLiesh C, Shleifer A (2007) Private credit in 129 countries. J Financ Econ 84:299–329
Djankov S, Hart OD, McLiesh C, Shleifer A (2008a) Debt enforcement around the world. J Polit Econ 116:1105–1149
Djankov S, La Porta R, Lopez-de-Silanes F, Shleifer A (2008b) The law and economics of self-dealing. J Financ Econ 88:430–465
Dollar D, Kraay A (2003) Institutions, trade and growth. J Monet Econ 50:133–162
Dupraz Y (2016) French and British colonial legacies in education: a natural experiment in Cameroon. Paris School of Economics working paper, Paris
Easterly W (2007) Inequality does cause underdevelopment: insights from a new instrument. J Dev Econ 84:755–776
Easterly W, Levine R (1997) Africa's growth tragedy: policies and ethnic divisions. Q J Econ 112 (4):203–250
Easterly W, Levine R (2003) Tropics, germs, and crops: how endowments influence economic development. J Monet Econ 50:3–39
Easterly W, Levine R (2016) The European origins of economic development. J Econ Growth 21 (3):225–257
Engerman SL, Sokoloff KL (1997) Factor endowments, institutions, and differential paths of growth among New World economies. In: Haber S (ed) How Latin America fell behind. Stanford University Press, Stanford, CA, pp 260–304
Engerman SL, Sokoloff KL (2000) Institutions, factor endowments, and paths of development in the New World. J Econ Perspect 14(3):217–232
Engerman SL, Sokoloff KL (2005) The evolution of suffrage institutions in the New World. J Econ Hist 65(4):891–921
Evans-Pritchard EE, Fortes M (eds) (1940) African political systems. Oxford University Press, London
Fage JD (2002) A history of Africa. Routledge, London
FAO/IIASA (2002) Global agro-ecological assessment for agriculture in the 21st century CD-ROM. International Institute for Applied Systems Analysis & FAO
Fenske J (2012) Land abundance and economic institutions: Egba land and slavery, 1830–1914. Econ Hist Rev 65(2):527–555
Fenske J (2013) Does land abundance explain African institutions? Econ J 123(573):1363–1390
Fenske J (2014) Ecology, trade and states in precolonial Africa. J Eur Econ Assoc 12(3):612–640
Feyrer J, Sacerdote B (2009) Colonialism and modern income: Islands as natural experiments. Rev Econ Stat 91(2):245–262
Fieldhouse DK (1966) The colonial empires: a comparative survey from the eighteenth century. Weidenfeld and Nicolson, London
Fieldhouse DK (1973) Economics and empire, 1830-1914. Weidenfeld and Nicolson, London
Firmin-Sellers K (2000) Institutions, context, and outcomes. Explaining French and British rule in West Africa. Comp Polit 32(3):253–272
Fisher MH (1991) Indirect rule in India: residents and the residency system 1764-1858. Oxford University Press, Delhi

Gallego FA (2010) Historical origins of schooling: the role of democracy and political decentralization. Rev Econ Stat 92(2):228–243
Gallego FA, Woodberry R (2010) Christian missionaries and education in former African colonies: how competition mattered. J Afr Econ 19(3):294–329
Gallup JL, Mellinger AD, Sachs JD (2001) Geographic datasets: Köppen-Geiger climate zones. Center of International Development, Harvard University
Galor O, Moav O, Vollrath D (2009) Inequality in landownership, the emergence of human-capital promoting institutions, and the great divergence. Rev Econ Stud 76:143–179
García-Jimeno C, Robinson JA (2011) The myth of the frontier. In: Costa DL, Lamoreaux NR (eds) Understanding long-run economic growth. University of Chicago Press, Chicago, pp 49–88
Gennaioli N, Rainer I (2007) The modern impact of precolonial centralization in Africa. J Econ Growth 12:185–234
Gennaioli N, La Porta R, de Silanes FL, Shleifer A (2013) Human capital and regional development. Q J Econ 128(1):105–164
Gennaioli N, La Porta R, López de Silanes F, Shleifer A (2014) Growth in regions. J Econ Growth 19:259–309
Glaeser EL, La Porta R, Lopez-de-Silanes F, Shleifer A (2004) Do institutions cause growth? J Econ Growth 9:271–303
Goldewijk KK, Beusen A, Janssen P (2010) Long-term dynamic modeling of global population and built-up area in a spatially explicit way, HYDE 3.1. Holocene 20(4):565–573
Grafe R, Alejandra Irigoin M (2006) The Spanish Empire and its legacy: fiscal redistribution and political conflict in colonial and post-colonial Spanish America. J Glob Hist 1:241–267
Grier RM (1999) Colonial legacies and economic growth. Public Choice 98:317–335
Grosjean P (2011a) The weight of history on European cultural integration: a gravity approach. Am Econ Rev 101(3):504–508
Grosjean P (2011b) The institutional legacy of the Ottoman Empire: Islamic rule and financial development in South Eastern Europe. J Comp Econ 39(1):1–16
Gwartney J, Lawson R (2006) Economic freedom of the world: 2006 annual report. The Fraser Institute, Vancouver
Hall RE, Jones CI (1999) Why do some countries produce so much more output per worker than others? Q J Econ 114(1):83–116
Hariri JG (2012) The autocratic legacy of early statehood. Am Polit Sci Rev 106(3):471–494
Hayek FA (1960) The constitution of liberty. University of Chicago Press, Chicago
Heldring L, Robinson JA (2014) Colonialism and economic development in Africa. In: Lancaster C, Van de Walle N (eds) Handbook on the politics of development. Oxford University Press, Oxford
Heritage Foundation (2012) Index of economic freedom. On-line publication. http://www.heritage.org/index/. Accessed on 05/01/2012
Hobsbawn EJ (1987) The age of empire: 1875–1914. George Weidenfeld and Nicolson, London
Hobson JA (1902) Imperialism: a study. James Pott, New York
Huillery E (2009) History matters: the long-term impact of colonial public investments in French West Africa. Am Econ J Appl Econ 1(2):176–215
Huntington SP (1991) The third wave: democratization in the late twentieth century. University of Oklahoma Press, Norman
Irigoin MA, Grafe R (2008) Bargaining for absolutism: a Spanish path to nation-state and empire building. Hisp Am Hist Rev 88(2):173–209
Iyer L (2010) Direct versus indirect colonial rule in India: long-term consequences. Rev Econ Stat 92(4):693–713
Iyigun M (2008) Luther and Suleyman. Q J Econ 123(4):1465–1494
Jones P (2013) History matters: new evidence on the long run impact of colonial rule on institutions. J Comp Econ 41:181–200

Kaufmann D, Kraay A, Mastruzzi M (2009) Governance matters VIII: aggregate and individual governance indicators for 1996–2008. World Bank Policy Research paper no. 4978

Kirk-Greene AHM (1980) The thin white line: the size of the British colonial service in Africa. Afr Aff 79(314):25–44

Kleibergen F (2005) Testing parameters in GMM without assuming that they are identified. Econometrica 73(4):1103–1123

Klerman D, Mahoney PG, Spanmann H, Weinstein M (2011) Legal origin or colonial history. J Legal Anal 3(2):379–409

Knack S, Keefer P (1995) Institutions and economic performance: cross-country tests using alternative measures. Econ Polit 7(3):207–227

Kumar K (2006) English and French national identity: comparisons and contrasts. Nations Nationalism 12:413–432

La Porta R, Lopez-de-Silanes F, Shleifer A, Vishny RW (1997) Legal determinants of external finance. J Financ 52:1131–1150

La Porta R, Lopez-de-Silanes F, Shleifer A, Vishny RW (1998) Law and finance. J Polit Econ 106:1113–1155

La Porta R, Lopez-de-Silanes F, Shleifer A, Vishny RW (1999) The quality of government. J Law Econ Organ 15(1):222–279

La Porta R, Lopez-de-Silanes F, Shleifer A (2002) Government ownership of banks. J Financ 57:265–301

La Porta R, Lopez-de-Silanes F, Pop-Eleches C, Shleifer A (2004) Judicial checks and balances. J Polit Econ 112:445–470

La Porta R, Lopez-de-Silanes F, Shleifer A (2006) What works in securities laws? J Financ 61:1–32

La Porta R, Lopez-de-Silanes F, Shleifer A (2008) The economic consequences of legal origins. J Econ Lit 46:285–332

Landes DS (1998) The wealth and poverty of nations: why some are so rich and some so poor. W.W. Norton, New York

Lang J (1975) Conquest and commerce, Spain and England in the Americas. Academic Press, New York

Lange M (2004) British colonial legacies and political development. World Dev 32(6):905–922

Lange M (2005) British colonial state legacies and development trajectories: a statistical analysis of direct and indirect rule. In: Lange M, Rueschemeyer D (eds) States and development: historical antecedents of stagnation and advance. Palgrave Macmillan Press, New York, pp 117–139

Lange M (2009) Lineages of despotism and development: British colonialism and state power. Chicago University Press, Chicago, IL

Lange M, Dawson A (2009) Dividing and ruling the world? A statistical test of the effects of colonialism on postcolonial civil violence. Soc Forces 88:785–818

Lange M, Mahoney J, vom Hau M (2006) Colonialism and development: a comparative analysis of Spanish and British colonies. Am J Sociol 111(5):1412–1462

Lee A, Schultz KA (2012) Comparing British and French colonial legacies: a discontinuity analysis of Cameroon. Q J Polit Sci 7:1–46

Lenin VI (1917) Imperialism, the highest stage of capitalism. Petrograd, 26 April 1917

Levine R (2005) Law, endowments and property rights. J Econ Perspect 19(3):61–88

Lewis MD (1962) One hundred million Frenchmen: the assimilation theory in French colonial policy. Comp Stud Soc Hist 4(2):129–153

Lugard FD (1919) 1970. Political memoranda. Frank Cass, London

Lugard FD (1922) The dual mandate in British Tropical Africa. William Blackwood and Sons, London

Maddison A (2010) Statistics on world population, GDP and per capita GDP, 1-2008 AD. University of Groningen

Mahoney J (2003) Long-run development and the legacy of colonialism in Spanish America. Am J Sociol 109(1):50–106
Mamdani M (1996) Citizen and subject. Princeton University Press, Princeton, NJ
Marshall MG, Gurr TR, Jaggers K (2010) Polity IV project: political regime characteristics and transitions, 1800-2009: dataset users' manual. Center for Systemic Peace, Vienna
Mauro P (1995) Corruption and growth. Q J Econ 110(3):681–712
Mayer T, Zignago S (2011) Notes on CEPII's distances measures: the GeoDist database. Working papers 2011-25, CEPII Research Center
McEvedy C, Jones R (1978) Atlas of world population history. Facts on File, New York
Michalopoulos S (2012) The origins of ethnolinguistic diversity. Am Econ Rev 102(4):1508–1539
Michalopoulos S, Papaioannou E (2013) Pre-colonial ethnic institutions and contemporary African development. Econometrica 81(1):113–152
Michalopoulos S, Papaioannou E (2014) National institutions and subnational development in Africa. Q J Econ 129(1):151–213
Michalopoulos S, Papaioannou E (2016) The long-run effects of the scramble for Africa. Am Econ Rev 106(7):1802–1848
Migdal JS (1988) Strong societies and weak states: state-society relations and state capabilities in the third world. Princeton University Press, Princeton, NJ
Migdal JS (1994) The state in society: an approach to struggles of domination. In: Migdal J, Kohli A, Shue V (eds) State power and social forces: domination and transformation in the third world. Cambridge University Press, New York, pp 7–36
Miles WFS (1987) Partitioned royalty: the evolution of Hausa chiefs in Nigeria and Niger. J Mod Afr Stud 25(2):233–258
Moreira MJ (2003) A conditional likelihood ratio test for structural models. Econometrica 71:1027–1048
Murdock GP (1967) Ethnographic atlas. Pittsburgh University Press, Pittsburgh
Murdock GP, White DR (1969) Standard cross-cultural sample. Ethnology 9:329–369
Naritomi J, Soares RR, Assunçao JL (2012) Institutional development and colonial heritage within Brazil. J Econ Hist 72(2):393–422
North DC (1981) Structure and change in economic history. W.W. Norton, New York
North DC (1989) Institutions and economic growth: a historical introduction. World Dev 17 (9):1319–1332
North DC (1991) Institutions. J Econ Perspect 5(1):97–112
North DC, Thomas RP (1973) The rise of the Western World: a new economic history. Cambridge University Press, Cambridge
Nunn N (2007) Historical legacies: a model linking Africa's past to its current underdevelopment. J Dev Econ 83:157–175
Nunn N (2008a) Slavery, inequality, and economic development in the Americas: an examination of the Engerman-Sokoloff hypothesis. In: Helpman E (ed) Institutions and economic performance. Harvard University Press, Cambridge, pp 148–180
Nunn N (2008b) The long term effects of Africa's slave trades. Q J Econ 123(1):139–176
Nunn N (2009) The importance of history for economic development. Annu Rev Econ 1(1):65–92
Nunn N (2014) Historical development, Chapter 7. In: Aghion P, Durlauf P (eds) Handbook of economic growth, vol 2. Elsevier, North-Holland, pp 347–402
Nunn N, Wantchekon L (2011) The slave trade and the origins of mistrust in Africa. Am Econ Rev 101(7):3221–3252
Olsson O (2009) On the democratic legacy of colonialism. J Comp Econ 37:534–551
Osafo-Kwaako P, Robinson JA (2013) Political centralization in pre-colonial Africa. J Comp Econ 41:6–21
Oto-Peralías D, Romero-Ávila D (2014a) Legal traditions and initial endowments in shaping the path of financial development. J Money Credit Bank 46(1):43–77
Oto-Peralías D, Romero-Ávila D (2014b) The distribution of legal traditions around the world: a contribution to the Legal Origins Theory. J Law Econ 57(3):561–628

Oto-Peralías D, Romero-Ávila D (2016) The economic consequences of the Spanish Reconquest: the long-term effects of medieval conquest and colonization. J Econ Growth 21(4):409–464
Oto-Peralías D, Romero-Ávila D (2017) Historical frontiers and the rise of inequality. The case of the Frontier of Granada. J Eur Econ Assoc 15(1):54–98
Perham M (1934) A re-statement of indirect rule. Africa J Int Afr Inst 7:321–334
PRS Group ICRG Methodology (2011) On-line publication. http://www.prsgroup.com/ICRG_Methodology.aspx. Accessed on 05/01/2012
Ramankutty N, Foley JA, Norman J, McSweeney K (2002) The global distribution of cultivable lands: current patterns and sensitivity to possible climate change. Glob Ecol Biogeogr 11:377–392
Richens P (2009) The economic legacies of the 'Thin White Line': indirect rule and the comparative development of sub-Saharan Africa. Afr Econ Hist 37:33–102
Robinson JA (2012) States and power in Africa by Jeffrey I. Herbst: a review essay. J Econ Lit 40:510–519
Rodrik D, Subramanian A, Trebbi F (2004) Institutions rule: the primacy of institutions over geography and integration in economic development. J Econ Growth 9(2):131–165
Schumpeter JA (1919) The sociology of imperialisms. Archivfür Sozialwissenshaft und Sozialpolitik 46 (Tubingen)
Spolaore E, Wacziarg R (2013) How deep are the roots of economic development? J Econ Lit 51 (2):325–369
Staiger D, Stock JH (1997) Instrumental variables regression with weak instruments. Econometrica 65:557–586
Teorell J, Hadenius A (2005) Determinants of democratization: taking stock of the large-N evidence. Department of Government, Uppsala University, Mimeo
Teorell J, Samanni M, Holmberg S, Rothstein B (2011) The quality of government dataset. Version 6 April 2011. The Quality of Government Institute, University of Gothenburg. http://www.qog.pol.gu.se
Treisman D (2000) The causes of corruption: a cross-national study. J Public Econ 76(3):399–457
Vanhanen T (2003a) Democratization: a comparative analysis of 170 countries. Routledge, London
Vanhanen T (2003b) Democratization and power resources 1850-2000 [computer file]. FSD1216, version 1.0 (2003-03-10)'. Finnish Social Science Data Archive, Tampere
von Strandmann HP (1969) Domestic origins of Germany's colonial expansion under Bismarck. Past Present 42:140–159
Weber M (1976) [1904–1905]. The Protestant ethic and the spirit of capitalism. Allen and Unwin, London
Whittlesey D (1937) British and French colonial technique in West Africa. Foreign Aff 15:362–373
Woodberry RD (2004) The shadow of empire: Christian missions, colonial policy, and democracy in post-colonial societies. Ph.D. dissertation. University of North Carolina, Chapel Hill, NC
Woodberry RD (2012) The missionary roots of liberal democracy. Am Polit Sci Rev 106 (2):244–274
World Bank (2002) World development Report 2002: building institutions for markets. Oxford University Press, New York
World Bank (2011) World development indicators 2011 database. World Bank Publishing Services, World Bank, Washington, DC
Wylie K (1977) Political kingdoms of the Temne. Holmes and Meier Publishers, London
Zweigert K, Kötz H (1998) An introduction to comparative law. Clarendon Press, Oxford

MIX
Papier aus verantwortungsvollen Quellen
Paper from responsible sources
FSC® C105338
FSC
www.fsc.org

If you have any concerns about our products,
you can contact us on
ProductSafety@springernature.com

In case Publisher is established outside the EU,
the EU authorized representative is:
Springer Nature Customer Service Center GmbH
Europaplatz 3, 69115 Heidelberg, Germany

Printed by Libri Plureos GmbH
in Hamburg, Germany